TH

TIMES RECONSIDERED

Carl Olof Jonsson

Second Edition

M. JAMES PENTON
Editor: English Edition

Commentary Press, Atlanta
1986

The Gentile Times Reconsidered

Published by Commentary Press, Atlanta, GA., with
permission of Hart Publishers Ltd. and Good News
Defenders

M. James Penton, Editor of the English edition
Swedish edition entitled: Slutade hedningarnas tider 1914?
Copyright by CKI-Förlaget, Göteborg, Sweden

Manufactured in the United States of America
ISBN: 0-914675-05-2
Library of Congress Catalog Card No.: 86-70168

TABLE OF CONTENTS

EDITOR'S FOREWORD

In the *Prologue,* which follows immediately, Carl Olof Jonsson tells some of the background of *The Gentile Times Reconsidered* and his attempts to have the Governing Body of Jehovah's Witnesses examine honestly the data which he placed before them in an earlier, unpublished form of this work. What he does not discuss, however, is how he was excommunicated in July 1982 by a Swedish Jehovah's Witness "judicial committee" or church court for having questioned the Witnesses' so-called Bible chronology when, according to the Swedish press, that body's members could not even read his typescript which had been written in English.

Jonsson's case bears a striking resemblance to the sixteenth-century inquisitorial trial of Galileo Galilei. For Jonsson's judges, like those of Galileo, were concerned more with doctrinal orthodoxy than truth. Thus all they wanted to do was force him to recant or, if that were not possible, to isolate him and declare his ideas heretical. So the present volume is definitely on the Witnesses' *Index Librorum Prohibitorum* and reading it is regarded as a serious sin.

Nevertheless, Jonsson's study has already had a profound effect on the Witness community. As he points out, some years ago he distributed photocopies of his typescript to scholarly-minded friends who in turn passed them on to other persons of like bent of mind within the Witness community. As a result, some photocopies of *The Gentile Times Reconsidered* reached such far away places as Australia, Canada and Latin America where much questioning of official Witness doctrine was already taking place. There, those photocopies served to add fuel to the fires of dissent and rebellion which have now blazed forth throughout much of the world within the ranks of Jehovah's Witnesses or what is often called the Watchtower movement.

The present volume should not be seen simply as an attack on the doctrinal system of Jehovah's Witnesses. It is, rather, an attempt to aid all thinking persons, whether Witnesses or not, to gain a greater understanding of the importance of archaeology, astronomy and, above all, history to a proper understanding of the Christian religion. For a faith which flies in the face of proven facts is not only blind credulity, it is nonsense. As Pope Leo XIII once noted, the study of church history reveals "*Un ensemble de faits dogmatiques qui s'imposent a la foi et qu'il n'est permis à personne de révoquer en doute*" (a body of dogmatic facts which are imposed on faith and which no one may call in question); and, as he also stressed in quoting Job 13:7 from the French, "*Dieu n'a pas besoin de nos mensonges*" (God has no need of our lies). Hence the readers of this work are clearly invited to study, evaluate and determine whether Jonsson has proven the case against a central doctrine of Jehovah's Witnesses or not. I believe firmly that he has.

In closing, a few points should be made with respect to

certain terms which appear in this work. Jonsson regularly uses the designations B.C.E. (Before the Common Era) and C.E. (Common Era) rather than the more traditional B.C. and A.D. The reason is that this is the practice of Jehovah's Witnesses today. He also ordinarily refers to their printing and publishing organization as the Watchtower Society which is the proper designation for the Watchtower Bible and Tract Society, Inc. of New York. Sometimes he also makes reference to the Watch Tower Society which is the name of the older Pennsylvania corporation. As the name of the Witnesses' official magazine has changed several times over the last century, he has, of necessity, given the correct titles for the various magazines he quotes. So the reader should be aware that *Zion's Watch Tower, The Watch Tower* and *The Watchtower* are the same journal.

M. James Penton
University of Lethbridge
Lethbridge, Alberta, Canada

PROLOGUE

As one of Jehovah's Witnesses for more than twenty-five years, I put great trust in the Watchtower Bible and Tract Society—the Witnesses' publishing corporation—and its leadership. Until very recently, I hoped that the current leaders of that organization would carefully and discreetly face the facts respecting their chronology, even if those facts should prove fatal to some of the central doctrines and unique claims of their organization. But when at last I realized that the Society's leaders—apparently for reasons of organizational or "ecclesiastical" policy—were determined to deceive millions of persons by suppressing information which they regarded and regard as undesirable, no other course seemed open to me but to publish my findings, thus giving every individual an opportunity to examine the evidence and draw his own conclusions.

The chronological calculation of the "times of the Gentiles" (Luke 21:24) which holds them to be a period of

2,520 years, beginning in 607 B.C.E. and ending in 1914 C.E., is a basic element in the doctrinal structure of the Watchtower Bible and Tract Society, whose central message is founded upon this calculation. It is asserted that God's kingdom was established in heaven in 1914 and that Christ's *parousia* or presence began in that year. Even the "good news" of the kingdom (Matt. 24:14), they hold, refers specifically to the Witnesses' proclamation that God's kingdom was established invisibly in 1914; the gospel preached by other confessed Christians, therefore, has never been the *true gospel.* Said *The Watchtower* of May 1, 1981, on page 17:

> Let the honest-hearted person compare the kind of preaching of the gospel of the Kingdom done by the religious systems of Christendom during all the centuries with that done by Jehovah's Witnesses since the end of World War I in 1918. They are not one and the same kind. That of Jehovah's Witnesses is really "gospel," or "good news," *as of God's heavenly kingdom that was established by the enthronement of his Son Jesus Christ at the end of the Gentile Times in 1914.* [Italics mine]

Because of the central importance attached to this chronological calculation for the unparalleled claims of the Watchtower Society, it is seen not merely as a theory or interpretation, but as an *established, indisputable fact*, stubbornly resisted by the nations of the earth, including those of Christendom. It is said that those who reject it incur the wrath of God.[1]

For one of Jehovah's Witnesses to doubt the validity of this basic prophetic calculation is, then, no easy matter. To many Witness believers, the doctrinal system based on the Gentile times chronology functions as a sort of "fortress" inside which shelter, in the form of spiritual and emotional security, is sought. If some part of that doctrinal structure is questioned, believers tend to react emotionally; they take a defensive attitude, sensing that their "fortress" is under attack and that their security is threatened. This defense mechanism makes it very difficult for them to listen to and examine what doubters may have to say on the matter *objectively*. Unwittingly, they often elevate their need for emotional security to a place *above* their respect for truth.

To reach behind this defensive attitude so common among Jehovah's Witnesses to find open, listening minds is extremely difficult—especially when so basic a tenet as the Gentile times chronology is being questioned. For such questioning rocks the very foundations of the Witness doctrinal system and, therefore, often causes Witnesses at all levels to become belligerently defensive. I have repeatedly experienced such reactions ever since 1977 when I first presented the material in this volume to the Governing Body of Jehovah's Witnessess.

The present study began in 1968. At the time, I was a "pioneer" or full-time evangelist for Jehovah's Witnesses. In the course of my ministry, one man with whom I was conducting a Bible study challenged me to prove the date the Watchtower Society had chosen for the desolation of Jerusalem by the Babylonians, that is 607 B.C.E. He pointed out that historians marked that event as having occurred in either 587 or 586 B.C.E. As a result of this challenge, I began periodic research on the matter which continued until the end of 1975, when the growing burden of evidence against the 607 B.C.E. date forced me reluctantly to conclude that the Watchtower Society was wrong. Then, for some time after 1975, the evidence was discussed with some close, research-minded friends. Since none of them could refute the evidence demonstrated by the data that I had collected, I decided to develop a systematically composed treatise on the whole question which I determined to send to the headquarters of the Watchtower Society at Brooklyn, New York. That treatise was prepared and sent to the Governing Body of Jehovah's Witnesses in 1977. The present work is based on that document, although since 1981 I have revised and expanded it somewhat.

In subsequent correspondence with the Governing Body, it became very evident that they too were unable to refute the evidence I had produced. In fact, no such attempt was made until February 28, 1980. In the meantime I was repeatedly cautioned not to reveal my findings to others. For example, in a letter dated January 17, 1978, officials of the Society wrote: "However, no matter how strong the argumentation may be in support of those views, they must, for the present, be regarded as your personal viewpoint. *It is not something that you should talk about or try to advance among other members of the congregation.*" And further, in a letter dated May 15, 1980, they stated: "We are sure you appreciate that *it would not be appropriate for you to begin to state your views and conclusions on chronology that are different than those published by the Society so as to raise serious questions and problems among the brothers.*"

I accepted such advice, as I was given the impression that my spiritual brothers at Watchtower headquarters needed time to re-examine the whole subject thoroughly. In their first reply to my treatise, dated August 19, 1977, they had stated: "We are sorry that the press of work here has not allowed us to give it the attention we would like up to the present time." And in a letter of January 17, 1978, they wrote:

> We have not had the opportunity of examining this material as yet, as other urgent matters are occupying our attention. However, we will look into this material when we have the opportunity.... You can be assured that your views will be examined by responsible brothers....In due course we hope to look into your treatise and evaluate what is contained therein.

Judging from these and similar statements, Watchtower officials at the Brooklyn headquarters seemed prepared to examine the data presented to them honestly and objectively. In a very short time, however, the whole matter took quite a different course.

Early in August, 1978, Albert D. Schroeder, a member of the Governing Body, held a meeting in Europe with representatives from European Watchtower branch offices. At that meeting, he told the audience that there was a campaign going on both inside the movement and from outside to have the Society's 607 B.C.E. - 1914 C.E. chronology overthrown.[2] *The Society, however, had no intention of abandoning it*, he stated.

Three weeks later, on September 2, I was summoned to a hearing before two representatives of the Watchtower Society in Sweden. I was told that they had been commissioned by the Society's branch office to hold such a hearing because "the brothers" at the Brooklyn headquarters were deeply concerned about my treatise. Once again I was cautioned not to spread the information I had gathered. I was also told that the Society did not need or want individual Jehovah's Witnesses to become involved in research of this kind.

Partly as a result of this meeting, I resigned from my position as an elder in the local congregation of Jehovah's Witnesses, explaining why in a lengthy letter to my fellow elders. Soon it became widely known among my Witness brothers in different parts of Sweden that I had rejected the chronology of the Society. In the following months I and others who had questioned the Society's chronology began to be condemned privately as well as from the platforms of kingdom halls (meeting houses) and at Witness assemblies or conventions. We were publicly defamed and characterized in the most negative terms as "rebellious," "presumptuous," "false prophets," "small prophets who work out their own little chronology," and "heretics." We were called "dangerous elements in the congregations," "evil slaves," "blasphemers," as well as "immoral, lawless ones." Privately, some of our Witness brothers, including a number of the Watchtower Society's travelling representatives, also intimated that we were "demon-possessed," that we had "drenched the Society with criticism" and that we "should have been disfellowshipped long ago." These are just a few examples of the widespread defamation which has gone on ever since, although no names, for obvious legal reasons, have ever been mentioned publicly. That such slander was not just a local phenomenon, but had the sanction of the Governing Body of Jehovah's Witnesses, was evident from the fact that similar statements were printed in *The Watchtower* magazine.[3]

In a letter to Albert Schroeder, dated December 6, 1978, I described the new turn of events, calling attention to the sad fact that although my treatise had been composed with the greatest thoughtfulness and sent to the Society in all sincerity, I had become the victim of backbiting, villification and character assassination:

> How tragically, then, to observe how a situation develops, where the attention is drawn away from the question raised—the validity of the 607 B.C.E. date—and directed to the person who raised it, and *he*—not the question—is regarded as the problem! This is really distressing. How is it possible that a situation of this kind develops in our movement?

The answer to this question, which was never given officially by the Society, is to be found in the psychological defense mechanism described by Dr. H. Dale Baumbach: "Insecure individuals, when faced with a problem which highlights their insecurity, instinctively respond by attempting to destroy that which addresses their insecurity or to banish it to the recesses of the mind."[4]

Eventually The Watchtower Bible and Tract Society did attempt to refute the evidence against the 607 B.C.E. date, but this was not done until a special representative of the Governing Body in Sweden had asked the Society in a letter to answer *the content* of the treatise sent to them, telling them that the author was still waiting for a reply. This representative was none other than the co-ordinator of the Society's work in Sweden, Bengt Hansson.

Hansson paid me a visit on December 11, 1979, to discuss the situation that had developed. During our discussion, he was brought to realize that the evidence I had presented to the Society against the 607 B.C.E. date—not me, my motives or attitude—was the real problem. Early in 1980, Hansson therefore wrote a letter to the Governing Body explaining the situation, telling them that I was still waiting for a reply to the evidence I had brought against their chronology. And so, at long last, in a letter dated February 28, 1980, an attempt was made to refute *some* of the arguments.

The "refutation" turned out, however, to be largely a repetition of earlier arguments presented in various places in the Watchtower Society's literature, arguments which had already been demonstrated to be unsatisfactory in the treatise. In a letter dated March 31, 1980, I answered its arguments and added two new lines of evidence against the 607 B.C.E. date. Thus the Society failed to defend its position successfully, and the evidence against it became considerably stronger.

No further attempt to deal with the whole matter was made by the Society until the summer of 1981, when a short discussion of it appeared as an appendix to the book "*Let Your Kingdom Come*" (pp. 186-189). This latest discussion added nothing new to the earlier arguments, and to anyone who has carefully studied the subject of ancient chronology, it appears to be no more than a feeble attempt to save an untenable position by concealing facts. Thus it became evident in final analysis that *the Society will not let facts interfere with fundamental doctrines.*

It may be noted that while the Society's officers feel perfectly free to *publish* any argument in support of their chronology, they have gone to extremes in trying to keep Jehovah's Witnesses at large *in ignorance* of the heavy burden of evidence against it. Thus they have not only repeatedly cautioned me not to share my evidence against the 607 B.C.E. date with others, but they have also supported the widespread defamation of any and all Jehovah's Witnesses who have questioned their chronology. This mode of procedure is not only unfair towards those who have questioned it; it is also most unfair towards Jehovah's Witnesses in general. They should have a right to hear *both* sides of the issue and learn *all* the facts. Thus it is that I have decided to publish *The Gentile Times Reconsidered*.

Interestingly, various arguments have been advanced by representatives of the Watchtower Society to the effect that facts and evidence that go contrary to its teachings should not be made known among Jehovah's Witnesses. One line of reasoning goes as follows: Jehovah reveals the truth gradually through his "faithful and discreet slave" class, whom Christ has appointed "over all his belongings." This "slave" class is represented by the writers of Watchtower literature. We should, therefore, *wait upon Jehovah*—wait, in other words, until the organization publishes "new truths." Anyone who runs ahead of the organization therefore, is *presumptuous*, for he thinks he knows better than "the faithful and discreet slave."

Such an argument, however, is invalid *if the Society's suppositions regarding Bible chronology are wrong*. The notion that it is possible today to identify a class of "faithful and discreet" slaves, whom Christ, as the "master" in the parable at Matthew 24:45-47, has appointed "over all his belongings," rests wholly on the chronological calculation that the "master" arrived in 1914 and made such an appointment a few years later in 1919.[5] If, as will be shown in this work, the Gentile times did not end in 1914, then certainly Christ did not return that year, and Watchtower leaders cannot claim to have been appointed "over all his belongings" in 1919. If this is so, neither can they rightfully claim a monopoly on publishing "the truth."

Also, it should be noted that it is the "master" of the parable who, on his arrival, decides who is "the faithful and discreet slave," *not the slaves themselves*. So, for a group of individuals to claim, before Christ's appointed time, to be "the faithful and discreet slave," elevating themselves over all the master's "belongings," *is grossly presumptuous*. On the other hand, an individual who claims no lofty position can hardly be regarded as presumptuous if he publishes some information that contradicts some of the teachings of the Watchtower Society.

To "wait upon Jehovah," of course, is the duty of every Christian. Unfortunately, the Watchtower Bible and Tract Society, like many other apocalyptic movements, has constantly run ahead of Jehovah and tried to "announce" the fulfillment of his prophecies before his due time. Relying on their chronological calculations, writers of *The Watchtower* magazine have, from its first issues in the late 1870s, run ahead of Jehovah. When they for more than fifty years (1876-1930) taught that Christ had arrived invisibly in 1874, did they wait upon Jehovah? When they taught that the "remnant" of Christ's church would be changed, first in 1878, then in 1881, then in 1914, then in 1915, then in 1918, and then again in 1925, did they wait upon Jehovah? If 1914 is not the terminal date of the "Gentile times" as the Watchtower Society continues to hold, then the numerous "prophetic" applications stemming from it are additional proofs that the Society *still* is not prepared to wait upon Jehovah. It is therefore preposterous for the Society to advise others to "wait upon Jehovah." A person who *really* wants to wait upon Jehovah has to rid himself immediately of all the premature assumptions of Watchtower chronology.

As pointed out above, the conclusions arrived at in this work upset a number of claims to authority and apocalyptic interpretations of the Watchtower Society. Such conclusions, therefore, may cause some unrest among Jehovah's Witnesses, and the leaders of the Society clearly fear that their publication will disrupt the unity of their flock. I am well aware that this publication will be greeted by Watchtower officials as an attempt to destroy faith and to disrupt the unity of the "true Christian congregation." But faith must be in harmony with historical facts. Thus I feel confident that publishing the facts on the subject at hand will not disturb peace and unity among those who are truly Christians. True unity is founded upon *love* among them, for love is the "perfect bond of union." (Col. 3:14)

Unfortunately, there is also a false unity, founded, not upon love, but upon fear. Such "unity" is characteristic of authoritarian organizations, political as well as religious. It is a *mechanical* unity enforced by the leaders of such organizations who want to maintain their authority and keep control over individuals—a unity that need not necessarily depend on truth. In such organizations, individuals surrender their rights and responsibilities to think, speak, and act freely to central authorities. Those who retain the ability or insist on their right to think—to weigh the evidence, to "examine these things" for themselves—are automatically in jeopardy; and this is certainly the case with Jehovah's Witnesses. Yet one can still hope that enough Witnesses have retained their God-given natural abilities to be able to challenge in a significant way the enforced "unity at all costs" of an organization determined to have its membership live a lie.

During the years that have passed since this research started, I have come to know, personally or by letter, a number of Jehovah's Witnesses at different levels of the Watchtower organization who have examined thoroughly the question of chronology and independently arrived at the same conclusions that are presented in this volume. Some of these men tried very hard to defend the Society's chronology before they were forced by biblical and historical evidence to abandon it. Among such were members of the Watchtower research committee appointed to produce the Society's excellent Bible dictionary, *Aid to Bible Understanding*. The section on chronology in this work on pages 322 through 348 is the most able and thorough discussion of Watchtower chronology ever published by that organization. Yet the individual who wrote the article in question ultimately came to realize that the Society's 607 B.C.E. date for the fall of Jerusalem to the Babylonians could not be defended, and later he abandoned it altogether, with all the calculations and teachings founded upon it. In a recent letter to me, he stated:

In developing the subject "Chronology" for *Aid to Bible Understanding*, the Neo-Babylonian period, extending from the reign of Nebuchadnezzar's father Nabopolassar to the reign of Nabonidus and the fall of Babylon, presented a particular problem. As Jehovah's Witnesses, we were obviously interested in finding and presenting some evidence, however small, in support of the year 607 B.C.E. as the date of the destruction of Jerusalem in Nebuchadnezzar's eighteenth year. I was well aware of the fact that historians consistently point to a time some twenty years later and that they place the start of Nebuchadnezzar's reign in 605 B.C.E. (his accession year) rather than 625 B.C.E., the date used in Watchtower publications. I knew that the 607 B.C.E. date was crucial to the Society's interpretation of the "seven times" of Daniel chapter four as pointing to the year 1914 C.E.

A large amount of research went into the effort. At that time (1968), Charles Ploeger, a member of the Watchtower headquarters staff, was assigned as an assistant to me. He spent many weeks searching through the libraries of New York City for any sources of information that might give some validity to the date of 607 B.C.E. as the time of Jerusalem's destruction. We also went to Brown University to interview Dr. A.J. Sachs, a specialist in astronomical texts relating to the Neo-Babylonian and adjoining periods. None of these efforts produced any evidence in support of the 607 B.C.E. date.

In view of this, in writing the article on "Chronology" I devoted a considerable portion of the material to efforts at showing the uncertainties existent in ancient historical sources, including not only Babylonian sources but also Egyptian, Assyrian and Medo-Persian. Though I still believe that a number of the points presented as to such uncertainties are valid, I know that the argumentation was born of a desire to uphold a date for which there was simply no historical evidence. If the historical evidence did, in fact, contradict some clear statement in Scripture I would not hesitate to hold to the Scriptural account as the more reliable. But I realize that the issue is not some contradiction of clear Scriptural statement but contradiction of an *interpretation* placed upon portions of Scripture, giving to them a meaning that is not stated in the Bible itself. The uncertainties that are to be found in such human interpretations are certainly equal to the uncertainties to be found in chronological accounts of ancient history.[6]

In conclusion, I would like to thank the many knowledgeable persons all over the world, many of whom are still active Jehovah's Witnesses, who, by their encouragement, suggestions, and questions have greatly contributed to this treatise. First of all, however, my thanks go to the true God, Jehovah, as this research has been done under constant prayer for his help and understanding. All honor goes to him, since it is his Word of truth that has been the basis of this study. Although certain theories have had to be rejected, his prophetic Word has been confirmed, over and over again, during the biblical and historical research connected with the subject under discussion. This faith-strengthening experience has been a real and lasting blessing to me. I hope that the reader will be blessed in a similar way.

Carl Olof Jonsson
Partille, Sweden
December 1982

CHAPTER I

THE HISTORY OF AN INTERPRETATION

All ideas have a history. Unfortunately, the adherents of a particular one may not be aware of its history. In fact, ignorance of the background, origin, and development of an idea may often tend to strengthen the conviction that it is true, even when it is not. Such ignorance provides fertile soil for fanaticism. It is true that knowledge of the historical development of an idea does not necessarily disprove it, but such knowledge does enable us to improve our judgment as to its veracity. Clearly one example of an idea or interpretation of an idea that is obscured by ignorance is the notion of the "Gentile times" referred to by Christ at Luke 21:24.

THE "YEAR-DAY PRINCIPLE"

The length of the period called "Gentile times" or "The appointed times of the nations," has been calculated to be

2,520 years. This calculation is founded upon the so-called "year-day principle." According to this principle, in biblical time-related prophecies, *a day always stands for a year*, "just as on a map one inch may stand for one hundred miles."[1] In the Bible there are two passages where prophetic periods are explicitly counted that way: Numbers 14:34 (as the spies had spied out the land for forty days, so Israel had to wander in the desert for forty *years*, "a day for a year") and Ezekiel 4:6 (Ezekiel was to lie on his left side for 390 days, and on his right side for 40 days, prophetically carrying the errors of Israel and Judah committed during just as many *years*, "a day for a year.") Note that these interpretations are given to us by the Bible itself.

This way of counting prophetic time was applied by some Jewish rabbis to the "seventy weeks" of Daniel 9:24-27,[2] but it was not stated as *a principle* until the first century C.E., by the famous rabbi, Akibah ben Joseph (c. 50-132 C.E.).[3] And not until the beginning of the ninth century was the year-day principle extended to the longer time periods of Daniel. This was done by a series of Jewish rabbis, beginning with Nahawendi, who considered the 2,300 days of Daniel 8:14 as years, counting from the destruction of Shiloh (942 B.C.E.) to 1358 C.E., the year in which he expected the Messiah would come. Likewise he counted the 1,290 days (Dan. 12:11) as a period of years, beginning with the destruction of the second temple (70 C.E.) and thereby arriving at the same date, 1358 C.E.[4]

Nahawendi was soon followed by others such as Saadia ben Joseph from the same century and Solomon ben Jeroham from the tenth century. The latter counted the 1,335 year-days (Dan. 12:12) from the time of Alexander the Great, which brought him to the year 968 C.E. as a speculative date for the redemption of Israel. The famous rabbi, Rashi (1040-1105), calculated that the 2,300 year-days ended in 1352 C.E. when he thought the Messiah would come. Abraham bar Hiyya Hanasi (c. 1065-1136) speculated that the 2,300-, the 1,290- and the 1,335-year periods would terminate on different dates in the fifteenth century. Many other Jewish scholars, even in the nineteenth century, continued fixing dates for the coming of the Messiah, using the year-day principle.

Joachim of Floris (c. 1130-1202), abbot of the Cistercian monastery in Corace, was probably the first *Christian* expositor to apply the year-day principle to the longer time periods of Daniel and Revelation. This was pointed out during the last century by Charles Maitland in a number of articles. For example, in refuting those holding that the 1,260 days of Revelation 11:3 were 1,260 *years*, he concluded, after a thorough investigation, that "the system of the 1260 years...was never heard of till dreamed into the world by a wild Abbot in 1190."[5] Though many nineteenth-century adherents of the year-day principle tried to refute Maitland's statement regarding the novelty of the principle, all such attempts proved unsuccessful. Thus, even the most learned of his opponents, the Reverend E.B. Elliott, after a very thorough examination of all available sources, had to admit that "for the *first four centuries* the days mentioned in Daniel's and the Apocalyptic prophecies respecting Antichrist were interpreted literally as *days*, not as *years*, by the Fathers of the Christian Church."[6] And although a number of expositors from the fourth century onward suggested a mystical or symbolic meaning for the 1,260 days, they never (before the twelfth century) applied the year-day rule to them, nor to any other time period, except for the 3 ½ days of Revelation 11:8, which a number of expositors—beginning with Victorinus in the fourth century—explained to mean 3 ½ years.[7] This, of course, was far from holding to a year-day *rule* or *principle*. Thus, Elliott, in his discussion of the 1,260 days, had to agree with Maitland that Joachim of Floris was the first Christian writer to apply the year-day principle to this period: "At the close of the 12th century Joachim Abbas, as we have just seen, made a first and rude attempt at it: and in the 14th, the Wycliffite *Walter Brute* followed."[8]

Joachim, who was probably influenced by Jewish rabbis, applied the year-day rule to the 1,260 years from the time of Christ and believed that they would soon end in an "age of the Spirit." Although he did not fix any specific date, it seems that he looked forward to the year 1260 C.E. After his death, that year came "to be considered among his followers as the fatal date that would begin the new age, so much so that when it passed without any notable event some ceased to believe any of his teachings.'"[9] Joachim's works initiated a new tradition of interpretation, a tradition in which the "year-day principle" was the very basis of prophetic interpretations. During the following centuries innumerable dates were fixed for the second advent, most of them built upon the year-day principle. Most of the reformers believed in that principle, and it was largely accepted among Protestant scholars far into the nineteenth century.

THE PRINCIPLE APPLIED TO THE GENTILE TIMES

Revelation 11:2,3 refers to a prophetic period of "forty-two months," or "a thousand two hundred and sixty days," during which "the temple...has been given to the nations, and they will trample the holy city underfoot for forty-two months." (Rev. 11:2, NW) It seemed plausible, therefore, to associate these words with the prophecy of the Gentile times at Luke 21:24, and this was done by some of Joachim's followers. But as Revelation 11:2,3 and 12:6,14 seemed to deal with the Christian church, Jerusalem or the "holy city" usually was interpreted to mean the church of Rome.[10] Some thought that the affliction of the holy city would expire in 1260 C.E.; others believed that this prophecy applied to the literal city of Jerusalem. Arnold of Villanova (c.1235-1313), the well known scholastic physician, identified the Gentile times with the 1,290 days of Daniel 12:11, and counting from the taking away of the Jewish sacrifices after the destruction of Jerusalem by the Romans, he expected the end of the Gentile times in the fourteenth century. The expiration of the Gentile times in the near future was also connected with the Crusades. As

Arnold stated: "Unless the end of the times of the Gentiles is near, how can the 'faithful people' regain the Holy Land from the unbelievers?"[11]

For Walter Brute, one of Wycliffe's followers in England at the end of the fourteenth century, the period of the Gentile times began "soon after the departure of the Apostles."[12] From the destruction of Jerusalem, Brute counted 1290 years:

> Now if any man will behold the Chronicles, he shall find, that after the destruction of *Jerusalem* was accomplished, and after the strong hand of the holy people was fully dispersed, and after the placing of the abomination; that is to say, the Idol of Desolation of *Jerusalem*, within the Holy place, where the Temple of God was before, there had passed 1290 days, taking a day for a year, as commonly it is taken in the Prophets. And the times of the Heathen people are fulfilled, after whose Rites and Customs God suffered the holy City to be trampled under foot for forty and two months.[13]

Since the times of the Gentiles already had expired according to his calculations, Brute thought that the second coming of Christ was imminent.

Time passed and left the many apocalyptic fixed dates behind. It was no longer possible to count the 1,260 or 1,290 years from the destruction of Jerusalem in 70 C.E., or from the death of the apostles. The starting-point had to be moved forward to a later date. Groups persecuted and branded as heretics by the Roman church commonly viewed themselves as "the true church"—pictured in Revelation 12 as a woman who had to flee into "the wilderness" for "a thousand two hundred and sixty days," the period of trampling spiritual Jerusalem. The starting-point was often put somewhere in the fourth century, a view that was very common among the Reformers. John Napier (1550-1617), the distinguished Scottish mathematician and student of prophecy, began the period about 300 or 316 C.E., thus ending it in the latter half of the sixteenth century.[14] The trampling Gentiles soon came to be identified with the papacy of Rome. Later, the starting-point was again moved forward into the sixth or seventh centuries, when the popes had reached a real position of power. George Bell, for example, writing in the London *Evangelical Magazine* of 1796, counted the 1,260 years from 537, or 553 C.E., and predicted the fall of the Antichrist (the Pope) in "1797, or 1813."[15] Of the 1,260 years Bell says:

> The holy city is to be trodden under foot by the Gentiles, or Papists, who, though they are Christians in name, are Gentiles in worship and practice; worshipping angels, saints, and images, and persecuting the followers of Christ. These Gentiles take away the daily sacrifice, and set up the abomination that maketh the visible church of Christ desolate for the space of 1260 years.[16]

This was written in 1795 in the midst of the French Revolution, just shortly before the Pope was taken captive by French troops and forced into exile. Very interestingly, these events in France and Italy had to some extent been predicted nearly a century in advance by several expositors, the best known of whom was the Scottish pastor, Robert Fleming, Jr. (c. 1660-1716).[17] Because of these remarkable predictions, the year 1798 was very soon rather commonly held among biblical commentators to be the terminal date for the 1,260 years. This view—with some differences—was also adopted by Charles Taze Russell and his followers prior to 1930; and it is still prevalent among the Seventh-Day Adventists.

The French Revolution of 1789–1798 and its chaotic aftermath in Europe greatly increased interest in prophetic study, especially as some of these upheavals had been partly predicted by expositors of the prophecies. The Revolution culminated in the violent removal of the French monarchy and the proclamation of the Republic in 1792. New, extremist leaders brought about a period of terror and chaos in France itself and inaugurated an almost unbroken period of wars of conquest, which lasted until 1815, when the Emperor Napoleon was defeated at Waterloo. Historians agree that the French Revolution marked an important turning-point in history. It brought to an end a long era of relative stability in Europe and uprooted the established order, and it deeply changed political and religious thought. As historian R.R. Palmer states on page v of Georges Lefebvre's *The Coming of the French Revolution* (New York: Vintage, 1947):

> Even today in the middle of the twentieth century, despite all that has happened in the lifetime of men not yet old, and even...in America or in any other part of a world in which the countries of Europe no longer enjoy their former commanding position, it is still possible to say that the French Revolution at the end of the eighteenth century was the turning point of modern civilization.

This uprooting of European political and social institutions impelled many to believe that they were living in *the last days*. Men of many backgrounds—ministers, politicians, lawyers, and laymen—became involved in prophetic study. A voluminous body of literature on the prophecies was produced, prophetic periodicals were started, and prophetic conferences were held on both sides of the Atlantic. The religious awakening commenced in England, but soon spread to the European Continent and the United States of America where, in the latter case, it culminated in the well-known Millerite movement. The predictions for the second advent generally pointed to 1843, 1844, or 1847, when the 2,300 year-days of Daniel 8:14 were supposed to end. It was in this feverish atmosphere that a new interpretation of the Gentile times was born, in which the 1,260 years were doubled to 2,520 years.

TABLE 1: APPLICATIONS OF THE 1,260 YEAR-DAYS

EXPOSITOR	*PUBLICATION DATE*	*APPLICATION OF THE 1260 YEARS*	*REMARKS*
Joachim of Floris	1195	A.D. 1 - 1260	

EXPOSITOR	*PUBLICATION DATE*	*APPLICATION OF THE 1260 YEARS*	*REMARKS*
Arnold of Villanova	1300	c. 74 - 1364	Gentile times = 1290 year-days
Walter Brute	1393	134 - 1394	
Martin Luther	1530	38 - 1328	= 1290 years
A. Osiander	1545	412 - 1672	
J. Funck	1558	261 - 1521	
G. Nigrinus	1570	441 - 1701	
Aretius	1573	312 - 1572	
John Napier	1593	316 - 1576	
D. Pareus	1618	606 - 1866	
J. Tilinghast	1655	396 - 1656	
J. Artopaeus	1665	260 - 1520	
Cocceius	1669	292 - 1552	
T. Beverley	1684	437 - 1697	
P. Jurieu	1687	454 - 1714	
R. Fleming, Jun.	1701	606 - 1848 758 - 2000	1260 years = 1242 Julian years
William Whiston	1706	606 - 1866	
Daubuz	1720	476 - 1736	
J. Ph. Petri	1768	587 - 1847	
Lowman	1770	756 - 2016	
John Gill	1776	606 - 1866	
Hans Wood	1787	620 - 1880	
J. Bicheno	1793	529 - 1789	
Fraser	1795	756 - 1998	1242 Jul. years
George Bell	1796	537 - 1797 553 - 1813	
Edward King	1798	538 - 1798	
Galloway	1802	606 - 1849	1242 Jul. years
W. Hales	1803	620 - 1880	
W. Cuninghame	1813	533 - 1792	

G.S. Faber	1814	606 - 1866	
J.H. Frere	1815	533 - 1792	
Lewis Way	1818	531 - 1791	
W.C. Davis	1818	588 - 1848	
J. Bayford	1820	529 - 1789	
John Fry	1822	537 - 1797	
John Aq. Brown	1823	622 - 1844	1260 *lunar* years

JOHN AQUILA BROWN

The first expositor known to have arrived at a period of 2,520 years was John Aquila Brown in 1823. He did not associate this period with the Gentile times of Luke 21:24, however; to him the Gentile times were a period of 1,260 *lunar* years, corresponding to 1,242 *Julian* years (see Table 1). Although no biographical data on Brown has been found, he strongly influenced the apocalyptic thinking of his time. Not only was he the originator of the 2,520 year calculation, but he was also the first to apply the 2,300 year-days of Daniel 8:14 from 457 B.C.E. to 1843 C.E. Brown first published his chronology in an article in the London monthly *The Christian Observer* of November 1810. The 1843 date for the end of the 2,300 years was to become the focal point of prophetic interest both in England and the U.S.A., although some commentators ended them in 1844 (as did Brown himself later) or in 1847. The 1843 date was unanimously accepted by all of Miller's followers in the United States.[18]

Brown's calculation that the "seven times" of Daniel 4, were a period of 2,520 years was first published in 1823 in his two-volume work *The Even-Tide: or, Last Triumph of the Blessed and Only Potentate, the King of Kings, and*

Lord of Lords: Being a Development of the Mysteries of Daniel and St. John, and of the Prophecies respecting the Renovated Kingdom of Israel, etc. He specifically states that he was the first to write on the subject.

> Although many large and learned volumes have been written on prophetical subjects during a succession of ages; yet, having never seen the subject, on which I am about to offer some remarks, touched upon by any author, I commend it to the attention of the reader, not doubtingly, indeed, but with strong confidence that it will be found still further to corroborate the scale of the prophetical periods, assumed as the basis of the fulfillment of prophecy.[19]

Brown's exposition of the "seven times" is based on Daniel 4. Nowhere does he refer to the "seven times" of prophetic punishment directed against Israel at Leviticus 26:12-28, as did other expositors after him. "Nebuchadnezzar was a type," Brown says, "of the kings of the tyrannical earth, and his kingdom of the three successive kingdoms which were to arise." The "seven times," or years, of Nebuchadnezzar's affliction, "would, therefore, be considered as a grand week of years, forming a period of two thousand five hundred and twenty years, embracing the duration of the four tyrannical monarchies; at the close of which they are to learn, like Nebuchadnezzar, that '*the Most High ruleth in the kingdom of men, and giveth it to whomsoever he will.*'" Brown calculates the 2,520 years from the beginning of the reign of Nebuchadnezzar (604 B.C.E.) to 1917 C.E., when "the *full glory* of the kingdom of Israel shall be perfected."[20]

The 2,520 years were soon identified by other expositors with the "Gentile times" of Luke 21:24. At the *Albury Park Prophetic Conferences*, held at Albury, south of London, England from 1826 onward, the times of the Gentiles was one of the topics discussed. Even at the first meeting they were connected with the 2,520 year period.[21] Many biblical commentators dated the "seven times of the Gentiles'' from the captivity of Manasseh, in 677 B.C.E., as did John Fry (1775-1849) in his *Unfulfilled Prophecies of Scripture*, published in 1835. This was obviously done to make them end at the same time as the 2,300 years, that is in 1843 or 1844. In the same year, 1835, William W. Pym published his work, *A Word of Warning in the Last Days*, in which he ended the ''seven times'' in 1847. Interestingly, he builds his calculation of the 2,520 years of Gentile times on the ''seven times'' mentioned in Leviticus 26 as well as the ''seven times'' of Daniel 4: ''In other words, the judgments threatened by Moses, which should last during the seven times, or 2,520 years; and the judgments revealed to Daniel, which should come to an end by the cleansing of the sanctuary after a portion of the greater number 2520.''[22]

Others, who looked forward to the year 1836 C.E., a year fixed by the German theologian J.A. Bengel (1687-1752), tried to end the ''seven times'' in the same year. So did W.A. Holmes, chancellor of Cashel, in his book *The Time of the End* which was published in 1833. He dated the captivity of Manasseh under Esarhaddon to 685 B.C.E., and counting the 2,520 years from that year, he ended the ''seven times'' in 1835-1836.

Edward Bickersteth (1786-1850), evangelical rector of Watton, Hartfordshire, tried different starting-points for the seven times of the Gentiles:

> If we reckon the captivity of Israel as commencing in 727 before Christ, Israel's first captivity under Salmanezer, it would terminate in 1793, when the French revolution broke out: and if 677 before Christ, their captivity under Esarhaddon (the same period when Manasseh, king of Judah, was carried into captivity, 2 Kings xvii. 23,24. 2 Chron. xxxiii. 11,) it would terminate in 1843: or, if reckoned from 602 before Christ, which was the final dethronement of Jehoiakim by Nebuchadnezzar, it would terminate in 1918. All these periods may have a reference to corresponding events at their termination, and are worthy of serious attention.[23]

THE GENTILE TIMES IN THE MILLERITE MOVEMENT

The leading British works on prophecy were extensively reprinted in the United States and strongly influenced the many American writers on the subject, including William Miller and his associates. Most, if not every position they held on the different prophecies was previously taught by other past or contemporary expositors. On the "Gentile times" Miller just followed others, ending the 2,520 years in 1843. At the First General Conference held in Boston on October 14 and 15, 1840, one of Miller's addresses dealt with Bible chronology. The "seven times," or 2,520 years, he placed from 677 B.C.E. to 1843 B.C.E.[24] Some years later, writing on page 11 in *Wm. Miller's Apology and Defence* (1845), he says: "From a further study of the Scriptures, I concluded that the seven Times of Gentile supremacy must commence when the Jews ceased to be an independent nation, at the captivity of Manasseh, which the best chronologers assigned to B.C. 677...."

Other Millerites that stressed the 2,520 years included Richard Hutchinson (editor of *The Voice of Elijah*) in an 1843 pamphlet, *The Throne of Judah Perpetuated in Christ*, and Philemon R. Russell (editor of the *Christian Herald and Journal*) in the March 19, 1840 issue of that periodical. The 2,520 years also appear on charts used by Millerite evangelists.[25]

NELSON H. BARBOUR

After the "Great Disappointment" of 1844, the Millerite movement broke into several Adventist groups. The parent movement, the "Evangelical Adventists," was gradually decimated by divisions. Some held that the time was right, but the event anticipated was wrong. They had expected "the wrong thing at the right time." This position was taken by another group which later came to be known as the Seventh-Day Adventists. Others, and among them Miller himself, openly confessed that the time was a mistake.[26] Many began to set new dates: 1845, 1846, 1847, 1853, 1854, 1866, 1867, 1868, 1873, etc.; and the Adventist movement became even more divided when different ones accepted different dates or no specific apocalyptic date at all. George Storrs, who had been one of the leaders in the last stages of the Millerite movement, started a group in 1863, called "The Life and Advent Union." One of the other leaders, Jonathan Cummings, declared in 1852 that he had received a "new light" on the chronology, and that the second advent was to be expected in the autumn of 1853 or the spring of 1854. Many Millerites joined Cummings, who edited the *World's Crisis.* They formed a new denomination, "The Advent Christian Association" (later "The Advent Christian Church"), today the most important Adventist denomination aside from the Seventh-Day Adventists.[27]

One of Miller's associates, Nelson H. Barbour, "lost his religion" completely after the "Great Disappointment" in 1844 and went to Australia where he became a miner during the gold rush there.[28] In 1859 he returned to America by way of London, England. "To while away the monotony of a long sea voyage, the English chaplain proposed a systematic reading of the prophecies; to which the brother readily assented."[29] During this reading Barbour thought he discovered the error in Miller's reckoning: Why did Miller start the 1,290 and 1,335 year-days of Daniel thirty years earlier than the 1,260? Should not all three periods start at the same date? Then the 1,290 years would end in 1828 and the 1,335 years in 1873! "On arriving in London (in 1860) he went to the library of the British Museum, and among many other extensive works on the prophecies found Elliott's *Horae Apocalypticae*, which at that time, 1860, was a standard work advocating 1866 as the time of the coming of the Lord."[30] In this work Elliott reproduced a table, "The Scripture Chronology of the World," as prepared by the Reverend Christopher Bowen, showing that 5,979 years since man's creation ended in 1851.[31] In adding up the remaining years, Barbour discovered that 6,000 years would terminate in 1873. This he saw as a remarkable confirmation of his own calculation of the 1,335-year period.

On returning to the United States, Barbour tried to interest others in his new date for the coming of the Lord. From 1868 onward he began to preach and publish his findings. In 1870 he published the pamphlet *Evidences for the Coming of the Lord in 1873: or the Midnight Cry*, the second edition of which has been quoted above.[32] He also published a series of articles on the chronology in the *World's Crisis*, at that time edited by Miles Grant. In 1873 he started a monthly of his own called *The Midnight Cry*, "the circulation of which soon ran up to 15,000 copies a month." This paper announced that "the Bridegroom was due in 1874."[33] But when that year came and went, Barbour and his followers experienced great concern:

> When 1874 came and there was no outward sign of Jesus in the literal clouds and in a fleshly form, there was a general re-examination of all the arguments upon which the "Midnight Cry" was made. And when no fault or flaw could be found, it led to the critical examination of the Scriptures which seem to bear on the *manner* of Christ's coming, and it was soon discovered that the expectation of Jesus in the *flesh* at the second coming was a mistake....[34]

One of the readers of the *Midnight Cry*, B.W. Keith (later one of the contributors to *Zion's Watch Tower*), "had been reading carefully Matt xxiv chapter, using the 'Emphatic Diaglott', a new and very exact word for word translation of the New Testament; when he came to the 37th and 39th verses he was much surprised to find that it read as follows, viz,: 'For as the days of Noah thus will be the *presence* of the son of man.' " He found this Greek word *parousia*, usually translated "coming," translated as "presence." Here was a possibility to save the date, 1874, and from then on Barbour and his associates taught that Christ really arrived in 1874, and since then had been "invisibly present": "It was evident, then, that though the *manner* in which they had expected Jesus was in error, yet the time, as indicated by the 'Midnight Cry', was correct, and that the Bridegroom *came* in the Autumn of 1874...."[35] "The wrong thing at the right time" once again, they held.

But most readers of the *Midnight Cry* could not accept this explanation, and the 15,000 readers "dwindled to about 200." Barbour himself was convinced that the Millennial morning had begun to dawn, and therefore he thought that the *Midnight Cry* no longer was a suitable name for his paper. He remarked: "Will some one inform me how a 'Midnight Cry' can be made in the *morning*?"[36] The paper, which had ceased publication in October 1874, was therefore restarted in June 1875 as the *Herald of the Morning*, a name which would better correspond to the ideas which Barbour held at that time. In one of the very first issues (September, 1875), he published his calculation of the Gentiles times, making them terminate in 1914 C.E.[37]

CHARLES TAZE RUSSELL

Charles Taze Russell, together with his father and a few other Bible students in Allegheny, Pennsylvania, formed a class for Bible study in 1870. This group had close contacts with certain Adventists, including a group under the leadership of Jonas Wendell in Allegheny and George Storrs' congregation in New York. Although Russell knew that some Adventists, including Jonas Wendell, expected Christ in 1873 or 1874, he rejected all time settings until 1876: "It was about January, 1876, that my attention was specifically drawn to the subject of prophetic times as it relates to these doctrines and hopes. It came about this way: I received a paper called *The Herald of the Morning*, sent by its editor, Mr. N.H. Barbour." Russell was surprised to find that Barbour's group had come to the same conclusion as his own group about the *manner* of Christ's return—that it would be "thieflike, and not in flesh, but as a spirit-being, invisible to men...."[38] Russell at once wrote to Barbour about the chronology, and later in 1876 he arranged for a meeting with him at Philadelphia where Russell had business engagements during the summer. Russell wanted Barbour to show him, "if he could, that the prophecies indicated 1874 as the date at which the Lord's *presence* and the 'harvest' began. He came," said Russell, "and the evidence satisfied me."[39]

It is apparent that during these meetings Russell accepted *all* of Barbour's time calculations, including his calculation of the Gentile times.[40] While still in Philadelphia, Russell wrote an article entitled "Gentile Times: When do They End?" which was published in George Storrs' periodical the *Bible Examiner* in the October 1876 issue. Referring to the "seven times" of Leviticus 26:27,33 and Daniel 4 on page 27 of the *Examiner*, he determines the length of the Gentile times to be 2,520 years which began in 606 B.C.E. and would end in 1914 C.E.: "when Jerusalem shall be delivered forever, and the Jew say to the Deliverer, 'Lo, this is our God, we have waited for Him and He will save us.' "

What, exactly, was expected to occur in 1914? In the book *The Time Is At Hand*, published in 1889 (later referred to as Vol. II of *Studies in the Scriptures*), pages 76-78, Russell's expectations are enumerated in seven points:

> Firstly, That at that date the Kingdom of God ... will obtain full, universal control, and that it will then be 'set up', or firmly established, in the earth, on the ruins of present institutions.
>
> Secondly, It will prove that he whose right it is thus to take the dominion will then be present as earth's new Ruler....
>
> Thirdly, It will prove that some time before the end of A.D. 1914 the last member of the divinely recognized Church of Christ, the "royal priesthood", "the body of Christ", will be glorified with the Head....
>
> Fourthly, It will prove that from that time forward Jerusalem shall no longer be trodden down of the Gentiles, but shall arise from the dust of divine disfavor, to honor....
>
> Fifthly, It will prove that by that date, or sooner, Israel's blindness will begin to be turned away; because their "blindness in

part" was to continue "*until* the fulness of the Gentiles be come in" (Rom. 11:25)....

Sixthly, It will prove that the great "time of trouble such as never was since there was a nation", will reach its culmination in a world-wide reign of anarchy ... and the "new heavens and the new earth" with their peaceful blessings will begin to be recognized by the trouble-tossed humanity....

Seventhly, It will prove that *before that date* God's Kingdom, organized in power, will be in the earth and then smite and crush the Gentile image (Dan. 2:34)—and fully consume the power of these kings.

These were indeed very daring predictions. Did Russell really believe that all these remarkable things would come true within the next twenty five years? Yes, he did; in fact, he believed his chronology to be *God's* chronology, not just his own. In 1894 he wrote of the 1914 date: "We see no reason for changing the figures—nor could we change them if we would. They are, we believe, God's dates, not ours. But bear in mind that the end of 1914 is not the date for the *beginning*, but for the *end* of the time of trouble."[41] Thus it was thought that "The time of trouble" was to commence some years *before* 1914, "not later than 1910," reaching its climax in 1914.[42]

But in 1904, just ten years before 1914, Russell changed his view on this matter. In an article in the July 1, 1904 issue of *Zion's Watch Tower*, entitled "Universal anarchy—just before or after October, 1914 A.D.," he argued that the time of trouble would begin *after* October, 1914:

> We now expect that the anarchistic culmination of the great time of trouble which will preceed the Millennial blessings will be after October, 1914 A.D.—very speedily thereafter, in our opinion—"in one hour," "suddenly," because "our forty years" harvest, ending October, 1914 A.D., should not be expected to include the awful period of anarchy which the Scriptures point out to be the fate of Christendom.[43]

This change caused some readers to think that there might be other errors in the chronological system, too—one reader even suggesting that Bishop Usher's chronology might be more correct when it dated the destruction of Jerusalem as having happened in 587 B.C.E. rather that in 606 B.C.E. This would end the 2,520 years in 1933 instead of 1914. But Russell strongly reaffirmed his belief in the 1914 date, referring to the other time parallels pointing to it: "We know of no reason for changing a figure: to do so would spoil the harmonies and parallels so conspicuous between the Jewish and Gospel ages."[44] And answering another reader he said, "The harmony of the prophetic periods is one of the strongest proofs of the correctness of our Bible chronology. They fit together like the cog-wheels of a perfect machine. To change the chronology *even one year would destroy all this harmony,*—so accurately are the various proofs drawn together in the *parallels* between the Jewish and Gospel ages."[45] (Italics mine) These arguments were further backed up by articles written by the Edgar brothers of Scotland.[46] So in 1904 Russell was still as convinced of his dates as he was in 1889, when he wrote that the understanding of these time features was the *"sealing of the foreheads"* mentioned at Revelation 7:3.[47]

As the 1914 date drew nearer, however, Russell became more and more cautious in his statements. Answering an inquiring Bible student in 1907, he said that "we have never claimed that they were *knowledge,* nor based upon indisputable evidence, facts, knowledge; our claim has always been that they are based on *faith.*"[48] The dates no longer seemed to be "God's dates,"as he had stated thirteen years earlier; they might be fallible. Russell even considered the possibility that 1914 (and 1915) could pass by with none of the expected events having occurred:

> But let us suppose a case far from our expectations: suppose that A.D. 1915 should pass with the world's affairs all serene and with evidence that the "very elect" had not all been "changed" and without the restoration of natural Israel to favor under the New Covenant. (Rom. 11:12,15) What then? Would not that prove our chronology wrong? Yes, surely! And would not that prove a keen disappointment? Indeed it would! ... What a blow that would be! One of the strings of our "harp" would be quite

broken! However, dear friends, our harp would still have all the other strings in tune and that is what no other aggregation of God's people on earth could boast.[49]

Another point of uncertainty was whether a year 0 (between 1 B.C.E. and 1 C.E.) was to be included in the calculation or not. This matter had been brought up by Russell as early as 1904, but gained in importance as the year 1914 approached. The 1914 date had been arrived at simply by subtracting 606 from 2,520, but gradually it was realized that no year 0 is allowed for in our present calendar. Consequently, from October 1, 606 B.C.E. to January, 1 C.E. was only 605 years and 3 months, and from January, 1 C.E. to October 1914 only 1913 years and 9 months, making a total of 2,519 years instead of 2,520. Thus this would cause the 2,520 years to end in October 1915, rather than October 1914.[50]

The cautiousness regarding the year 1914 increased in 1913. In the article "Let Your Moderation Be Known," which appeared in the June 1, 1913 issue of *The Watch Tower*, Russell warned his readers against spending "valuable time and energy in guessing what will take place this year, next year, etc." His confidence in his earlier published scheme of events was gone: "This is the good tidings of God's grace in Christ—whether the completion of the church shall be accomplished before 1914 or not."[51] He expressed himself still more vaguely in the October 15 issue of the same year:

> We are waiting for the time to come when the government of the world will be turned over to Messiah. We cannot say that it may not be either October 1914 or October 1915. It is possible that *we might be out of the correct reckoning on the subject a number of years*. We cannot say with certainty. We do not know. It is a matter of faith, and not of knowledge.[52]

Earlier, 1914 had been one of "God's dates," and "to change the chronology even one year would destroy all this harmony." But now they "might be out of the correct reckoning on the subject a number of years," and nothing on the matter could be said "with certainty." This really was a *volte-face*!

Russell's tottering faith in his chronology was further brought to light in *The Watch Tower* of January 1, 1914: "As already pointed out, we are by no means confident that this year, 1914, will witness as radical and swift changes of dispensation as we have expected."[53] The article "The Days Are at Hand" in the same issue is especially disclosing:

> If later it should be demonstrated that the church is not glorified by October, 1914, we shall try to feel content with whatever the Lord's will may be.... If 1915 should go by without the passage of the church, without the time of trouble, etc., it would seem to some to be a great calamity. It would not be so with ourself.... If in the Lord's providence *the time should come twenty-five years later*, then that would be our will.... If October, 1915, should pass, and we should find ourselves still here and matters going on very much as they are at present, and the world apparently making progress in the way of settling disputes, and there were no time of trouble in sight, and the nominal church were not yet federated, etc., we would say that evidently we have been out somewhere in our reckoning. In that event we would look over the prophecies further, to see if we could find an error. And then we would think, *Have we been expecting the wrong thing at the right time*? The Lord's will might permit this.[54]

Again, in the May 1, 1914 issue, Russell, forgetting his earlier statements, told his readers that "in these columns and in the six volumes of STUDIES IN THE SCRIPTURES we have set forth everything appertaining to the times and seasons *in a tentative form*; that is to say, not with positiveness, not with the claim that we knew, but with the suggestion that 'thus and so' seems to be the teaching of the Bible."[55]

Two months later Russell seemed to be on the point of rejecting his chronology altogether. Answering a colporteur, who wanted to know if the STUDIES IN THE SCRIPTURES were to be circulated after October, 1914, "since you have some doubts respecting the full accomplishment of all expected by or before October, 1914,"

Russell said:

> It is our thought that these books will be on sale and read for years in the future, provided the Gospel age and its work continue.... We have not attempted to say that these views are infallible, but have stated the processes of reasoning and figuring, leaving to each reader the duty and privilege of reading, thinking, and figuring for himself. *That will be an interesting matter a hundred years from now*; and if he can figure and reason better, he will still be interested in what we have presented.[56]

Thus Russell now seemed ready to accept the thought that the 1914 date probably was a failure, and that his writings on the matter were going to be merely of historical interest to Bible students a hundred years later!

But then the First World War broke out, and Russell's wavering confidence in the chronology began to recover. Although the war itself did not exactly fit into the predicted pattern of events—that the time of trouble would be a class struggle between capital and labor, leading up to a period of worldwide anarchy—he saw in the World War the prelude to that situation: "Socialism is, we believe, the main factor in the war now raging and which will be earth's greatest and most terrible war—and probably the last."[57] And later in 1914, he wrote:

> We think that the present distress amongst the nations is merely the beginning of this time of trouble....The anarchy that will follow this war will be the real time of trouble....Our thought is that the war will so weaken the nations that following it there will be an attempt to bring in Socialistic ideas, and that this will be met by the governments—etc., leading up to worldwide class struggle and anarchy.[58]

Further, although the *city* of Jerusalem was still trodden down by the Gentiles, Russell argued that the Gentile times had ended:

> The treading down of the Jews has stopped. All over the world the Jews are free—even in Russia. On September 5, the Czar of Russia issued a proclamation to all the Jews of the Russian Em-

pire; and this was before the times of the Gentiles had expired. It stated that the Jews might have access to the highest ranks in the Russian army, and that the Jewish religion was to have the same freedom as any other religion in Russia. Where are the Jews being trodden down now? Where are they being subjected to scorn? At present they are receiving no persecution whatever. We believe that the treading down of Jerusalem has ceased, because the time for the Gentiles to tread down Israel has ended.[59]

Although Russell partly foresaw the Socialist revolution in Russia in 1917 and the Jews' return to Palestine, he did not, of course, foresee the coming persecutions of the Jews in Germany, Poland, and other countries during the Second World War.

From the outbreak of the First World War and up to his death on October 31, 1916, Russell's restored confidence in his chronology remained unshaken, as demonstrated by the following extracts from various issues of *The Watch Tower* during the period:

January 1, 1915: ... the war is one predicted in the Scriptures as associated with the great day of Almighty God—'the day of vengeance of our God.'[60]

September 15, 1915: Tracing the Scriptural chronology down to our day, we find that we are now living in the very dawn of the great seventh day of man's great week. This is abundantly corroborated by the events now taking place about us on every hand.[61]

February 15, 1916: In STUDIES IN THE SCRIPTURES, Vol. IV, we have clearly pointed out the things now transpiring, and the worse conditions yet to come.[62]

April 15, 1916: We believe that the dates have proven to be quite right. We believe that Gentile Times have ended, and that God is now allowing the Gentile Governments to destroy themselves, in order to prepare the way for Messiah's kingdom.[63]

September 1, 1916: It still seems clear to us that the prophetic period known as the Times of the Gentiles ended chronologically in October, 1914. The fact that the great day of wrath upon the

> nations began there marks a good fulfillment of our expectations.[64]

But in 1918 the First World War ended without being followed by a worldwide Socialist revolution and anarchy. The last member of the Church of Christ had not been glorified, the city of Jerusalem was still trodden down by the Gentiles, the Kingdom of God had not crushed "the Gentile image," and the "new heavens and the new earth" could not be seen anywhere by trouble-tossed humanity. Not one of the seven predictions enumerated in the book *The Time Is at Hand* had come true.[65]

Yet, something *had* happened: The World War. So it was felt that the time was right, and once again it could be maintained that Russell's followers—like the Adventists and Millerites before them—had expected "the wrong thing at the right time."[66] But how could the time be right, when all predictions had failed? For years many of Russell's followers experienced deep perplexity because of the non-arrival of the predicted events. After the lapse of some years, J.F. Rutherford, Russell's successor as president of the Watch Tower Society, began, step by step, to explain what "really" had been fulfilled from 1914 onward.

In the address "The Kingdom of Heaven is at Hand" at the Cedar Point Convention, September 5-13, 1922, Rutherford told his audience that the Kingdom of God *really had been established in 1914*, not on earth but *in the invisible heavens*![67] And three years later, in 1925, he applied Revelation 12 to this event, stating that God's Kingdom was *born in heaven* according to this prophecy.[68] Also at the Cedar Point Convention in 1922, Rutherford for the first time presented his view that "in 1918, or thereabouts, the Lord came to his (spiritual) temple."[69] Earlier, Russell and his associates had held the view that the heavenly resurrection took place in 1878. But in 1927 Rutherford transferred that event to 1918.[70] Likewise in the early 1930s, Rutherford changed the date for the beginning of *Christ's invisible presence* from 1874 to 1914.[71] Thus Rutherford gradually replaced the unfulfilled predictions with *a series of invisible and spiritual events* associated with the years 1914 and 1918. Sixty-three years after 1914 Rutherford's "explanations" are still held by Jehovah's Witnesses.

SUMMARY

The interpretation of the "Gentile times" as having been of 2,520 years, beginning in 607 B.C.E. (earlier, 606 B.C.E.) and ending in 1914 C.E., was not miraculously revealed to Pastor Charles T. Russell in the autumn of 1876. On the contrary, this idea had a long history of development, with its roots far back in the past. It had its origin in the "year-day principle," first posited by Rabbi Akibah ben Joseph in the first century C.E. From the ninth century onward this principle was applied to the time periods of Daniel by several Jewish rabbis. Among Christians, Joachim of Floris in the twelfth century probably was the first to pick up the idea, applying it to the 1,260 days of Daniel and Revelation. After Joachim's death, his followers soon identified the 1,260 year period with the Gentile times of Luke 21:24, and this interpretation was then common among groups branded as heretics by the church of Rome during the following centuries, including the Reformers. As time passed, and expectations failed when earlier explanations proved to be wrong, the starting-point of the 1,260 (or 1,290) years was moved forward, in order to make them end in a then near future.

The first to arrive at the period of 2,520 years was apparently John Aquila Brown in 1823. Although his calculation was founded upon the "seven times" of Daniel 4, he did not equate those periods with the "Gentiles times" of Luke 21:24. But this was very soon done by other expositors. Fixing the starting-point at 604 B.C.E., Brown reached the year 1917 as the seven times' termination date. By using different starting-points, other biblical commentators in the following decades arrived at a number of different terminal dates. Some writers, who experimented with biblical "Jubilee cycles," arrived at a period of 2,450 (or 2,452) years ($49 \times 49 + 49$), which they held to be the period of the Gentile times. The accompanying table presents a selection of applications of the 2,520 (and 2,450) years made by different authors during the last century. As is seen from that table, some of them came very close to the 1914 date which was first published by Nelson H. Barbour in 1875. This date would most probably have drowned in the sea of other failed dates and been forgotten by now had it not happened to fall close to the outbreak of the First World War. Barbour's calculation was accepted by C.T. Russell at their meeting in 1876. Barbour was then fifty-two years old while Russell was twenty-four—still very young. Although their ways parted again in the spring of 1879, Russell stuck to Barbour's time calculations, and since that time the 1914 date has been the pivotal point in prophetic explanations among Russell's followers.

TABLE 2: Applications of the 2,520 (or 2,450 years)

Expositor	Publication	Date	Applications of the 2,520 (or 2,450) yrs.	Comments
John Aq. Brown	The Even-Tide . . .	London 1823	B.C. 604-1917 A.D.	= "seven times" of Dan. 4
Wm. Cuninghame	Dialogues on prophecy, Vol. I	London 1827	728-1792	= report from the prophetic
H. Drummond	"	1827	722-1798	conference at Albury Park 1826-1830
G.S. Faber	The Sacred Calendar of Prophecy	London 1828	657-1864	
Alfred Addis	Heaven Opened	1829	680-1840	
William Digby	A Treatise on the 1260 Days	1831	723-1793	
W.A. Holmes	The Time of the End	1833	685-1835	
M. Habershon	A Dissertation . . .	1834	677-1843	
John Fry	Unfulfilled Prophecies . . .	1835	677-1843	
William W. Pym	A Word of Warning . . .	1835	673-1847	
William Miller	The First Report of the General Conference	1842	677-1843	
Th. R. Birks	First Elements of Sacred Prophecy	1843	606-1843	Gentile times = 2,450 years
Wm. Cuninghame	The Fulfilling	London 1847	606-1847	Gentile times = 2,452 years (a change in his position 1827)
J.H. Frere	The Great Continental Revolution	London 1848	603-1847	Gentile times = 2,450 years
E. Bickersteth	A Scripture Help	London 1850	727-1793	another of his calculations
"	"	London 1850	602-1918	was 677-1843
E.B. Elliott	Horae Apocalypticae, Vol. IV	London 1851	727-1793	

- - -	The Watch Tower	London 1856	727-1793	a periodical
R.C. Shimeall	Our Bible Chronology,	N.Y. 1859	652-1868	
J.S. Phillips	The Rainbow, March 1,	London 1865	652-1867	a periodical published by
"J.M.N."	" April 1,	London 1865	658-647-1862-1873	William Leask, edited later
W. Farrar	" Nov. 1,	London 1865	654-1866	by J. B. Rotherham
Joseph Baylee	The Times of the Gentiles	1871	623-1896	
"P.H.G."	The Quarterly Journal of Prophecy, April,	London 1871	652-649-1868-1871	a periodical edited by Horatius Bonar
Edward White	Our Hope, June,	London 1874	626-1894	a periodical edited by William Maude. White's article was a reprint from 1866
N.H. BARBOUR	HERALD OF THE MORNING, Sept., Oct.,	N.Y. 1875	606-1914	periodical published by Nelson H. Barbour
C.T. RUSSELL	THE BIBLE EXAMINER, October,	N.Y. 1876	606-1914	published by George Storrs
E.H. Tuckett	The Rainbow, Aug.	London 1877	651/650-1869/1870	
M.P. Baxter	Forty Coming Wonders	London 1880	620-1900	= 5th edition (1st, 1866)
H.G. Guinness	Light for the Last Days	London 1886	606-1915	These are only
	"	1886	604-1917	some of his many,
	"	1886	598-1923	diverse analyses
	"	1886	587-1934	
W.E. Blackstone	The Weekly Evangel, May 13	1916	606-1915	This article sums up his
	"	1916	595-1926	viewpoint as published
	"	1916	587-1934	many years earlier

CHAPTER II

THE CHRONOLOGY OF THE NEO-BABYLONIAN PERIOD

The validity of the 1914 date is intimately connected with the length of the Neo-Babylonian period. This period ended when Babylon was captured by Cyrus in 539 B.C.E., a year which has been firmly established by modern astronomers.[1] In the first year of his reign over Babylon, Cyrus issued an edict which permitted the Jews to return to Jerusalem. According to the Watchtower Society this ended the seventy-year period mentioned at Jeremiah 25:11; 29:10; Daniel 9:2, and 2 Chronicles 36:21. If the Jewish remnant returned to Jerusalem in 537 B.C.E., as has been calculated,[2] this period would have begun seventy years earlier, or in 607 B.C.E. As the Watchtower Society holds this seventy-year period to be a period of *complete desolation* of Judah and Jerusalem, we are told that it was in the year 607 B.C.E. that Nebuchadnezzar destroyed Jerusalem, in his eighteenth regnal year. (Jer. 52:12; 2 Kings 25:8; Jer. 52:29) This event, it is assumed, started the 2,520 years, called the Gentile times. But this starting-point is incompatible with a number of historical facts.

ANCIENT HISTORIANS

Up to the latter part of the nineteenth century the length of the Neo-Babylonian period had to be determined solely by consulting ancient Greek and Roman historians. Those historians lived hundreds of years after the Neo-Babylonian period, and unfortunately their statements are often contradictory. The two held to be most reliable are Berossus and Claudius Ptolemy.

Berossus was a Babylonian priest who lived in the third century B.C.E. In about 281 B.C.E. he wrote a history of Babylonia known as *Babyloniaca* or *Chaldaica* which he dedicated to King Antiochus I. Later he abandoned Babylon and settled on the Ptolemaic island of Cos.[3] Unfortunately, his writings have been lost, and all that is known about them comes from the twenty-two quotations or paraphrases of his work by other ancient writers and eleven statements about Berossus made by classical, Jewish, and Christian writers.[4] The longest quotations deal with the reigns of the Neo-Babylonian kings and are found in the Chronicle of Eusebius (c. 303 C.E.),[5] Flavius Josephus' *Against Apion, Antiquities of the Jews*[6] and other late works. It is known that Eusebius and Josephus both quoted Berossus indirectly via the Greco-Roman scholar Cornelius Alexander Polyhistor (first century B.C.E.).

Where did Berossus get his information on the Neo-Babylonian kings? According to his own words he "translated many books which had been preserved with great care at Babylon and which dealt with a period of more than 150,000 years."[7] These "books" included accounts of the legendary kings before the Flood with their very exaggerated lengths of reign. But it has also been established that he used the very reliable Babylonian chronicles, for example, for the Neo-Babylonian period, and "that he reliably reported their contents in Greek."[8]

Claudius Ptolemy (70-161 C.E.) was a distinguished scholar, astronomer, geographer, historian and chronologist who lived in Egypt during the reigns of Hadrian and Antoninus Pius. In about 142 C.E. he wrote his *Hē Mathematikē Syntaxis*, better known as the *Almagest* (the Latin title), to which he added his famous *canon*, a list of kings and their lengths of reign beginning with the reign of Nabonassar in Babylon, 747 B.C.E., through the Babylonian, Persian, Greek (Ptolemaic), and Roman rulers to his contemporary, Antoninus Pius (C.E. 138-161).[9]

Where did Ptolemy get his king list? The book *Aid to Bible Understanding* states that "Ptolemy is thought to have used the writings of Berossus."[10] This, though, is not very likely. On the contrary, scholars have concluded that Ptolemy's canon "represents a Babylonian tradition about the first millennium B.C. that is *independent of Berossus* as can be seen from the order and forms of the names of the kings."[11] F. Schmidtke explains:

> With respect to the dependence of the sources, the Canon of Ptol. has certainly to a great extent taken its stuff from the Bab. Chron. This is clear from the characteristic *abasileuta ete* [years of interregnum] 688-681, which is also found in the Chronicle (IV,23), while the King List A at this place introduces Sennacherib instead, as well as for the two *abasileuta ete* 704-703. The Canon of Ptol. like the Chronicle reproduces here the Babylonian tradition, which did not recognize Sennacherib as the legitimate king, as he had sacked and destroyed Babylon.[12]

There is also some evidence that Ptolemy used Babylonian king lists. Thus he had access to Babylonian chronicles and king lists, probably through intermediary sources, but *evidently independent of Berossus!* This is a very important conclusion, as Ptolemy's figures for the Neo-Babylonian kings are in agreement with Berossus' figures. Thus we have two independent witnesses to the length of the Neo-Babylonian era according to the chronicles, and even if these chronicles are only partly preserved on cuneiform tablets, their figures for the lengths of reign of the Neo-Babylonian kings have been correctly transmitted to us via Berossus and Ptolemy!

The reigns of the Neo-Babylonian kings, according to Berossus and Ptolemy, are as follows:

	YEARS OF REIGN ACCORDING TO:		
	BEROSSUS	*PTOLEMY*	*B.C.E.*
Nabopolassar	21 years	21 years	625 - 605
Nebuchadnezzar	43 years	43 years	604 - 562
Evil-merodach	2 years	2 years	561 - 560
Neriglissar	4 years	4 years	559 - 556
Labashi-Marduk	9 months	—	556
Nabonidus	17 years	17 years	555 - 539

Ptolemy omits Labashi-Marduk, as he always reckons *whole* years only. Labashi-Marduk's short reign of only a few months[13] was included in Neriglissar's last year (which was also the accession-year of Nabonidus). Ptolemy, therefore, could leave him out of his account.

If these lists by two of the oldest and most reliable historians are correct, the first year of Nebuchadnezzar would be 604/603 B.C.E. and his eighteenth year, when he desolated Jerusalem, would be 587/586 B.C.E. But even if Berossus and Ptolemy both give a true representation of the length of reigns given in the original Neo-Babylonian chronicles, how do historians know that the chronological information originally contained in these chronicles is reliable?

One important reason why they place such confidence in Ptolemy's canon is that in his *Almagest* he records a large number of ancient astronomical observations from the periods covered by the canon. As these observations were dated to different kings mentioned in the king list, Ptolemy could attach the list to a series of astronomically fixed dates, thus turning it into a kind of "absolute chronology" for the periods it covered. Bible chronologist Edwin R. Thiele explains:

> What makes the canon of such great importance to modern historians is the large amount of astronomical material recorded by Ptolemy in his *Almagest,* making possible checks as to its accuracy at almost every step from beginning to end. Over eighty solar, lunar, and planetary positions, with their dates, are recorded in the *Almagest* which have been verified by modern astronomers. The details concerning eclipses are given with such minuteness as to leave no question concerning the exact identification of the particular phenomenon referred to, and making possible the most positive verification.[14]

For example, the three oldest eclipses of the moon that Ptolemy made use of were observed, he says, at Babylon in the first and second years of the reign of Mardokempados.[15] Of the first one, he wrote "that it took place in the first year of Mardokempados, on [the night] of the Egyptian [month] Thot 29/30. It began, so it is said, a good hour after the rising of the moon and was total."[16] And similarly, he described the second and third eclipses as taking place in the second year of the same Mardokempados, the second on the night between the eighteenth and nineteenth of the Egyptian Thot, and the third in the night between the fifteenth and sixteenth of the month Pamenoth. The two last mentioned eclipses were partial only.[17]

These descriptions are accurate enough to enable modern astronomers to identify them; and their identifications are in agreement with Ptolemy's own. The first eclipse took place on March 19, 721 B.C.E., the second on March 8/9, 720 B.C.E., and the third on September 1, 720 B.C.E., Julian calendar.[18] Thus, the evidence is clear that the year 721/20 B.C.E. was the first year of Mardokempados' reign. This conclusion is also supported by other kinds of evidence quite independent of Ptolemy's eclipses.[19] Yet it may not have as much astronomical support as historians have traditionally accepted as being the case; most seem to be unaware of the fact that astronomers for centuries have questioned Ptolemy's observations. As early as 1008 C.E., ibn Yunis concluded that they contained serious errors, and by about 1800, astronomers had recognized that *almost all* of Ptolemy's observations were in error. In 1817, Delambre asked: "Did Ptolemy do any observing? Are not the observations that he claims to have made merely computations from his tables, and examples to help in explaining his theories?"[20] Two years later Delambre also concluded that Ptolemy fabricated some of his solar observations and demonstrated how the fabrication was made.[21] In recent years certain astronomers have re-examined Ptolemy's observations and arrived at similar results. The most sensational are those of Dr. Robert R. Newton. In his book, *The Crime of Claudius Ptolemy*,[22] Newton claims that Ptolemy fudged, not only a large body of the observations he says he had made himself, but also a number of the observations Ptolemy attributes to other astronomers, including at least one of the three observations he records from the reign of Mardokempados.[23] If Newton's conclusions are correct, Ptolemy's king list cannot be verified by his astronomical data.

In the ensuing debate a number of scholars have repudiated Newton's conclusions. They have argued that Newton's arguments "are marred by all manner of distortions,"[24] that his case collapses because "it is based on faulty statistical analysis and a disregard for the methods of early astronomy,"[25] and similar comments.[26] Most of these critics, though, are historians without particular expertise in the field of Greek astronomy. Some reviews written by well-informed astronomers have been favorable to Newton's conclusions, and one historian who is also well acquainted with Greek astronomy, K.P. Moesgaard, agrees that Ptolemy fabricated his astronomical data, though he feels it was done for some honest reason.[27]

Dr. Newton is a noted physicist who has published a series of outstanding works on the secular accelerations of the moon and the earth. His conclusion that Ptolemy fudged his observations and also a number of those he ascribed to earlier astronomers might very well be correct. As noted above, the astronomical verification claimed for his king list, then, cannot be accepted quite simply. But what about the claim that not only the astronomical data recorded in the *Almagest* but, also, the king list itself was invented by Ptolemy?

In a review of Newton's book on Ptolemy, published in the *Scientific American* of October 1977, on pages 79 through 81, it was also stated that "Ptolemy's forgery may have extended to inventing the length of reigns of Babylonian kings." Anyone acquainted with the ancient history of Babylonia knows, however, that this statement is completely erroneous. Ptolemy's king list bears clear marks of the older sources it was derived from, expecially the Babylonian chronicles, and it is in complete agreeement with ancient chronicles and king lists from the Neo-Babylonian period. Yet the statement by the reviewer in *Scientific American* was quickly picked up and published in *The Watchtower*.[28] Newton himself seems to share this attitude towards Ptolemy's canon. In his work on Ptolemy he says: "It follows that Ptolemy's king list is useless in the study of chronology, and that it must be ignored. What is worse, much Babylonian chronology is based upon Ptolemy's king list. All relevant chronology must now be reviewed and all dependence upon Ptolemy's list must be removed."[29]

Newton is not a historian and he is not an expert on Babylonian chronology. He also admits that he has not studied sources other than Ptolemy for the years prior to Nebuchadnezzar.[30] His thoughts on the relations between chronology and the work of Ptolemy were influenced by a Mr. Philip G. Couture of Santee, California, as he states in the Preface of his book.[31] The same Mr. Couture also induced Dr. Newton to reject the Assyrian eponym canon in his recent work, *The Moon's Acceleration and Its Physical Origins*, using an argument that is clearly based on a misunderstanding of this Assyrian source.[32] As Couture is a member of Jehovah's Witnesses, the chronological arguments he passed on to Newton seem to have aimed at supporting the chronology of the Watchtower Society, and some of them may be shown to be identical to those presented in *Aid to Bible Understanding*. For this reason Newton's views on the relations between ancient chronology and Ptolemy's king list should not be used by Watchtower writers to buttress their chronology, as his views were at least partly formed by certain untenable arguments taken from their own Bible dictionary!

Anyone who feels it is possible to invalidate the Neo-Babylonian chronology by trying to prove that Ptolemy invented his king list and fabricated a number of astronomical observations in support of it is lost in a delusion. Such a person fails to realize that the length of the Neo-Babylonian era given in Ptolemy's canon is in *complete* agreement with the figures given by Berossus 400 years earlier, and that their figures in turn agree with those given by the ancient Neo-Babylonian historical records unearthed during the last hundred years. If it could be proved that Ptolemy invented his king list, we must conclude that he was very fortunate, for his "invented" figures happen to be in complete agreement with actual reigns of the Neo-Babylonian kings!

Further, even if it could be proved that the astronomical observations Ptolemy used in support of his king list were fabricated, the length of the Neo-Babylonian era as given in his king list would still have astronomical verification. As R.R. Newton himself points out, "the later part of his king list has independent verification."[33] In his *Almagest*, V. 14, Ptolemy refers to a lunar eclipse observed at Babylon in the seventh year of Cambyses which has been astronomically fixed to the year 523 B.C.E. Even if Ptolemy fabricated this observation, as Newton claims, a cuneiform text has been found ("Strm. Kambys, 400"; see note 1), in which this eclipse is also described and dated to Cambyses' seventh year. Another text from the thirty-seventh year of Nebuchadnezzar which records a number of lunar and planetary observations has enabled modern astronomers to fix his thirty-seventh year to 568/567 B.C.E. (This text will be dealt with later in the study.) After having mentioned these two cuneiform texts, Newton concludes: "Thus we have quite strong confirmation that Ptolemy's list is correct for Nebuchadnezzar, and reasonable confirmation for Kambyses."[34] To use Newton's theory that Ptolemy forged his observations and invented his canon as an argument against the correctness of the generally accepted Neo-Babylonian chronology is, therefore, not honest. Such an argument denies Newton's own conclusions because he holds that Ptolemy's king list gives the correct length for the Neo-Babylonian period.

The conclusive argument against the theory that Ptolemy may have invented his kinglist, however, is the fact that the so-called "Ptolemy's canon" is *a misnomer*. This is a fact very little known outside the circle of a few experts. As professor Otto Neugebauer has pointed out, the kinglist was compiled from Babylonian sources by Alexandrian astronomers long before Ptolemy, to be used in their astronomical calculations. The attempts to prove that Ptolemy forged his observations cannot, therefore, cast any shadow on the kinglist that erroneously bears his name. (See Otto Neugebauer, "'Years' in Royal Canons," in *A Locust's Leg*; Studies in the honour of S. H. Taqizadeh, London, 1962)

Today, historians do not need Ptolemy's canon or his astronomical data in order to fix the length of the Neo-Babylonian period. Its length is firmly established by at least *seven lines of evidence* which are independent of Ptolemy's canon and his eclipses, consisting of chronicles and other historical records, business and administrative documents, astronomical diaries, and synchronisms with contemporary Egyptian chronology. Much of the evidence in question has been unearthed in Mesopotamia and Egypt since the middle of the last century.

CHRONICLES AND OTHER HISTORICAL RECORDS

On page 327, paragraph 5, *Aid to Bible Understanding*

states: "Babylonian historical records that could either substantiate or undermine Ptolemy's figures for the lengths of the reigns of certain kings are largely lacking." But the author (or authors) of the article in that book fails to mention that *this does not hold true for the history of the Neo-Babylonian period.* There are enough historical texts to establish the length of the Neo-Babylonian era independent of Ptolemy's canon. These historical records consist of (A) Chronicles, (B) King Lists, and (C) Royal Inscriptions.

(A) Several chronicles covering parts of Neo-Babylonian history have been discovered, all of which are kept in the British Museum, London. The most recent translation of them has been published by A.K. Grayson in *Assyrian and Babylonian Chronicles*. The chronicles relevant for our study are as follows:

CHRONICLE	*B.M. NO.*	*RULER*	*REGNAL YEARS COVERED*
No. 2	25127 etc.	Nabopolassar	acc. year - 3
3	21901	Nabopolassar	10 - 17
4	22047	Nabopolassar	18 - 20
5	21946	Nabopolassar-	21
		Nebuchadnezzar	acc. year - 10
6	25124	Neriglissar	3
7	35382	Nabonidus	acc. year - 17

As can be seen, most of these chronicles are incomplete. But from B.M. 21946 it may be learned that Nabopolassar ruled Babylon for twenty-one years, as is also stated in Ptolemy's canon. That part of the text says: "For twenty-one years Nabopolassar ruled Babylon. On the eighth day of the month Ab he died. In the month Elul Nebuchadnezzar (II) returned to Babylon and on the first day of the month he ascended the royal throne in Babylon."[35]

The last chronicle (B.M. 35382), the famous "Nabonidus Chronicle," covers the whole reign of Nabonidus, but unfortunately it is damaged. The portion covering his twelfth year to his sixteenth year of rule is lacking, and the portion where the words for "seventeenth year" no doubt originally could be read, is damaged.[36] Yet other information in this chronicle confirms that a seventeen-year reign for Nabonidus must be very close to the truth. For the sixth year it is stated that Cyrus, king of Anshan, defeated Astyages, king of Media, and further, in Nabonidus' ninth year, Cyrus (now called "king of Parsu," that is, Persia) marched against the country of Lydia, "defeated its king, took its possessions, (and) stationed his own garrison (there)."[37] Thus Cyrus is clearly stated to be the king of Media and Persia in the sixth and ninth years of Nabonidus and well on his way towards expanding his empire.

Cyrus' first year as king of Anshan (Elam) cannot be put earlier that 560/59 B.C.E. According to Herodotus (fifth century B.C.E.), Cyrus reigned twenty-nine years, the last nine of which he ruled Babylon. Ktesias, Dinon, Diodorus, Africanus and Eusebius all give the same length of reign for Cyrus.[38] Cuneiform tablets (business documents), too, give Cyrus a rule of nine years over Babylon (538 - 530 B.C. E.), which puts his accession to the throne of Elam in 560 or 559 B.C.E.

Suppose now that some twenty years have to be added to the Neo-Babylonian era, which is required if the destruction of Jerusalem is set at 607 rather than 587 B.C.E., and that we add these twenty years to the reign of Nabonidus, making it some thirty-seven years instead of seventeen. Then his first year must have been 575 B.C.E. instead of 555, as is commonly held. Nabonidus' sixth year, when Astyages was defeated by Cyrus, must have been 570 and his nineth year 567 B.C. Those dates, however, are impossible, as Cyrus did not come to power until 560/59 B.C.E., as was shown above. He clearly could not have defeated Astyages ten years before he came to power! This is why the Watchtower Society's book *"Babylon the Great had Fallen!" God's Kingdom Rules!* correctly dates this battle in 550 B.C.E.,[39] thereby indicating Nabonidus' reign of seventeen years to be correct, as is held by all authorities and classical authors.

Though the chronicles available do not furnish a complete chronology for the Neo-Babylon period, the information which they preserve supports the dates for the lengths of the reigns of the Neo-Babylonian kings given by Berossus and Ptolemy. As both of these authors derived their information from the Babylonian chronicles independent of each other, as was shown above, and as their figures for the Neo-Babylonian reigns agree, it is logical to conclude that the chronological information originally given in the Neo-Babylonian chronicles has been preserved for us in an unaltered condition by Berossus and Ptolemy. But even if this is agreed upon, can the information given by these Babylonian chronicles be trusted?

It is often pointed out that the Assyrian scribes distorted history in order to glorify their kings and gods. "It is a well known fact that in Assyrian royal inscriptions a serious military set-back is never openly admitted."[40] Sometimes scribes garbled the narration by changing the date of a defeat and weaving it into an account of a later battle.[41] Do the Neo-Babylonian chronicles treat history in this way, too? Dr. A.K. Grayson, a well-known authority on the Assyrian and Babylonian chronicles, concludes: "Unlike the Assyrian scribes the Babylonians neither fail to mention Babylonian defeats nor do they attempt to change them into victories. The chronicles contain a reasonably reliable and representative record of important events in the period with which they are concerned."[42] And in *Assyrian and Babylonian Chronicles* he says: "Within the boundaries of their interest, the writers are quite objective and impartial."[43] In this respect the chronicles closely resemble the historical parts of the Old Testament books.[44]

We may rest assured, then, that the figures for the reigns of the Neo-Babylonian kings given by these chronicles and preserved to our time thanks to Berossus and Ptolemy represent the actual reigns of these kings. This conclusion will be confirmed, over and over again, in further discussion.

(B) A *king list* usually is a list of royal names with the addition of regnal years, similar to the king list composed by Ptolemy at a later time. Though a number of king lists both from Assyria and Babylonia have been unearthed, only one of them covers the Neo-Babylonian era: the Uruk King List. Unfortunately, it is badly preserved, and some portions of it are missing. The preserved portions cover the periods from Kandalanu to Darius I (647 - 486 B.C.E.) and on the reverse side from Darius III to Seleucus II (335 - 226 B.C.E.). It was evidently composed from older sources sometime after the reign of Seleucus II.

The Uruk King List was discovered during the excavation campaign at Uruk (modern Warka) in 1959/60 together with about 1,000 other cuneiform texts (mostly economic texts) from different periods. It was translated and published by Van Dijk in UVB 18, Berlin 1962, pages 53-60.[45] The portion covering the Neo-Babylonian period gives the following information:

21 years: Nabopolassar

43 [ye]ars: Nebuchadnezzar (II)

2 [ye]ars: Amel-Marduk

[X] + 2 years, 8 months: Neriglissar

[...] 3 months: Labashi-Marduk

[X] + 15 years: Nabonidus

As is seen, the royal names and the preserved figures agree with Berossus' and Ptolemy's: Nabopolassar 21 years, Nebuchadnezzar 43 years, Evil-merodach 2 years. The only deviation is the length of Labashi-Marduk's reign, which is given as 3 months against Berossus' 9 months. The smaller figure is without doubt closer to the truth, as is proved by the economic documents (see below). Anyway, Labashi-Marduk's reign was swallowed up by Neriglissar's fourth year, which was also Nabonidus' assession-year, and the total length of the era is not affected.

In contrast to Ptolemy, the Uruk King List gives both years and months for the reigns of Neriglissar and Labashi-Marduk. The damaged figures for Neriglissar and Nabonidus may be restored as [1] + 2 years, 8 months, and [2] + 15 years, respectively. The economic texts, too, show Neriglissar's reign to have been 3 years and 8 months (August 560 - April 556 B.C.E.).[46] As he died early in his fourth regnal year, his reign would normally have been counted chronologically as 4 years, according to the Babylonian accession-year system.[47] The Uruk King List deviates from this method at this point.

Thus we find Berossus' and Ptolemy's figures confirmed once again by this ancient document. Admittedly, it was composed more that 300 years after the end of the Neo-Babylonian era. Thus it is possible that scribal errors may have crept into it. So it is important to ask: Are there then no historical records preserved from the Neo-Babylonian era itself which establishes its chronology? Yes, there are, as is immediately evident.

(C) *Royal inscriptions* of different kinds (building inscriptions, annals, etc.) have been found in Assyria and Babylonia in great numbers. A German translation of then-known Neo-Babylonian royal inscriptions was published in 1912 by S. Langdon,[48] but since then many new ones from the period in question have been unearthed. A new translation of all the Neo-Babylonian royal inscriptions is therefore being prepared for publication by P.R. Berger.[49] For the chronology, *three* are especially valuable: (1) *Nabon. No. 18* (Nbd Zyl. II, 7 according to Berger's arrangement), (2) *Nabon. No. 8* (also known as the Hillah stele), and (3) *Nabon. H 1, B* (also known as the Adda-Guppi' stele). All of them are original documents from the reign of Nabonidus.

1. Nabon. No. 18 is a cylinder inscription from an unnamed year of Nabonidus. Fulfilling the desire of Sin, the moon-god, Nabonidus dedicated a daughter of his to this god as priestess at the Sin temple of Ur. An eclipse of the moon, dated in the text to Elul 13 and observed in the morning watch, led to this dedication. When, during Nabonidus' reign, did such an eclipse take place?

In 1949 Hildegard Lewy examined the eclipse and concluded that it referred to the eclipse of September 26, 554 B.C.E. (Julian calendar).[50] If Nabonidus ruled for seventeen years and his first year was 555/54 B.C.E., as is shown by Berossus and Ptolemy, the eclipse and the dedication of Nabonidus' daughter took place in his *second* regnal year (554/53 B.C.E.), according to Lewy's calculation. A remarkable confirmation of this dating was brought to light twenty years later, when W. G. Lambert published his translation of four fragments of an inscription from Nabonidus' reign. The inscription established that the dedication of Nabonidus' daughter took place shortly before his third year, and obviously in his second, precisely as Lewy had concluded.[51] The lunar eclipse of Elul 13, then, definitely fixed the second year of Nabonidus to 554/53 B.C.E. and his first year to 555/54, thus giving a very strong confirmation to Berossus' and Ptolemy's figures for Nabonidus' reign.[52]

2. *Nabon. No. 8*, or the Hillah stele, was discovered in the neighbourhood of Hillah, south-east of the ruins of Babylon, at the end of the last century. A transcription of the text was first published by Messerschmidt in 1896, and in 1912 Langdon published his translation of it.[53] The information given in this stele alone helps us to establish the length of the *whole* Neo-Babylonian era from Nabopolassar to the reign of Nabonidus. This inscription, too, contains a record of astronomical observations which enable us to fix the reign of Nabonidus. Columns VI - VIII, relating the occurrences of Nabonidus' accession year and his first full year, contain a description of a constellation of planets and stars observed by Nabonidus in an unnamed

evening during this period. It is stated that Venus, Saturn, and Jupiter were visible after dusk while Mars and Mercury were absent. Stars mentioned as visible were: α Bootis, ε Virginis, and α Lyrae. If, as has been established earlier, Nabonidus ascended to the throne in 556 B.C.E. and his first full year was 555/554 (Nisan-Nisan), we should find this constellation of stars and planets during that period. Hildegard Lewy, in the article quoted above, calculated the date for this constellation and concluded: "The only time within the given interval when this constellation occurred was the period of 3 days comprised between Simânu 2 and Simânu 6 of Nabû-na'id's first full year (May 31 to June 4, 555 B.C.E.), during which period, in fact, also the fixed stars enumerated by the king were visible in the evening sky."[54] So again, we find Nabonidus' reign astronomically fixed and his seventeen years of rule confirmed.

In several of his royal inscriptions (*Stelenfrgm*. III,1 and XI, *Nabon*. H 1,B, and *Zyl*. III, 2) Nabonidus says that in a dream in his accession-year, he was commanded by the gods Marduk and Sin to rebuild the temple é.hul.hul in Harran. In connection with this the text under discussion (*Nabon*. No. 8) provides a very interesting piece of information: "As to the temple é.hul.hul. in Harran which was in ruins for 54 years—through a devastation by the Manda-hordes the(se) sanctuaries were laid waste—the time (predestined) by the gods, the moment for the appeasement (to wit) 54 years, had come near, when Sin should have returned to his place."[55] The date when the temple é.hul.hul in Harran was ruined by the "Manda-hordes" is known to us from two different reliable sources: The Babylonian chronicle *B.M. 21901* and the Harran inscription *Nabon. H 1, B.* The chronicle states that in the sixteenth year of Nabopolassar, in the month of Marcheswan, "the Umman-manda (the Medes), [who] had come [to help] the king of Akkad, put their armies together and marched to Harran.... The king of Akkad reached Harran and [...] he captured the city. He carried off the vast booty of the city and the temple."[56] The Nabonidus stele H 1, B gives the same information: "Whereas in the 16th year of

Nabopolassar, king of Babylon, Sin, king of the gods, with his city and his temple was angry and went up to heaven—the city and the people that (were) in it went to ruin."[57] Thus it is obvious that Nabonidus reckons the fifty-four years from the sixteenth year of Nabopolassar to the beginning of his own reign when the gods commanded him to rebuild the ruined temple.[58] This is in excellent agreement with the figures for the Neo-Babylonian reigns given by Berossus and Ptolemy. As Nabopolassar reigned for twenty-one years, five years remained from his sixteenth year to the end of his reign. After that Nebuchadnezzar ruled for forty-three, Evil-Merodach for two, and Neriglissar for four years before Nabonidus came to power (Labashi-Marduk's few months may by neglected). Summing up these regnal years (5 + 43 + 2 + 4) we get fifty-four years—exactly as Nabonidus states on his stele. If, as has been established, Nabonidus' first year was 555/554 B.C.E., Nabopolassar's sixteenth year must have been 610/609, his first year 625/624 and his twenty-first year 605/604 B.C.E. Nebuchadnezzar's first year, then, was 604/603, and his eighteenth year, when he desolated Jerusalem, was 587/586 B.C.E. These dates agree completely with the dates arrived at from Ptolemy's king list and Berossus' figures.

Consequently, this stele alone establishes the length of the whole Neo-Babylonian era. It fixes the reign of Nabonidus astronomically, and it gives the total length of the reigns of all the Neo-Babylonian kings prior to Nabonidus. The strength of this evidence, produced during the Neo-Babylonian era itself cannot be insisted upon too strongly.

3. In order to demonstrate the fragmentary condition of the Babylonian historical records, *Aid to Bible Understanding* quotes from an inscription of Nabonidus' mother on a stele, discovered by H. Pognon at Eski Harran in 1906. This stele, entitled *Nabon. H 1, A,* by C.J. Gadd was described by Professor B. Landsberger in 1947 and is now in the Archeological Museum at Ankara. The inscrip-

tion on the stele includes a biographical sketch of the life of Nabonidus' mother from the time of Ashurbanipal and on to the ninth year of Nabonidus (when she died), giving the length of reign of each of the Neo-Babylonian kings except, of course, of Nabonidus. Unfortunately this portion of the text is damaged, and the only readable figures are the forty-three years of Nebuchadnezzar's reign and the four years of Neriglissar's reign.[59]

Obviously, the author (or, authors) of the article in *Aid to Bible Understanding* did not know about the recent discovery at Harran by Dr. D.S. Rice in August-September 1956 of three other stelae, *one of which bore a duplicate inscription of the one discovered in 1906*! In 1958 a translation of this inscription was published by C.J. Gadd. Fortunately, the portions containing the chronological information were undamaged. The portion discussed in *Aid to Bible Understanding* reads as follows according to the new inscription, *Nabon. H 1, B:*

> From the 20th year of Assurbanipal, King of Assyria, that I was born (in) until the 42nd year of Assurbanipal, the 3rd year of Assur-etillu-ili, his son, the 21st year of Nabopolassar, the 43rd year of Nebuchadnezzar, the 2nd year of Awel-Murduk, the 4th year of Neriglissar, in 95 years of the god Sin, king of the gods of heaven and earth ....[60]

Further on in the text a complete summary of the long life of the queen, Adda-Guppi', is given:

> From the time of Assurbanipal, king of Assyria, until the 9th year of Nabu-na'id king of Babylon, the son, offspring of my womb, 104 years of happiness, with the reverence which Sin, king of the gods, placed in me, he made me flourish, my own self ....[61]

This queen died in the ninth year of Nabonidus, and the mourning for the deceased Mother is described in the last column of the inscription. Interestingly, the same information is also given in the *Nabonidus Chronicle* (B.M. 35382). "Ninth year: ... In the month Nisanu the 5th day, the mother of the king died in Dur-karashu which is on the banks of the Euphrates, above Sippar."[62]

All the reigns of the Neo-Babylonian kings are given in this royal inscription, from Nabopolassar and on to the ninth year of Nabonidus, and the lengths of reign are *in complete accordance with Ptolemy's canon*—a very significant fact, because the corroboration comes from a witness *contemporary with all these Neo-Babylonian kings* and intimately connected with all of them![63]

The results from our discussion of the Neo-Babylonian historical records are summarized in the table below.

TABLE 3: THE NEO-BABYLONIAN HISTORICAL RECORDS

NEO-BABYLONIAN KINGS	*THE CHRONICLES AS PRESERVED VIA BEROSSUS AND PTOLEMY*	*THE URUK KING LIST*	*THE ROYAL INSCRIPTIONS*	*B.C.E. DATES*
Nabopolassar	21 years	21 years	21 years	625 - 605
Nebuchadnezzar	43 years	43 years	43 years	604 - 562
Evil-merodach	2 years	2 years	2 years	561 - 560
Neriglissar	4 years	damaged	4 years	559 - 556
Labashi-Marduk	some months	(3 months)	—	556
Nabonidus	17 years	damaged	17 years	555 - 539

As may be seen from the table, the Neo-Babylonian chronology adopted by secular historians is very strongly supported by the ancient cuneiform sources, some of which were produced during the Neo-Babylonian era. Yet this is just a beginning. We must still wait to be introduced to the four strongest lines of evidence in support of the chronology presented in the table above. These will establish once and for all the historical facts of the matter.

Hundreds of thousands of cuneiform texts have been excavated in Mesopotamia since the middle of the last century. The overwhelming majority of them concern economic and administrative items such as contract tablets, official letters from the temple archives and legal records. These texts are to a great extent dated just as are commercial letters today, giving the year of the reigning king, the month, and the day of the month. A text concerning ceremonial salt from the archives of the temple Eanna in Erech, dated in the first regnal year of Evil-merodach, is given here as an example:

> One and one-half talents of salt,
> the fixed offering of the month Sivan
> of the god Usur-amatsu,
> Ina-sillis brought.
> The sixth day of the month Sivan,
> the first year of
> Amel-Marduk, the king of Babylon.[64]

Thousands of such dated cuneiform texts have been unearthed from the Neo-Babylonian period. During the 1920s alone, more than five-hundred tablets dated in the reign of Nabonidus were published, according to Raymond P. Dougherty.[65] Thus there exist many such dated tablets *from every year during the whole Neo-Babylonian era*! Because of this abundance of dated texts modern scholars are able to determine not only the length of the reign of each king, but also the time of the year when each change of reign occurred, sometimes almost to the day! This has been demonstrated by R.A. Parker and W.H. Dubberstein in their work, *Babylonian Chronology*.[66] The last text from the reign of Nabonidus, for example, is dated VII/17/17 (October 13, 539, Julian Calendar) although the Nabonidus Chronicle states that Babylon fell VII/16/17, or one day earlier. The last tablet dated to Nabonidus comes from Uruk, about which Parker and Dubberstein give the following comment: "Interestingly enough, the last tablet dated to Nabunaid from Uruk is dated the day after Babylon fell to Cyrus. News of its capture had not yet reached the southern city some 125 miles distant."[67] Another interesting business document, published by R.H. Sack, mentions both the forty-third year of Nebuchadnezzar and the accession-year of his son, Evil-merodach. A slave-girl, lady Lit-ka-idi, was placed at the disposal of Nabu-ahhe-iddina "in the month of Ajaru, forty-third year of Nebuchadnezzar, king of Babylon." Some months later, "in the month of Kislimu, accession year of (Amel)-Marduk," full payment was given for the girl.[68] This text, then, fixes the length of Nebuchadnezzar's reign and shows that he was succeeded by Evil-merodach. Other business documents show that Nebuchadnezzar's rule ended at the end of the month Ululu of his forty-third year, which dates his death to the first days of October, 562 B.C.E. The latest text from Evil-merodach's reign is dated V/17/2 (Aug. 7, 560), and the earliest text from the reign of Neriglissar is dated V/21/acc. (Aug. 11, 560). Evil-merodach's death, then, may be fixed between August 7 and August 11, 560.[69]

If twenty years have to be added to the Neo-Babylonian era in order to place the destruction of Jerusalem in 607 B.C.E., where are the thousands of business and administrative texts dated in those missing years? Why do we, for instance, have many tablets dated in each of Nabonidus' first seventeen regnal years, but not one single tablet from his later years, if he reigned for more than seventeen years? Twenty years are about one fifth of the whole Neo-Babylonian period. Among the many thousands of dated tablets from this period, hundreds or thousands ought to have been found from those missing twenty years. If one casts a die many thousands of times without ever getting a 6, he must logically conclude: "There is no number 6 on this die." The same is true of the twenty missing "ghost years" which one must look for in vain during the Neo-Babylonian period.

But suppose that a number of missing years really existed, and that the hundreds or thousands of dated tablets from them, by some incredible chance, have not been found. Why should those missing years amount to exactly twenty years? Why not a period of seventeen, or thirteen, or seven years, or perhaps different years distributed throughout the Neo-Babylonian period? Why do the lengths of reign according to the dated tablets *which have been unearthed* happen to agree completely with Berossus' and Ptolemy's figures, the Uruk King List, the contemporary royal inscriptions and all the other evidence that will be presented below? Why are the missing hundreds or thousands of dated tablets from *just the same period of twenty years* that is also missing in all the other sources, and not from another period of twenty years? From time to time, new quantities of dated tablets are unearthed, translated, and *sometimes* published, but the twenty missing years never turn up. Even improbability has a limit.

The family of Egibi. A great number of the business documents come from the archives of "banking-houses" in Babylonia. The "banking" firm "The Sons of Murašu" had its center in Nippur and reached its highest position during the reigns of Artaxerxes I and Darius II. Two of the best known banking houses from the Neo-Babylonian era were owned by the families *Nur-Sin* and *Egibi.* "The Family of Egibi," centered in Babylon, appears in the documents as early as at the end of the eighth century B.C.E. It prospered from the time of Nebuchadnezzar up to the time of Darius I, controlling the finances of that time. Of this banking house Bruno Meissner says: "From the firm *the Sons of Egibi* we possess such an abundance of documents that we are able to follow nearly all business transactions and personal experiences of its head from the time of Nebuchadnezzar up to the time of Darius I."[70] The discovery of the archive of dated verifications of this firm, covering a period of more than a hundred years, has proved to be of great help in establishing the chronology of this period.

The business documents from the Egibi-house were discovered by Arabs during the wet season of the year 1875-76 in a mound in the neighbourhood of Hillah, a town about four miles south-east of the ruins of Babylon. Some three or four thousand tablets were discovered enclosed in a number of earthern jars, resembling common water jars, covered over at the top with a tile, and cemented with bitumen. The discoverers brought the tablets to Bagdad and sold them to a dealer there. In that same year George Smith visited Bagdad and acquired about 2,500 of these important documents for the British Museum.

The tablets were examined during the following months by W. St. Chad Boscawen, and his report appeared in the *Transactions of the Society of Biblical Archaeology,* Vol. VI, January 1878, pages 1-78.[71] The information which follows immediately below is taken from that report.

Boscawen states that the tablets "relate to the various monetary transactions of a Babylonian banking and financial agency, trading under the name of Egibi and Sons." The tablets "relate to every possible commercial transaction; from the loan of a few shekels of silver, to the sale or mortgage of whole estates whose value is thousands of *manas* of silver."[72]

After a very short examination, Boscawen realized the importance of following the sequence of the heads of the Egibi firm, and after a more careful analysis he ascertained the main lines of the succession to be as follows: From the third year of Nebuchadnezzar a person named Sula acted as head of the Egibi firm, and continued to act as its head for a period of twenty years, up to the twenty-third year of Nebuchadnezzar when he died and was succeeded by his son, Nabu-ahi-idina. Nabu-ahi-idina continued as the head of affairs for a period of thirty-eight years, that is, from the twenty-third year of Nebuchadnezzar to the twelfth year of Nabonidus when he was succeeded by his son Itti-Marduk-Balatu.[73] Itti-Marduk-Balatu in his turn remained head of the firm until the first year of Darius Hystaspis (521 B.C.E.), which was the twenty-third year of his headship of the firm:[74]

> Now, summing up these periods, we get the result that from the 3rd year of Nebuchadnezzar II to the 1st year of Darius Hystaspis was a period of eighty-one years:
>
> | | |
> |---|---|
> | Sula at the head of the firm . . . . | 20 years |
> | Nabu-ahi-idina . . . . | 38 years |
> | Itti-Marduk-Balatu . . . . | 23 years |
> | | 81 years |
>
> This would give an interval of eighty-three years from the 1st year of Nebuchadnezzar II to the 1st year of Darius Hystaspis.[75]

This agrees exactly with Berossus, Ptolemy, and the Neo-Babylonian historical records. Counting backwards eighty-three years from the first year of Darius Hystaspis (521 B.C.E.; see *Aid to Bible Understanding*, pp. 421, 422) brings us to 604 B.C.E. as the first year of Nebuchadnezzar, which agrees completely with the other lines of evidence presented above.

The archive of the Egibi-house alone would suffice to establish the length of the Neo-Babylonian period. With this complete set of dated commercial tablets from the archive of one of the "Rothschilds" of Babylon "there ought to be but little difficulty in establishing once and for ever the chronology of this important period of ancient history."[76] The evidence of these documents leaves no room for a gap in Neo-Babylonian history from Nebuchadnezzar onward. The archive, containing tablets dated up to the forty-third year of Nebuchadnezzar, the second year of Evil-merodach, the fourth year of Neriglissar and the seventeenth year of Nabonidus, gives a complete confirmation of the chronology as stated by Berossus and Ptolemy. Since the last century still other collections of tablets belonging to the Egibi family have been discovered.[77] Yet the Egibi tablets are *only a part of* the many thousands of business and administrative documents discovered from the Neo-Babylonian era.[78]

The importance of the business and administrative texts for the chronology of the Neo-Babylonian period cannot be overestimated. In 1929, R.P. Dougherty published a Neo-Babylonian king-list, based upon more than two thousand dated documents. He gives this king-list priority over all other sources and says that it must be "accepted as the ultimate criterion in the determination of Neo-Babylonian questions ...."[79] This king-list is presented below:

THE NEO-BABYLONIAN CHRONOLOGY ACCORDING TO BUSINESS TEXTS.[80]

Nabu-apal-usur	21 years	(625 - 605 BC)
Nabu-kudurru-usur	43 years	(604 - 562 BC)
Amel-Marduk	2 years	(561 - 560 BC)
Nergal-sar-usur	4 years	(559 - 556 BC)
Labasi-Marduk	a few months	(556 BC)
Nabu-naid	17 years	(555 - 539 BC)

THE ASTRONOMICAL DIARIES

A group of documents recording astronomical observations by astronomers at Babylon have been termed "astronomical diaries" by Professor A.J. Sachs. A "diary" usually covers the six or seven months of the first or second half of a particular Babylonian year and gives the position of the moon at its first and last visibility on a specific day, along with the positions of the planets Mercury, Venus, Mars, Jupiter and Saturn. Much additional information is added, such as meteorological events, earthquakes, market prices, etc. More than 1,200 fragments of astronomical diaries of various sizes have been discovered, but because of their fragmentary condition only about a third of the number are datable. Most of these texts had already been discovered in the 1870s and 1880s, and almost all of them are kept in the British Museum. Most of them cover the period from 385 to about 60 B.C.E. and contain astronomical observations from about 180 of these 325 years, thus firmly establishing the chronology of this period. Half a dozen of the diaries are dated in the fifth, sixth, and seventh centuries B.C.E. The most important text for our discussion is designated *VAT 4956* and is kept in the "Vorderasiatischen Abteilung" in the Berlin Museum. This diary is dated from Nisan 1 of Nebuchadnezzar's thirty-seventh regnal year to Nisan 1 of his thirty-eighth regnal year, recording observations of the moon and the planets from his entire thirty-seventh year. A translation and careful examination of the text was published by P.V. Neugebauer and E.F. Weidner in 1915.[81]

Among the many observations recorded on *VAT 4956*, there are about thirty which are so exactly described that modern astronomers can easily fix the exact dates when they were made. By doing so they have been able to show that all these observations (of the moon and the five planets) must have been made during the year 568/67 B.C.E. (In astronomical computations, which include a year 0 between 1 B.C.E. and 1 C.E., the date is written as −567/66). If Nebuchadnezzar's thirty-seventh regnal year was 568/67 B.C.E.,[82] then his first year must have been 604/03 B.C.E., and his eighteenth, during which he desolated Jerusalem, 587/86 B.C.E. This is the same date indicated by Berossus, by Ptolemy, by the royal inscriptions, and by the business documents!

Could all these observations also have been made twenty years earlier, in the year 588/87 B.C., which according to the chronology presented in the *Aid* book corresponded to Nebuchadnezzar's thirty-seventh regnal year?[83] As is also noted in that Bible dictionary on page 331 (Where *VAT 4956* obviously is alluded to), "Modern chronologers point out that such a combination of astronomical positions would not be duplicated again in thousands of years." Let us consider one example. According to this "diary," on Nisan 1 and Airu 1 of Nebuchadnezzar's thirty-seventh year, the planet Saturn could be observed "opposite the

Southern Fish [south of the constellation of Aquarius] of the Zodiac."[84] As Saturn has a revolution of c. 29.5 years, it moves through the whole Zodiac in 29.5 years. This means that it can be observed opposite each of the twelve constellations of the Zodiac for about 2.5 years on the average. It means also that it could be observed in opposition to the Southern Fish 29.5 years prior to 568/67 B.C.E., or in 597/96, but certainly not twenty years earlier, in 588/87! Add to this the *different* revolutions of the other four planets mentioned in the text, along with the positions given for the moon, and it becomes easily understood as to why such a *combination* of observations could not be made again in thousands of years. The observations recorded in *VAT 4956* must have been made in the year 568/67 B.C.E., because they fit no other situation which occurred either thousands of years before or after that date! Thus *VAT 4956* gives very strong support to the chronology of the Neo-Babylonian era as established by the historians. Nonetheless, on page 331, *Aid to Bible Understanding* presents arguments against accepting the "secular" chronology outlined above:[85]

> (a) [The] observations made in Babylon may have contained errors. The Babylonian astronomers showed greatest concern for celestial events of phenomena occuring close to the horizon, at the rising or setting of the moon or of the sun. However, the horizon as viewed from Babylon is frequently obscured by sandstorms.

Then Professor Otto Neugebauer is quoted as saying that Ptolemy complained about "the lack of reliable planetary observations [from ancient Babylon]."[86]

Although the description of the meteorological conditions at Babylon is undoubtedly correct, this does not mean that unreliable planetary observations were commonly made. The horizon as viewed from Babylon was not obscured by sandstorms every day, and some planetary events could be observed many days in succession, e.g., the position of Saturn which, according to our text, could be observed "opposite the Southern Fish of the Zodiac." As was pointed out above, Saturn can be observed opposite each of the twelve constellations of the Zodiac for about 2.5 years on the average. Saturn's positions in the vicinity of the Southern Fish, then, could have been observed for several months in succession, which would have made it impossible for Babylonian astronomers to make any mistake as to where this planet was observed during the thirty-seventh year of Nebuchadnezzar, *in spite of frequent sandstorms.* And further, Babylonian astronomers made regular and systematic observations of the moon and planets, following their movements through the Zodiac day by day. As early as during the Neo-Babylonian period, they had devised computational methods for *predicting* certain celestial events;[87] some "observations" recorded in the diaries are actually not observations, but celestial events calculated in advance. These calculations are usually found to be correct when checked by modern astronomers. For example, *VAT 4956* records an eclipse of the moon which occurred on the fifteenth day of the month Sivan. An astronomer or astronomers had calculated this eclipse with the help of a known eclipse period and therefore it is designated in the text as *atalu Sin* which means "calculated lunar eclipse." Then were probably added the words (the text is somewhat damaged): *sa etelik (LU)*, "which did not take place," i.e., it was invisible in Babylon.[88] This has been confirmed by modern computations: The eclipse took place on July 4, 568 B.C.E. (Julian calendar), but as it began in the afternoon it was not visible at Babylon.[89] That the observations recorded in *VAT 4956* are substantially correct may be seen from the fact that all of them (except one or two containing scribal errors) fit the same year. This would not have been the case if the observations were erroneous. Besides, Professor Otto Neugebauer, who is quoted in *Aid to Bible Understanding*, does not himself seem to distrust the information given in the diaries.[90]

(b) Secondly, the fact is that the great majority of the astronomical diaries found were written, not in the time of the Neo-Babylonian or Persian Empires, but in the Seleucid period (312 - 64 B.C.E.), although they contain data relating to those earlier periods. Historians assume that they are copies of earlier documents.[91]

But historians do not only "assume" that they are copies of earlier documents. The earliest dated diaries frequently reflect the struggle of the copyists to understand the ancient documents they were copying, some of which were broken or otherwise damaged, and often the documents used an archaic terminology which the copyists tried to "modernize." This is clearly true of *VAT 4956*, too. Twice in the text the copyist added the comment "broken off, erased," indicating he was unable to decipher a word in the copy. Also, the text reflects his attempt to change the archaic terminology. But did he change the *content* of the text, too? On this Neugebauer and Weidner conclude: "As far as the contents are concerned the copy is of course a faithful reproduction of the original."[92] Suppose that some of the material in the thirty completely received observations recorded in *VAT 4956* had been distorted by later copyists. How great is the possibility that *all* these "distorted" observations would fit into one and the same year—the very one corroborated by the royal inscriptions, the business documents, the chronicles, Berossus, and Ptolemy—that is Nebuchadnezzar's thirty-seventh regnal year? Accidental errors of this kind do not "co-operate" to such a great extent. So there is no reason to doubt that the original observations have been correctly preserved in our copy.

(c) Finally, as in the case of Ptolemy, even though the astronomical data (as now interpreted and understood) on the texts discovered is basically accurate, this does not prove that the historical data accompanying it is accurate. Even as Ptolemy used the reigns of ancient kings (as he understood them) simply as a framework in which to place his astronomical data, so, too, the writers (or copyists) of the astronomical texts of the Seleucid

> period may have simply inserted in their astronomical texts what was then the accepted or 'popular' chronology of that time.[93]

What is suggested is that the later copyists falsified the documents they were copying, in order to adapt them to their own concepts of the ancient Babylonian and Persian chronology. Thus a writer in the *Awake!* magazine imagines that the copyists may have "inserted the 'thirty-seventh year of Nebuchadnezzar' " in the diary *VAT 4956*.[94] Is this a plausible theory?

As was pointed out above, *VAT 4956* is dated from Nisan 1 of Nebuchadnezzar's thirty-seventh year to Nisan 1 of his thirty-eighth year. Further, almost all events mentioned in the text are dated, with the month, the day and the time of the day given. About *forty* dates of this kind are given in the text, though the year, of course, is not repeated at all these places. All known diaries are dated in the same way. In order to change the years in the text, the copyists would also have been forced to change the name of the reigning king, because if Nebuchadnezzar's thirty-seventh year fell in 588/87 B.C.E., as the Watchtower Society holds, he must have been dead for many years by 568/67 when the observations of *VAT 4956* were made. Is it really likely that the Seleucid copyists devoted themselves to such large-scale forgeries? What do we know about the "popular" chronology of their time, which is proposed as the motive for this deliberate fraud?

Berossus' chronology for the Neo-Babylonian era was published during the Seleucid period and evidently represents the contemporary, "popular" concept of Neo-Babylonian chronology. Berossus' figures for the reigns of Neo-Babylonian kings place Nebuchadnezzar's thirty-seventh year in 568/67 B.C.E. as does *VAT 4956*. More importantly, Berossus' Neo-Babylonian chronology, as has been shown above, *is in complete agreement with the chronology given by the many documents contemporary with the Neo-Babylonian era itself* such as chronicles, royal inscriptions, business documents, and (as will be demonstrated below) with contemporary Egyptian documents! The "popular" Neo-Babylonian chronology of the Seleucid era, then, was a true and correct chronology, and there was no need for copyists to alter the ancient documents in order to adapt them to it. The theory that they falsified these documents, therefore, is thoroughly groundless. Besides, it is refuted completely by another diary, still unpublished.

In an article published in 1974,[95] Professor Abraham J. Sachs, considered to be the foremost authority on the astronomical diaries, gives a brief presentation of them. Mentioning that the oldest datable diary contains observations from the year 652 B.C.E., he explains how he was able to fix its date: "I found the astronomical contents to be just barely adequate to make this date virtually certain. It was a great relief when *I was able to confirm the date by matching up a historical remark in the diary with the corresponding statement for −651 in a well-dated historical chronicle.*"[96] As this diary seemed to be of great importance for the question of Babylonian chronology, I wrote to Professor Sachs and asked two questions:

> 1. What information in the diary makes the date −651 "virtually certain"?
>
> 2. What kind of historical remark in the diary corresponds with what statement in which well-dated chronicle?

In his answer, dated February 10, 1980, Professor Sachs enclosed an IBM copy of the diary in question, *B.M. 32312*, and added information which fully answered my two questions. The astronomical contents of the diary clearly establish the year as 652/51 B.C.E. when the observations were made. Sachs writes: "the preserved astronomical events (Mercury's last visibility in the east behind Pisces, Saturn's last visibility behind Pisces, both around the 14th of month I; Mars' stationary point in Scorpio on the 17th of month I; Mercury's first visibility in Pisces on the 6th of month XII) *uniquely determine the date.*" (Italics mine)

Interestingly, it cannot be claimed that this diary was redated by later copyists, because the name of the king, his regnal year, and month names *are broken away*. Yet these data may be supplied because of a historical remark in the diary. For *month 12, day 27*, the diary states that the king of Babylon was involved in a battle at a place called Hirit. Fortunately, this battle is also mentioned in a well-known Babylonian chronicle.

The chronicle is the so-called "Akitu Chronicle," B.M. 86379, which covers a part of Shamashshumukin's reign, especially his last five years (the sixteenth to the twentieth). The battle at Hirit is dated in his sixteenth year as follows:

> The sixteenth year of Shamash-shuma-ukin ... On the twenty-seventh day of Adar (the 27th day of the 12th month!) the armies of Assyria and Akkad did battle in Hirit. The army of Akkad retreated from the battlefield and a major defeat was inflicted upon them.[97]

The astronomical events described in the diary fix the battle at Hirit on Adar 27 to 651 B.C.E.[98] The "Akitu Chronicle" shows that this battle at this place on this day (Adar 27) was fought in the sixteenth year of Shamashshumukin. Thus Shamashshumukin's sixteenth year was 652/51 B.C.E.. His entire reign of twenty years, then, may be dated to 667 - 648 B.C.E.. Now this is how historians have dated Shamashshumukin's reign for a long time, and that is why Professor Sachs concludes his letter by saying: "I should perhaps add that the absolute chronology of the regnal years of Shamash-shuma-ukin was never in doubt, and that it is *only confirmed again* by the astronomical diary." (Italics mine)

Shamashshumukin's reign has been known, for example, through Ptolemy's canon which gives him twenty years and his successor Kandalanu twenty-two years. Thereafter Nabopolassar, Nebuchadnezzar's father, succeeded to the throne. These figures agree completely with ancient cuneiform sources. Business documents, as well as the

"Akitu Chronicle" and the "Uruk King List," all show that Shamashshumukin ruled for twenty years, and that from the first year of Kandalanu to the first year of Nabopolassar was a period of twenty-two years.[99]

The diary B.M. 32312, then, again corroborates the chronology of the Neo-Babylonian era established above:

Shamashshumukin	20 years	667 - 648 BC
Kandalanu	22 years	647 - 626 BC
Nabopolassar	21 years	625 - 605 BC
Nebuchadnezzar	43 years	604 - 562 BC
etc.		

This diary confirms, once again, Ptolemy's king list, and adds another witness to the increasing amount of evidence against the 607 B.C.E. date. A change of Nebuchadnezzar's eighteenth year from 587 to 607 B.C.E would also change Shamashshumukin's sixteenth year from 652 to 672 B.C.E. But the diary B.M. 32312 makes such a change impossible. And, as already pointed out, no one can claim that later copyists inserted "the 16th year of Shamashshumukin" in this diary, because the text is damaged at this point and that datum is broken away! The unique historical information in the text, repeated in the "Akitu Chronicle," fixes the diary to Shamashshumukin's sixteenth year. This diary, therefore, may be regarded as an independent witness, which upholds the authenticity of the dates given in *VAT 4956* and other diaries.

SYNCHRONIC LINKS TO THE CHRONOLOGY OF EGYPT

An excellent proof of the correctness of a chronology is the fact that it is in agreement with the chronologies of other contemporary nations, provided that these other chronologies are independently established and there are synchronisms, that is, dated connecting links, to them. During the Neo-Babylonian period there are at least *four* such synchronisms between Egypt and the kingdoms of Judah and Babylon. Three of these are given in the Bible, in 2 Kings 23:29 (where Egyptian pharaoh Nechoh and Judean king Josiah appear), Jeremiah 46:2 (Nechoh, Nebuchadnezzar and Jehoiakim all appearing), and Jeremiah 44:30 (Pharaoh Hophra, Zedekiah and Nebuchadnezzar listed). The fourth is given in a cuneiform text, *B. M. 33041*, which refers to a campaign against Amasis, king of Egypt, in Nebuchadnezzar's thirty-seventh regnal year.[100] The meaning of these synchronisms will be unravelled further on.

The kings reigning in Egypt during the Neo-Babylonian period belonged to the *Twenty-Sixth Dynasty*. The period of this dynasty is also referred to as the *Saite Period*. If the four synchronisms mentioned above are to be of any help to our study, it must first be shown that the chronology of the Twenty-Sixth Dynasty of Egypt is fixed independently from the contemporary Neo-Babylonian chronology. Of this F.K. Kienitz writes:

> The chronology of the kings of the 26th Dynasty, from Psammetichus onwards, is completely established through a series of death stelae and stelae of holy Apis bulls, which list the birth date in 'Day x, Month y, Year z, of King A' and the death date in 'Day x, Month y, Year z, of King B', and also the length of life of the [bull or person] in question in years, months, and days.[101]

This means that, if a death stele says that a sacred Apis bull or a person was born in the 10th year of King A and died at the age of 25 in the 20th year of King B, we know that King A ruled for *15 years*. This is the kind of contemporary evidence Dr. Kienitz refers to. A translation of Kienitz' presentation of this material is given here.[102]

1. GRAVE STELE OF THE 3RD APIS OF THE 26TH DYNASTY.

Date of Birth: Year 53 of Psammetichus I, Month 6, Day 19
Installation: Year 54 of Psammetichus I, Month 3, Day 12
Date of Death: Year 16 of Nechoh II, Month 2, Day 6
Date of Burial: Year 16 of Nechoh II, Month 4, Day 16
Length of Life: 16 years, 7 months, 17 days.
Result: Length of reign of Psammetichus I = 54 years.

2. GRAVE STELE OF THE 4TH APIS OF THE 26TH DYNASTY.

Date of Birth: Year 16 of Nechoh, Month 2, Day 7
Installation: Year 1 of Psammetichus II, Month 11, Day 9
Date of Death: Year 12 of Apries, Month 8, Day 12
Date of Burial: Year 12 of Apries, Month 10, Day 21
Length of Life: 17 years, 6 months, 5 days
Result: As the date of Psammetichus II's death is elsewhere attested as Year 7, Month 1, Day 23,[103] the length of Nechoh's reign amounts to 15 years, that of Psammetichus II to 6 years.

3. TWO GRAVE STELAE OF A PRIEST NAMED PSAMMETICHUS

Date of Birth: Year 1 of Nechoh II, Month 11, Day 1
Date of Death: Year 27 of Amasis, Month 8, Day 28
Length of Life: 65 years, 10 months, 2 days
Result: The sum of the lengths of reign of Nechoh II, Psammetichus II, and Apries = 40 years. As Nechoh II reigned for 15 years, and Psammetichus II for 6 years, Apries' reign amounts to 19 years.

4. GRAVE STELE OF ANOTHER PSAMMETICHUS

Date of Birth: Year 3 of Nechoh II, Month 10, Day 1 or 2
Date of Death: Year 35 of Amasis, Month 2, Day 6
Length of Life: 71 years, 4 months, 6 days
Result: The same as under 3.

5. GRAVE STELE OF ONE BESMAUT

Year of Birth: Year 18 of Psammetichus I
Year of Death: Year 23 of Amasis
Length of Life: 99 years
Result: The total of 94 years for the lengths of reign from Psammetichus I to Apries inclusive is once more confirmed.

Consequently, these contemporary death stelae conclusively establish the lengths of reign of the first four kings of the twenty-sixth dynasty of Egypt as follows:

Psammetichus I	54 years
Nechoh II	15 years
Psammetichus II	6 years
Apries (=Hophra)	19 years

Unfortunately, material of this kind is lacking for the last two kings of the Twenty-Sixth Dynasty, Amasis and Psammetichus III, but both Herodotus (c. 484-425 B.C.E.) and the Egyptian priest Manetho (of the third century B.C.E.) give forty-four years to Amasis and six months to Psammetichus III.[104] These lengths of reign have been confirmed by modern discoveries. In the papyrus *Rylands IX*, also called the "Petition of Petiese," dating from the time of Darius I (521-486 B.C.E.), the forty-fourth year of Amasis is mentioned in a context indicating it was his last full year. A prophet of Amun of Teuzoi, Psammetkmenempe by name, who lived in the Delta, used to send a representative each year to fetch his stipend. This he did until the forty-fourth year of Amasis. In the "Demotic Chronicle," a report on the compilation of Egyptian laws written under Darius I, there are two references to the forty-fourth year of Amasis as some sort of terminal point. The same figure is also given in an inscription from Wâdi Hammâmât.[105] For some time it was held among authorities that Amasis died in his forty-fourth regnal year, and because of the Egyptian nonaccession-year system, whereby a king's accession year is reckoned as his first regnal year, they gave Amasis only forty-three full years.[106] But in 1957 R.A. Parker demonstrated conclusively that Amasis reigned for forty-four full years.[107] We will return to this evidence shortly.

As to Psammetichus III, the highest date available for this king is Year 2. Three documents (papyri) dated to the third, fourth, and fifth months of his second year have been discovered. This is no contradiction to the statement that this king ruled six months only. According to the Egyptian nonaccession year system the year in which a king came to power was reckoned as his first regnal year. Psammetichus III was dethroned by the Persian king Cambyses during his conquest of Egypt in May/June 525 B.C.E., a date firmly established and accepted by all authorities.[108] If Psammetichus III ruled for six months, his reign began at the end of 526 B.C.E., probably only a few days or weeks before the end of that year. At this time the Egyptian civil calendar year almost coincided with the Julian calendar year, and Psammetichus III, therefore, ascended to the throne at the end of the Egyptian civil calendar year, too. Though he ruled for only a fraction of that year, this fraction of a few days or weeks was reckoned as his *first* regnal year according to the Egyptian nonaccession-year system. His *second* regnal year, then, began only a few days or weeks after his accession to the throne. If he ruled for only six months, as Herodotus and Manetho say, documents dated up to the fifth month of his second year are only what we should expect to find.[109] The following illustration makes the matter plain:

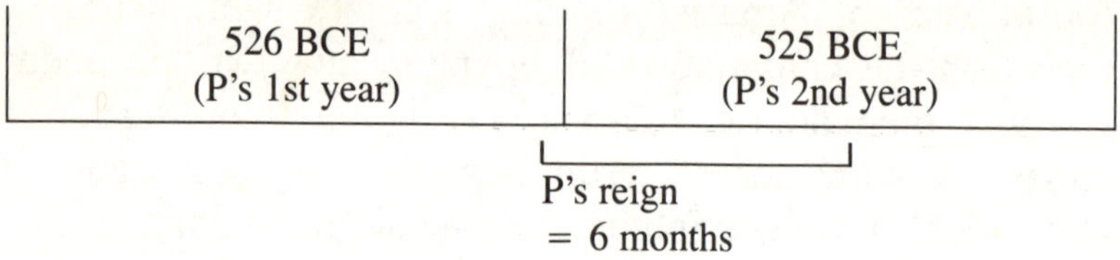

If Amasis, the predecessor of Psammetichus III, ruled for 44 years, his reign must have started in 570 BCE (526 + 44 = 570). It was this that Dr. R. A. Parker demonstrated in 1957, as mentioned earlier.

That year Parker examined a document in the Louvre collection in Paris, papyrus No. 7848, dated in the *12th year of Amasis*. At that time the Egyptians used two calendars of different lengths. Events, therefore, were sometimes dated according to both calendars. Interestingly, an event mentioned in Parker's Amasis document was dated this way, "in Year 12, II šmw 13 [= 13th day of month 10], being the 15th lunar day of I šmw [= month 9]."[110] The first date refers to the Egyptian *civil* calendar, the second date to the *lunar* calendar.

The civil calendar had 365 days, which is about a quarter of a day short of the true solar year, which has 365.2422 days. The lunar calendar was fixed to the moon, and as it was 11 days shorter than the solar year a 13th month had to be added to it every second or third year.[111] The resultant effect was that a date in the lunar calendar seldom fell on the same date in the civil calendar. This occurred only at intervals of 25 years.[112] These circumstances helped Parker demonstrate that Amasis' 12th year was 559, not 558 B.C.E. His first regnal year, therefore, must have been 570 (559 + 11), not 569 as had been thought previously.[113] (For details, see Parker's article.) The combined reigns of Amasis and Psammetichus III, then, extended from 570 to 525, or for a period of 45 years.

This was a remarkable confirmation of the dates for Amasis and Psammetichus III given by the most ancient historians, Herodotus and Manetho, as well as of the dates given on contemporary documents. Since 1957, Parker's conclusions have obtained general acceptance among scholars. One of them has even added further evidence in support of his dates. If Amasis' first year was 570 B.C.E. instead of 569, as was held by most scholars prior to 1957, this also moved the beginning of the Twenty-Sixth Dynasty from 663 to 664 B.C.E. This was the first year of Psammetichus I. As he ruled for 54 years, he died in 610 B.C.E. In 1966 Erik Hornung directed his attention to the *Demotic Papyrus Berlin 13588*, written in the first century B.C.E., but relating an event from the time of the Twenty-Sixth Dynasty. A priest named Amasis reports to the Egyptian king that he had heard that "heaven has devoured the sun disk," after which he had gone away to the place where King Psammetichus was being embalmed. Evidently this solar eclipse took place shortly after the death of king Psammetichus. But which Psammetichus? The evidence presented above shows king Psammetichus I to have died in 610; Psammetichus II died in 589 B.C. No solar eclipse took place in 589 B.C., but in 610 a solar eclipse occurred on September 30, Julian calendar, giving an additional support to this date for the death of Psammetichus I and the correctness of the chronology for the Twenty-Sixth Dynasty of Egypt established above.[114]

The discussion above has clearly demonstrated that the chronology of the Twenty-Sixth Dynasty of Egypt is firmly and independently established. The results are summarized in the following table:

	YEARS OF REIGN	*YEARS BCE*
Psammetichus I	54	664 - 610
Nechoh II	15	610 - 595
Psammetichus II	6	595 - 589
Apries (= Hophra)	19	589 - 570
Amasis	44	570 - 526
Psammetichus III	1	526 - 525
Cambyses' conquest of Egypt		May/June 525

Does this chronology square with that of the Neo-Babylonian era as established above, or with the chronology of the Watchtower Society as presented, for example, in *Aid to Bible Understanding*? The four synchronisms to the Egyptian chronology mentioned earlier decide the matter:

> *(1) 2 Kings 23:29:* In his [king Josiah's] days Pharaoh Nechoh the king of Egypt came up to the king of Assyria by the river Euphrates, and King Josiah proceeded to go to meet him; but he put him to death at Megiddo as soon as he saw him. (NW)

Here it is clearly shown that King Josiah of Judah died at Megiddo in the reign of Pharaoh Nechoh of Egypt. According to the chronology of the Watchtower Society Josiah's death took place about 629 B.C.E. (See *Aid to Bible Understanding*, p. 968). But Nechoh's reign did not begin until nineteen years later, in 610 B.C.E. (see table above.) So Josiah's death did not take place in 629 B.C.E. or thereabouts, but twenty years later, in 609.[115]

> *(2) Jeremiah 46:2:* For Egypt, concerning the military force of Pharaoh Nechoh the king of Egypt, who happened to be by the river Euphrates at Carchemish, whom Nebuchadnezzar the king of Babylon defeated in the fourth year of Jehoiakim the son of Josiah, the king of Judah. (NW)

This battle in the fourth year of Jehoiakim is placed in the year 625 B.C.E. by the Watchtower Society (See *Aid to Bible Understanding*, p. 347, footnote "u"), which again cannot be harmonized with the contemporary chronology of Egypt. But if this battle at Carchemish took place twenty years later, in the accession-year of Nebuchadnezzar, that is, in June, 605 B.C.E. according to all the lines of evidence presented earlier, we find this date to be in perfect harmony with the reign of Pharaoh Nechoh, 610 - 595 B.C.E.

> *(3) Jeremiah 44:30:* This is what Jehovah has said: 'Here I am giving Pharaoh Hophra, the king of Egypt, into the hand of his enemies and into the hand of those seeking for his soul, just as I have given Zedekiah the king of Judah into the hand of Nebuchadnezzar the king of Babylon, his enemy and the one seeking for his soul'. (NW)

As the context shows (verse 1ff.) these words were uttered not long after the destruction of Jerusalem and its temple, when the rest of the Jewish population had fled to Egypt after the assassination of Gedaliah. At that time Egypt was ruled by Pharaoh Hophra, or Apries, as he is named by Herodotus.[116] If Apries ruled Egypt at the time when the Jews fled there some months after the desolation of Jerusalem, this desolation cannot be dated to 607 B.C.E., for Apries did not begin his reign until 589 B.C.E. (See the table above). But a dating of the desolation of Jerusalem to 587 B.C.E. is in good agreement with the reign historically established for him: 589 - 570 B.C.E.

> *(4) B.M. 33041:* As mentioned earlier, this text refers to a campaign against king Amasis ([Ama]-a-su) in Nebuchadnezzar's thirty-seventh year. A.L. Oppenheim's translation of this scanty

> fragment reads in part as follows: "...[in] the 37th year, Nebuchadnezzar, king of Bab[ylon], mar[ched against] Egypt (Misir) to deliver a battle. [Ama]sis (text: [...]-a(?)-su), of Egypt [called up his [a]rm[y]... [...]*ku* from the town Putu-Iaman...distant regions which (are situated on islands) amidst the sea ..."[117]

This text is badly damaged, but it clearly states that the campaign took place in Nebuchadnezzar's thirty-seventh year. The name of the Pharaoh is only partly legible, but the signs preserved seem only to fit Amasis, and no other king of the Twenty-sixth Dynasty. The Watchtower Society dates the thirty-seventh year of Nebuchadnezzar to 588/87 B.C.E. (*Aid to Bible Understanding*, p. 498:13), but this was during the reign of Apries (see the table). On the other hand, if Nebuchadnezzar's thirty-seventh year was 568/67 B.C.E., as is established by the astronomical diary *VAT 4956* and all the other lines of evidence presented earlier, this date is in excellent agreement with the reign of Amasis (570 - 526 B.C.E.).

Consequently, not one of the four synchronisms with the independently established chronology of Egypt agrees with the chronology of the Watchtower Society. The discrepancy in that Society's reckoning is consistently about twenty years out of harmony. But interestingly, all four synchronisms are in perfect harmony with the dates arrived at from the other lines of evidences discussed above. These synchronisms to the Egyptian chronology, therefore, add yet *another* line of evidence to the others, which point to 587 B.C.E. as the definitive date for the destruction of Jerusalem.

SUMMARY AND CONCLUSION

Seven lines of evidence have been presented above against dating the destruction of Jerusalem in 607 B.C.E., all of which agree in dating that event twenty years later. This evidence has been presented above as *four* lines of evidence that are *independent of one another*:

1. *Chronicles and other historical records*: (a) *The Neo-Babylonian chronicles* unearthed hitherto are still incomplete. But it was demonstrated that both *Berossus* and *Ptolemy*—independently of each other—got their figures for the reigns of the Neo-Babylonian kings *from the Neo-Babylonian chronicles*. As their figures agree, we have strong reason to believe that the chronological information originally given in those chronicles has been preserved for us in an unaltered condition by Berossus and Ptolemy. Both agree as to the length of the Neo-Babylonian era. Their figures point to 604/03 B.C.E. as the first year of Nebuchadnezzar's reign, and 587/86 B.C. as his eighteenth year when he desolated Jerusalem.

b) *The royal inscription Nabon. No. 8* (the Hillah stele), probably inscribed in the second year of Nabonidus, gives the information that the temple *é.hul.hul* in Harran was in ruins for fifty-four years, until Nabonidus in his accession-year was commanded to rebuild it. The chronicle B.M. 21901 and the Harran stele Nabon. H 1, B both state that the Medes ruined Harran and its temple *in the sixteenth year of Nabopolassar*, the father of Nebuchadnezzar. Thus Nabonidus reckons the fifty-four years from that year to his own accession-year. The figures preserved by Berossus and Ptolemy also show this period to have been fifty-four years. Further, Nabon. No. 8 (as well as the cylinder Nabon. No. 18) records astronomical observations that help us to fix Nabonidus' first year to 555/554 B.C.E. The fifty-four years, therefore, began in 610/09 B.C.E. If this was Nabopolassar's sixteenth year, Nebuchadnezzar's first was 604/03 B.C.E. and his eighteenth year 587/86.

c) *The royal inscription Nabon. H 1. B* (the Adda-Guppi'stele) gives the length of all the reigns of the Neo-Babylonian kings up to the ninth year of Nabonidus (except for Labashi-Marduk's short reign which is ignored). The figures given on the stele are in complete agreement with the figures given by Berossus and Ptolemy. Again, the 587/86 B.C.E. date for the destruction of Jerusalem in the eighteenth year of Nebuchadnezzar is confirmed.

These three sources have been grouped together as *one* line of evidence because it cannot be clearly established that these documents are independent of one another. It has already been pointed out that Berossus and Ptolemy both got their information from the Babylonian chronicles. It is also possible that the chronological information given on the royal inscriptions was derived from the chronicles, although this cannot be proved.[118] Further, there is some evidence that the chronicles were composed with the help of the chronographical information given in the astronomical diaries.[119] This possible interdependence of these sources does not weaken their conclusive power. On the contrary it strengthens it. As the royal inscriptions preserve chronological information that is *contemporary with* the Neo-Babylonian era itself, we have every reason to accept it as *factual* and *true* information. If the royal inscriptions, Berossus, and Ptolemy all got their information from the Babylonian chronicles, Berossus' and Ptolemy's figures are proved to be correctly preserved by their agreement with the royal inscriptions.

2. *Business and Administrative Documents*: Thousands of business and administrative documents, dated to the year, the month, and the day of the reigning king, have come down to us from the Neo-Babylonian period. Thus we have many tablets from each year during this whole period. The length of reign of each king may, then, be established by these documents, sometimes almost to the day. The results arrived at are in good agreement with the figures given by Berossus and Ptolemy, the chronicles, and the contemporary royal inscriptions from the reign of Nabonidus. This is, for instance, excellently demonstrated by the thousands of tablets from the archive of the banking house called "the Sons of Egibi." The twenty years demanded by the chronology of the Watchtower Society, which dates the destruction of Jerusalem to 607 B.C.E., are totally missing. The business and administrative documents are original documents, *contemporary with* the

Neo-Babylonian era itself, which makes this line of evidence exceedingly stong. These documents definitely point to 587/86 B.C.E. as Nebuchadnezzar's eighteenth regnal year, when he desolated Jerusalem.

3. *Astronomical diaries*: (a) *The astronomical diary VAT 4956* contains about thirty completely verified astronomical observations from Nebuchadnezzar's thirty-seventh regnal year. The combination of these astronomical positions is not duplicated again in thousands of years. Consequently, there is only one year which fits this situation: 568/67 B.C.E. If this was Nebuchadnezzar's thirty-seventh regnal year, as is twice stated on this tablet, then 587/86 B.C.E. must have been his eighteenth year, in which he desolated Jerusalem.

(b) The oldest preserved astronomical diary, *B.M. 32312*, records astronomical observations that enable scholars to date this tablet to 652/51 B.C.E. A historical remark in the text, repeated in the Babylonian chronicle B.M. 86379 (the "Akitu Chronicle") shows this to have been the sixteenth year of Shamash-shuma-ukin. The diary, then, fixes his twenty-year reign to 667-648 B.C.E., Kandalanu's twenty-two-year reign to 647-626, Nabopolassar's twenty-one-year reign to 625-605, and Nebuchadnezzar's forty-three-year reign to 604-562 B.C.E. This, again, sets his eighteenth year and the destruction of Jerusalem at 587/86 B.C.E.

Strictly, these two diaries could have been dealt with as two independent lines of evidence. But as *B.M. 32312* is separated from the Neo-Babylonian era by the reigns of two kings (Shamash-shuma-ukin and Kandalanu), it is being treated here as a supporting evidence to *VAT 4956*, confirming the genuineness of the information given in the latter text.

4. *Synchronisms with Contemporary Egyptian Chronology*: The independently established chronology of contemporary Egyptian kings provides an excellent test of Neo-Babylonian chronology, as there are four synchronisms tied to it, three of which are given in the Bible.

These synchronisms are of the utmost importance, as the contemporary chronology of Egypt has been established *independently* of the chronologies of the other nations of that time. Yet it was shown that it is in complete harmony with the data given by Berossus, Ptolemy, the Babylonian chronicles, the royal inscriptions, the business and administrative documents, and the astronomical diaries, while a comparison with the chronology of the Watchtower Society shows a consistent difference of about twenty years. These four synchronisms to Egyptian chronology all refute the 607 B.C.E. date for the desolation of Jerusalem and once again uphold 587/86 B.C.E. as the correct date for that event.

The evidence from all this material is overwhelming *and conclusive*. Suppose for a moment that Berossus' figures for the reigns of the Neo-Babylonian kings contain an error of twenty years, as is required by the chronology of the Watchtower Society. Then about 400 years later Ptolemy must have made exactly the same mistake, evidently independently of Berossus! It might be argued, though, that both simply repeated an error contained in the sources they used, namely the Neo-Babylonian chronicles. Then the scribes of Nabonidus, too, who possibly used the same sources, would have had to have dropped twenty years from the reign of the same king (or kings) when they made the inscriptions of the Hillah stele and the Adda-Guppi' stele. But is it really likely that those scribes, who *wrote during the Neo-Babylonian era*, did not know the lengths of the reigns of the kings under whom they lived, especially since those reigns also functioned as calendar years by which they dated different events? If they really made such a strange mistake, how is it possible that contemporary scribes in Egypt also made the same mistake, dropping the same period of twenty years when making inscriptions on death stelae and other documents? Curiously, the Babylonian astronomers, too, must have made a similar "mistake" when dating the diary *VAT 4956*, changing not only the regnal year, but also the name of the reigning king—unless of course changes were purposely made by later copyists from the Seleucid era, as the Watchtower Society posits. But still more incredible is the idea that scribes and astronomers could remove any reference to twenty years from the Neo-Babylonian era several years *prior to* that era—as is shown by the oldest diary, *B.M. 32312*, which sets Shamash-shuma-ukin's sixteenth year as occurring in 652/51 B.C.E. instead of 672/71 as required by the chronology of the Watchtower Society. But the most remarkable "coincidence" of all is this: Thousands of dated business and administrative documents have been excavated from the Neo-Babylonian period, covering every year of this period—except, as the Watchtower Society would have it, for a period of twenty years from which not one tablet has been found. Again, most curiously, according to this logic, that period happens to be exactly the same as that lost through a series of other "mistakes" by scribes in Babylon and Egypt, and by later copyists and historians. Either there was an international agreement during several centuries to erase this twenty-year period from the recorded history of the world—or it never existed! If such an international "plot" ever took place it was so successful that of all the thousands of documents unearthed from the Neo-Babylonian era there is not one, not even a line in any of them, that indicates that such a twenty-year period ever existed. We can safely assume, then, that the Watchtower Society's chronology is unquestionably in error.

In an article on chronology published in *The Watch Tower* of July 15, 1922, entitled "The Strong Cable of Chronology," the strength of a chronology is described on page 217 in an excellent way:

> When a date is indicated by several lines of evidence it is strongly established. The scientific law of probabilities imparts a united strength to the strands of the cable of chronology far greater than the sum of the individual lines of evidence. This is a law which is implicitly relied upon in important affairs: viz., that when a thing is indicated in only one way it may be by chance; if it is indicated

> in two ways, it is almost certain to be true; and if in more than two ways, it is usually impossible that it is by chance, or that it is not true, and the addition of more proofs removes it entirely from the realm of chance into that of proven certainty.

Above, *seven* lines of evidence have been presented, four of which are clearly independent of one another, and all of them point to the year 587/86 B.C.E. as the date of the destruction of Jerusalem in Nebuchadnezzar's eighteenth regnal year. According to the principle described in *The Watch Tower* as just quoted, this cannot be by a mere chance; instead the matter must be regarded as a "proven certainty."

But if this is the conclusion of our study, how are we to harmonize this fact with the biblical prophecy of the seventy years, during which the land of Judah and Jerusalem would lay desolate according to the Watchtower Society? And how are we to view the year 1914 C.E., the supposed terminal date for the times of the Gentiles according to the prophetic time scale of the Watchtower Society? Do not world events clearly show that Bible prophecies have been fulfilled since that year? These questions will be dealt with in Chapter III.

CHAPTER III

EXEGETICAL PROBLEMS AND SUGGESTED SOLUTIONS

The date 607 B.C.E. as given by Watchtower chronologists for the destruction of Jerusalem and its temple by the Babylonians is determined by adding seventy years to 537 B.C.E., the date when the Jewish remnant are thought to have returned from exile. It is held that the seventy years were a period of *complete desolation* for Judah and Jerusalem:

> The Bible prophecy does not allow for the application of the seventy-year period to any time other than that between the destruction of Judah, accompanying Jerusalem's destruction, and the return of the Jewish exiles to their homeland as a result of Cyrus' decree. It clearly specifies that the seventy years would be years of *devastation of the land of Judah.*[1]

If no other understanding of the seventy-year period is allowed for by Bible prophecy, then a choice has to be made between the date determined by this application and the one established by several lines of historical evidence.

When a certain interpretation of a biblical prophecy contradicts historical evidence, this indicates that an error has been made. It is true that a certain application sometimes looks very convincing, so much so that no other appears feasible. It seems to the reader to be given by the Bible itself. In such a case it may also seem to be a sound Christian position to discard the historical evidence and "just stick to what the Bible says." But when this position is taken, those taking it often overlook the fact that the fulfillment of a prophecy cannot be demonstrated *aside from history*, because history shows whether, and—if it was—when and how it was fulfilled. Actually, prophecy is not generally understood until after it has been fulfilled historically through events in time. Serious mistakes have sometimes been made by sincere Bible students because historical evidence *contrary* to a certain application or interpretation has been rejected. One example will be given below to illustrate this fact.

HISTORY AND TIME PROPHECIES—A LESSON

Most scholars agree that Daniel's prophecy of the seventy weeks refers to a period of 490 years. But various opinions have been held regarding the starting-point of this period. Although it is stated at Daniel 9:25 that "from the going forth of [the] word to restore and rebuild Jerusalem until Messiah [the] leader, there will be seven weeks, also sixty-two weeks" (NW), different views are held regarding when and by whom this "word" was sent forth.[2] But if we "just stick to the Bible," it seems to point clearly to Cyrus. At Isaiah 44:28 Jehovah "saith of Cyrus, He is my shepherd, and shall perform all my pleasure, even saying of Jerusalem, She shall be built; and of the temple, Thy foundation shall be laid" (ASV). And further, in Chapter 45, verse 13: "I myself have roused up someone in righteousness [Cyrus], and all his ways I shall straighten out. *He is the one that will build my city*, and those of mine in exile he will let go, not for a price nor for bribery" (NW).

Thus it would seem clear, that according to the Bible itself the "word to restore and rebuild Jerusalem" was issued by Cyrus. But this application limits the period from Cyrus' edict (Ezra 1:1-4) until Messiah to 483 years ("seven weeks, also sixty-two weeks") and fixes Cyrus' first year as king of Babylon to c. 455 B.C.E. instead of 538 B.C.E. Several Christian commentators from Tertullian in the second century and onward have chosen this application, contrary to all historical evidence, and it is still adhered to by some expositors.[3] The idea was popularized by Martin Anstey in his work *The Romance of the Bible Chronology*, London 1913.[4] Dr. E.W. Bullinger accepted the same position, as may be seen in the chronolgical table in his *The Companion Bible*. Among present Bible commentators, David L. Cooper, founder of the Biblical Research Society and editor of the *Biblical Research Monthly*, holds this same thesis.

The reasoning underlying this unhistorical position is clearly demonstrated by George Storrs, a Bible student from the last century and editor of the periodical *Bible Examiner*. In an article dealing with the seventy weeks, he states: "In examining this point, we have nothing to do with profane chronology, or the chronology of the historians. The Bible must settle the question, and if profane chronology does not tally with it, we have a right to conclude such chronology is false, and not to be trusted."[5] Like Tertullian, and later Anstey, Bullinger and Cooper, Storrs tried to cut off nearly 100 years from the Persian period, holding that a number of the Persian kings mentioned in Ptolemy's canon and other historical sources never existed! George Storrs surely was an honest and sincere Christian Bible student, but his (and others') rejection of historical sources proved to be a grave mistake. That the Persian kings mentioned in Ptolemy's canon really existed has been proved beyond all doubt by archeological discoveries in modern times.[6] This is an instructive illustration of the necessity of considering the historical evidence in relation to biblical time prophecies. Although this special application of the seventy weeks seemed *very biblical* and very convincing, it has been refuted by historical facts and therefore cannot be correct. The same is also true of the application of the seventy-year prophecy made by the Watchtower Society. Although on the surface it may *seem to* be supported by some passages in the Bible, it should be abandoned because it is incompatible with historical facts established by a multitude of modern discoveries. Is it possible, then, to find an application of the seventy years that is in accordance with the historical evidence? It is, and a close examination of biblical texts dealing with the seventy years will demonstrate that there is no real conflict between the Bible and secular history in this matter. As will be shown below, *it is the application made by the Watchtower Society that conflicts, not only with secular history, but also with the Bible itself.*

THE SEVENTY YEARS: DESOLATION OR SERVITUDE—WHICH?

There are seven scriptural texts referring to a period of seventy years which the Watchtower Society applies to one and the same period: Jeremiah 25:10-12; 29:10, Daniel 9:1,2; 2 Chronicles 36:20,21; Zechariah 1:7, 12; 7:1-7, and Isaiah 23:15-18. These will now be examined one by one.[7]

> *1. Jeremiah 25:10-12*: And I will destroy out of them the sound of exultation and the sound of rejoicing, the voice of the bridegroom and the voice of the bride, the sound of the hand mill and the light of the lamp. And all this land must become a devastated place, an object of astonishment, and *these nations will have to serve the king of Babylon seventy years*. And it must occur that when seventy years have been fulfilled I shall call to account against the king of Babylon and against the land of the Chaldeans, and I will make it desolate wastes to time indefinite. (NW)[8]

Two things are predicted in this prophecy: (1) "all this land [Judah] must become a *devastated place*" (Hebr.

chorbáh), and (2) "*these nations* [that is, "all these nations round about," according to verse 9] will have to *serve* the king of Babylon seventy years." Although it is predicted that the land of Judah would be a devastated place, this devastation is not directly equated with the period of the seventy years.[9] What is clearly and unambiguously stated in the text is that the *nations surrounding Judah would serve* the king of Babylon. The seventy years, then, should be understood to mean years of *servitude* for Judah and the surrounding nations. This conclusion is so obvious that the Watchtower Society, at the head of page 826 of its large-print edition of the *New World Translation* (1971 ed.), automatically describes the seventy years as "70 years' *servitude*." Yet, in their discussions of this text, Watchtower writers never point out that Jeremiah included *many nations* in the servitude or that he predicted seventy years of *servitude* for them. They try always to give the impression that the seventy years referred to Judah only, and they always describe the seventy years as a period in which Judah suffered *complete desolation, "without an inhabitant*." This they reckon as having happened from the destruction of Jerusalem and its temple. But their application is in direct conflict with the exact wording of Jeremiah's prediction, and it can be upheld only by ignoring what the text actually says.

"Servitude" should not be taken to mean the same thing as "captivity" or "desolation" "without an inhabitant," although it sometimes may include such things. For the nations surrounding Judah the servitude first of all meant *vassalage*, even if Nebuchadnezzar's conquests of those nations often included the devastation of cities and deportation of captives. As time and again Judah revolted and attempted to throw off the Babylonian yoke, its servitude came to include wave after wave of devastating military ravages and deportations until the country was at last completely desolated and depopulated after the destruction of Jerusalem in 587 B.C.E. That such a fate was not the same thing as "servitude," but would come upon any nation that *refused to serve* the king of Babylon, had been clearly predicted by Jeremiah, at chapter 27, verse 8:

> And it must occur that the nation and the kingdom that *will not serve him*, even Nebuchadnezzar the king of Babylon; and the one that will not put its neck under the yoke of the king of Babylon, *with the sword and with the famine and with the pestilence I shall turn my attention upon that nation*, is the utterance of Jehovah, until I have finished them off by his hand. (NW)

Jeremiah, therefore, warned the people of attempting to throw off the Babylonian yoke and admonished them: "Serve the king of Babylon and keep on living. Why should this city become a devastated place?" (verse 17) Thus, the nations that accepted the Babylonian yoke would *serve* the king of Babylon seventy years. But the nation that *refused to serve* the Babylonian king would become *devastated*. This fate at last befell Judah after about eighteen years of servitude, interrupted by repeated rebellions. The devastation or desolation, though, is nowhere stated to have lasted for seventy years.[10] Other nations, too, that refused to accept the Babylonian yoke, were punished, cities were ruined, and captives were brought to Babylon. For example, one of the Philistine cities, probably Ashkelon, was "plundered and sacked" and "turned...into a ruin heap," according to the *Babylonian Chronicle* (B.M. 21946). This was in the first year of Nebuchadnezzar according to the chronicle, that is, in 604 B.C.E. (Grayson, *Assyrian and Babylonian Chronicles*, p. 100. "Ashkelon" is only partly legible.)

That the seventy years refer to the period of Babylonian supremacy, and not to the period of Jerusalem's desolation reckoned from its destruction in Nebuchadnezzar's eighteenth year, is also confirmed by verse 12 of Jeremiah 25: "And it must occur that *when seventy years have been fulfilled* I shall call to account against the king of Babylon and against that nation, is the utterance of Jehovah." When did Jehovah "call to account against the king of

Babylon and against that nation"? All will agree that this began to be fulfilled when Babylon fell to Cyrus' army in 539 B.C.E. At that time the seventy years had "been fulfilled," according to Jeremiah's prophecy. Did the Jewish *captivity* end in 539 B.C.E.? No! Did the *desolation* of Jerusalem end in 539 B.C.E.? No! Did the Babylonian *supremacy* and the *servitude* to the Babylonian king end that year? Yes! As the seventy years ended in 539 B.C.E., they clearly refer, not to the captivity or the desolation, but to the *servitude*. Thus, again we find the application of the seventy years made by the Watchtower Society in conflict with Jeremiah's prophecy. And if the seventy years ended in 539, as Jeremiah clearly indicates, how can they be counted from 607 B.C.E., and still be regarded as an *exact* figure, (as they are by the Watchtower Society)? The exact length of the period from 607 to 539 was sixty-eight years, not seventy! So how are we to apply these seventy years of servitude?

First of all, it is important to establish the date when this prophecy was uttered and the historical background against which it was given. Jeremiah 25 opens with these words: "The word that occurred to Jeremiah concerning all the people of Judah *in the fourth year of Jehoiakim* the son of Josiah, the king of Judah, that is, *the first year of Nebuchadnezzar* the king of Babylon." (NW) The prophecy, then, was given eighteen years before the destruction of Jerusalem and its temple, or in 605 B.C.E. That year saw a very important event take place, with momentous consequences to Judah and the nations surrounding it. It was the year of the well known *battle of Carchemish* when Nebuchadnezzar decisively defeated the Egyptian Pharaoh Necho and his military force. This important victory opened the way for the Babylonian king to the areas in the west, Syria and Palestine, which for a few years previous had been controlled by Egypt.

This famous battle is also referred to and dated at Jeremiah 46:2:

For Egypt, concerning the military force of Pharaoh Necho the king of Egypt, who happened to be by the river Euphrates at Carchemish, whom Nebuchadrezzar the king of Babylon defeated *in the fourth year of Jehoiakim* the son of Josiah, the king of Judah. (NW)

The prophecy of the seventy years, which was given in that same year (Jer. 25:1), was thus given at a crucial point of time. Could it be that Judah and the surrounding nations were made vassals to and began to serve the king of Babylon in that year? Research does find evidence to show that Judah and a number of the surrounding nations *began to be made subservient to the king of Babylon very soon after the battle of Carchemish, in the fourth year of Jehoiakim and thereafter*.

In 1956 Professor D.J. Wiseman published a translation of the Babylonian Chronicle *B.M. 21946,* covering the period from the last (21st) year of Nabopolassar up to and including the tenth year of his son and successor, Nebuchadnezzar.[11] This tablet commences with a concise description of the battle at Carchemish and the subsequent events. The opening portion is quoted here in full because of its importance for our examination:[12]

> [The twenty-first year]: The king of Akkad stayed home (while) Nebuchadnezzar (II), his eldest son (and) the crown prince, mustered [the army of Akkad]. He took his army's lead and marched to Carchemish which is on the bank of the Euphrates. He crossed the river [*to encounter the army of Egypt*] which was encamped at Carchemish. [...] They did battle together. The army of Egypt retreated before him. He inflicted a [defeat] upon them (and) finished them off completely. In the district of Hamath the army of Akkad overtook the remainder of the army of [Egypt which] managed to escape [from] the defeat and which was not overcome. They (the army of Akkad) inflicted a defeat upon them (so that) a single (Egyptian) man [did not return] home. At that time Nebuchadnezzar (II) conquered all of Ha[ma]th.[13]
>
> For twenty-one years Nabopolassar ruled Babylon. On the eighth day of the month Ab he died. In the month Elul

Nebuchadnezzar (II) returned to Babylon and on the first day of the month Elul ascended the royal throne in Babylon.[14]

In (his) accession-year Nebuchadnezzar (II) returned to Hattu. Until the month Shebat he marched about victoriously in Hattu. In the month Shebat he took the vast booty of Hattu to Babylon.... The first year of Nebuchadnezzar (II): In the month Sivan he mustered his army and marched to Hattu. Until the month Kislev he marked about victoriously in Hattu. *All the kings of Hattu came into his presence and he received their vast tribute.*[15]

The far-reaching consequences of Egypt's defeat at Carchemish are evident from the chronicle. Immediately after the battle, Nebuchadnezzar began to take over the areas in vassalage to Egypt, beginning with Hamath in Syria. His father died during these operations, so he had to return to Babylon to secure the throne, evidently leaving his army in Hatti (Syro-Palestine) to continue the conquests there. In the month of Sebat of his accession-year (February 604) Nebuchadnezzar went back to the Hatti territory, which now was under Babylonian control. He could, therefore, take a heavy tribute to Babylon, and in his first regnal year (still in 604 B.C.E.) he led another campaign to Hatti to maintain his rule over the conquered territories. Similar campaigns are also recorded for the following years. Clearly, the nations in the Hatti area (Judah and surrounding nations) became vassals to Babylon very soon after the battle at Carchemish. The seventy years of servitude had evidently begun to run their course.

Not only did Nebuchadnezzar bring a number of the nations surrounding Judah under his dominion in his accession year, but he also laid siege to Jerusalem and brought some Jewish captives to Babylon in that very year. This is clear from Daniel 1:1-6. Daniel, in recording the event, states that it occurred "in the *third* year of the kingship of Jehoiakim," although the siege and deportation apparently followed the battle at Carchemish "in the *fourth* year of Jehoiakim." (Jer. 46:2) This seeming contradiction has caused much debate, and different solutions have been proposed in order to resolve the difficulty. But if, as is pointed out in note 14, the different methods of reckoning regnal years in Judah and Babylon are taken into consideration, the whole matter is easily cleared up. Daniel, as a Jewish exile living in Babylon and as an official at the Babylonian court, quite naturally conformed to the Babylonian calendar system and adopted the accession-year method, and even did so when referring to Jewish kings. This would make Jehoiakim's fourth year his third, according to the accession-year system.

Daniel 1:2 states that at this time Jehoaikim was given into the hand of Nebuchadnezzar—which indicates that he was made a *vassal* to the king of Babylon. He also paid a tribute to Nebuchadnezzar in the form of utensils from the temple. As this clearly points to a beginning of the servitude of Judah early in the reign of Jehoiakim, the Watchtower Society has advanced several arguments against a natural and direct reading of this text. Thus it holds that the "third year" should be understood as *the third year of Jehoiakim's vassalage* to Nebuchadnezzar, which, it is argued, was his *eleventh* and last regnal year (and the eighth year of Nebuchadnezzar). But this explanation is in conflict with Daniel 2:1, which shows Daniel at the court of Nebuchadnezzar and interpreting his dream of the image already in the "second year" of this king. If Daniel was brought to Babylon in Nebuchadnezzar's *eighth* year, how could he be there interpreting his dreams in his *second* year? So this text, too, had to be changed and made to say something else besides what it *clearly* says. Two different explanations have been offered through the years, the last one being that in this verse Daniel reckons Nebuchadnezzar's years from the destruction of Jerusalem in his eighteenth year. Nebuchadnezzar's *second* year, then, should be understood as his *twentieth* year! Thus, once again we find that the application of the seventy years held to by the Watchtower Society is in glaring conflict with the Bible, this time with Daniel 1:1 and 2:1. In order to uphold its theory, it is forced to *reject* the easiest and most direct reading of these texts.[16]

That some Jewish captives had already been brought to Babylon in the accession-year of Nebuchadnezzar is also confirmed by Berossus in his Babylonian history written in the third century B.C.E. His account of the events during Nebuchadnezzar's accession-year reads as follows:

> Nabopolassaros, his father, heard that the satrap who had been posted to Egypt, Coele Syria, and Phoenicia, had become a rebel. No longer himself equal to the task, he entrusted a portion of his army to his son Nabouchodonosoros, who was still in the prime of life, and sent him against the rebel. Nabouchodonosoros drew up his force in battle order and engaged the rebel. He defeated him and subjected the country to the rule of the Babylonians again. At this very time Nabopolassaros, his father, fell ill and died in the city of the Babylonians after having been king for twenty-one years.
>
> Nabouchodonosoros learned of his father's death shortly thereafter. After he arranged affairs in Egypt and the remaining territory, he ordered some of his friends *to bring the Jewish, Phoenician, Syrian, and Egyptian prisoners* together with the bulk of the army and the rest of the booty to Babylonia. He himself set out with a few companions and reached Babylon by crossing the desert.[17]

Thus Berossus gives support to Daniel's statement that Jewish captives were brought to Babylon in Nebuchadnezzar's accession-year. This confirmation of Daniel 1:1 is important because, as was shown in Chapter II, Berossus derived his information from the Babylonian chronicles, or sources close to those documents, originally written during the Neo-Babylonian era itself.

That the servitude of "these nations" (Jer. 25:11) began long before the destruction of Jerusalem in 587 B.C.E. is also clear from Jeremiah, chapters 27, 28, and 35. In chapter 27, dated early in the reign of Zedekiah (verse 1 says "Jehoiakim," but a comparison with vv. 3 and 12 indicates that the original reading probably was "Zedekiah"), Jeremiah urges Zedekiah not to revolt, but to bring his neck under the yoke of the king of Babylon and serve him; otherwise the city (Jerusalem) would become a "devastated place." (Jer. 27:6-8, 11-13, 17) The background of this "word... from Jehovah" was, according to verse 2, that messengers had come to Zedekiah from Edom, Moab, Ammon, Tyre, and Sidon, apparently in order to enlist him in an extensive revolt against the Babylonian yoke. Obviously all these nations were *vassals* to Babylon at this time, as was Judah. The revolt plans aroused unfounded hopes and enthusiasm among the people, and the prophet Hananiah even foretold that the Babylonian yoke would be broken within two years: "This is what Jehovah of armies, the God of Israel, has said, 'I will break the yoke of the king of Babylon. Within two full years more I am bringing back to this place all the utensils of the house of Jehovah that Nebuchadnezzar the king of Babylon took from this place that he might bring them to Babylon.' "[18] (Jer. 28:2, 3) This prophecy, of course, presupposed that the Babylonian yoke had already been put on the neck of the nations. That is why Hananiah could take the yoke bar from the neck of Jeremiah, break it and say: "This is what Jehovah has said, 'Just like this I shall break the yoke of Nebuchadnezzar the king of Babylon within two full years more *from off the neck of all the nations!*' " (Jer. 28:10, 11) In the fourth year of Zedekiah (Jer. 28:1) the Babylonian yoke lay on "the neck of all the nations." The servitude was a hard-felt reality for "all these nations" at that time, and had evidently been so for a number of years.

The Babylonian invasion of Judah soon after the battle at Carchemish is also reflected in Jeremiah chapter 35, dated in "the days of Jehoiakim the son of Josiah." (v. 1) The Rechabites, who normally dwelt in tents in obedience to the command of their forefather, Jehonadab the son of Rechab, lived in Jerusalem at that time. Why? They explained to Jeremiah: "But it came about when *Nebuchadnezzar the king of Babylon came up against the land* that we began to say, 'Come, and let us enter into Jerusalem because of the military force of the Chaldeans and because of the military force of the Syrians, and let us dwell in Jerusalem.' " (Jer. 35:11, NW) Thus, some time earlier in the reign of Jehoiakim, the Babylonian army had invaded the territory of Judah, forcing the Rechabites to seek refuge inside the walls of Jerusalem. Either this invasion was the one described in Daniel 1:1,2, or the one that took place in the following year, when, according to the Babylonian chronicle, "all the kings of Hattu (Syro-Palestine)" presented their tribute to the Babylonian king as a sign of their vassalage.

That Judah became a vassal of Babylon early in the reign of Jehoiakim is clearly stated in 2 Kings 24:1: "In his (Jehoiakim's) days Nebuchadnezzar the king of Babylon came up, and so *Jehoiakim became his servant* for three years. However, he turned back and rebelled against him." (NW) This rebellion caused the king of Babylon "to send against him marauder bands of Chaldeans and marauder bands of Syrians and marauder bands of Moabites and marauder bands of the sons of Ammon" (see verse 2; these surrounding nations were now under the control of the king of Babylon), in order to bring Jehoiakim back under the Babylonian yoke.

It has been demonstrated above that Jeremiah's prediction of the seventy years in Jeremiah 25:10-12 did not refer to a period of complete desolation of Jerusalem, but a period of *servitude*, not only for Judah, but also for "these nations," that is, the nations surrounding Judah. It was further shown that the Bible and secular historical sources, such as the Babylonian chronicle and Berossus, all agree that the servitude for these nations began long before the destruction of Jerusalem in 587 B.C.E. The Babylonian chronicle *B.M. 21492* shows that Nebuchadnezzar started to conquer these areas immediately after the battle at Carchemish in 605 B.C.E. Daniel 1:1-6 relates that Nebuchadnezzar, in the same year, laid siege to Jerusalem and brought Jewish captives to Babylon. Berossus confirms Daniel 1:1 with respect to this first deportation (which evidently was very small). Jeremiah, chapters 27,

28, and 35 all show that Judah was a vassal to Babylon as early as in the reign of Jehoiakim, and this is also directly stated in 2 Kings 24:1,2. For Judah and a number of the surrounding nations, the servitude evidently began in the same year Jeremiah uttered his prophecy, that is in 605 B.C.E.

The application of the seventy years made by the Watchtower Society, on the other hand, is in direct conflict with the prophecy of Jeremiah. It applies the seventy years to Judah only, ignoring the fact that Jeremiah's prophecy refers to a period of *servitude* for *a number of nations*, not a state of complete desolation "without an inhabitant" of Jerusalem and Judah alone. The next text which deals with the seventy years, will be seen to be in direct conflict with the Society's application as well.

> 2. *Jeremiah 29:10*: For this is what Jehovah has said, 'In accord with the fulfilling of seventy years at Babylon I shall turn my attention to YOU people, and I will establish toward YOU my good word in bringing YOU back to this place.' (NW)

This second text which mentions the seventy years seems to depict them as a period of *captivity*: "seventy years *at* Babylon." But the Hebrew preposition *le*, here translated "at," generally means "for, to, in regard to, with reference to," and is so rendered by most modern translations. The following are a number of examples:

Revised Version (1885): "After seventy years be accomplished *for* Babylon."

American Standard Version (1901): "After seventy years are accomplished *for* Babylon."

New American Standard Version (1973): "When seventy years have been completed *for* Babylon."

Rotherham's *The Emphasized Bible*: "That as soon as there are fulfilled *to* Babylon seventy years."

The Jerusalem Bible (1966): "Only when the seventy years granted *to* Babylon are over."

Other translations give expression to the same thought in other words:

Goodspeed's *The Complete Bible* (1923): "As soon as Babylon has finished seventy years."

The New English Bible (1970): "When a full seventy years has passed over Babylon."

Byington's *The Bible In Living English* (1972): "As soon as Babylon has had a full seventy years."

The Anchor Bible (John Bright: Jeremiah): "Only when Babylon's seventy years have been completed."

All these translations express the same thought, namely, that the seventy years refer to *the Babylonian supremacy*, not to the Jewish captivity or to the desolation following the destruction of Jerusalem in 587 B.C.E. That this is what the Hebrew text meant to say is also evident from the fact that it is in agreement with Jeremiah's prophecy at Jeremiah 25:11 on the seventy years' *servitude*. As long as the Babylonian king held supremacy, other nations had to serve him.[19]

It is important to note *when* and *to whom* Jeremiah's words at Jeremiah 29:10 were uttered. In verse 2 the time is said to be "after Jeconiah the king and the lady and the court officials, the princes of Judah and Jerusalem, and the craftsmen and the builders of bulwarks had gone forth from Jerusalem." (NW) This would date the prophecy to the beginning of the reign of Zedekiah and probably about the same time as the preceeding chapter, i.e., to the fourth year of Zedekiah. (Jer. 28:1) The background situation seems to have been the same in both chapters: The widespread revolt plans which stirred up hopes of liberation from the Babylonian yoke in Judah and the surrounding nations also reached the exiles at Babylon. As in Judah, false prophets arose among the Jews at Babylon and promised release in a short time. (Jer. 29:8,9) This was the reason why at this time, *several years prior to the destruction of Jerusalem*, Jeremiah sent a letter to the exiles at Babylon, calling their attention to the prophecy of the seventy years "for Babylon": "Do not be deceived by the prophets among you or by your diviners .... For Yahweh says this: Only when the seventy years granted to Babylon are over, will I visit you and fulfill my promise in your favour by bringing you back to this place." (Jerusalem Bible) This utterance clearly presupposed that the seventy years "for Babylon" were in progress at the time. If the period had not commenced, why did Jeremiah connect it with the exiles' staying on at Babylon? If the seventy-year period was not already in progress, what relevance is there in Jeremiah's reference to it? Jeremiah did not urge the exiles to wait until the seventy years would *begin*, but to wait until the period *had been completed*. As Jeremiah sent his message to the exiles some six or seven years *before* the destruction of Jerusalem, it is obvious that he reckoned the beginning of the seventy years from a point many years *prior to* that event. Jeremiah 29:10, therefore, further supports the earlier conclusion that the seventy years should be reckoned from a point some years before the destruction of Jerusalem.

Jeremiah 25:10-12 and 29:10 contain the *prophecy* of the seventy years. The next two texts to be discussed, Daniel 9:2 and 2 Chronicles 36:20, 21, are just *brief references* to Jeremiah's prophecy. Neither of them pretends to be a thorough discussion of the prophecy nor gives a detailed application of the period. Every attempt to find an application of the seventy-year period, therefore, must *proceed from the prophecy*, not from the references to it. It is only the prophecy that gives detailed information on the seventy years: That they refer to "these nations," that they were to be a period of *servitude* for these nations, that they refer to the period of Babylonian supremacy, and that the period would be fulfilled when the king of Babylon was punished is evident. Such detailed information is missing in the latter references to the prophecy by Daniel and Ezra. The discussion of these references, then, should always be done in the light of what the prophecy actually is about.

> *3. Daniel 9:1,2:* In the first year of Darius the son of Ahasuerus ... I myself, Daniel, discerned by the books the number of the years concerning which the word of Jehovah had occurred to Jeremiah the prophet, for fulfilling the devastations of Jerusalem, [namely] seventy years. (NW)

What had aroused Daniel's interest in Jeremiah's prophecy of the seventy years "for Babylon"? It was evidently the fact that the Babylonian supremacy had suddenly come to an end, in the night of October 5-6, 539 B.C.E. (Gregorian calendar). "In that very night Belshazzar the Chaldean king was killed and Darius the Mede himself received the kingdom, being about sixty-two years old." (Dan. 5:30, 31, NW)

Daniel, of course, realized what this event meant. From Jeremiah 25:12 he knew that "when seventy years have been fulfilled I [Jehovah] shall call to account against the king of Babylon and against that nation," and from Jeremiah 29:10 he knew that the seventy years referred to the Babylonian supremacy. Now the king of Babylon had been punished, and the Babylonian supremacy had ended. From that Daniel could draw only one conclusion: The seventy years had ended! But of greater importance was what the end of these seventy years "for Babylon" could mean for Daniel's own people, the Jewish exiles at Babylon and for the devastated city of Jerusalem and its ruined temple. From the prophecy of Jeremiah, Daniel knew also that Jehovah had promised that "when the seventy years granted to Babylon are over, will I *visit you and fulfill my promise in your favour by bringing you back to this place*.... Then when you call to me, and come to plead with me, I will listen to you. When you seek me you shall find me, when you seek me with all your heart, I will let you find me.'' (Jer. 29:10-13, *Jerusalem Bible*) This was precisely what Daniel did: ''and I proceeded to set my face to Jehovah the [true] God, in order to seek [him] with prayer and entreaties, with fasting and sackcloth and ashes.'' (Dan. 9:3, NW)

From Daniel's prayer, recorded in the subsequent verses (4-19), it is clear that his main interest was in seeking forgiveness for his people in order that they might be returned to their homeland. He knew that the ''devastations of Jerusalem'' and the desolation of the land were the curse predicted ''in the law of Moses'' (Dan. 9:13), in Leviticus 26 and Deuteronomy 28, because of their violating Jehovah's law. (Dan. 9:11) By reading Deuteronomy 30:1-6 he knew that Jehovah would bring them back to their land only when they returned to him and began to listen to his voice. This knowledge is reflected in Daniel's prayer. Obviously, his interest in Jeremiah's prophecy of the seventy years was motivated by the exciting discovery that the ''devastations of Jerusalem'' were close to their end, as the seventy years ''for Babylon'' now had been completed.

An interesting detail in Daniel 9:2 is that Daniel uses the Hebrew ''devastation'' (*chorbah*) in the *plural* number, although Jeremiah 25:11 , uses the *singular* form: ''And all this land must become a devastated place (*lechorbah* ''to a devastation, to a ruin, to a desert''). If this means that there was more than one devastation of Jerusalem, Daniel could have had in mind the successive desolation and depopulation of Jerusalem caused by the series of sieges and deportations beginning in the accession-year of Nebuchadnezzar in 605 B.C.E. and ending with the complete destruction of Jerusalem in 587 B.C.E. This seems to have been how the translators of the *Jerusalem Bible* understood this passage, as they render Daniel's words in 9:2 as follows:

> In the first years of his reign I, Daniel, was perusing the scrip-

> tures, counting over the number of years—as revealed by Yahweh to the prophet Jeremiah—that were to pass before *the successive devastations of Jerusalem* would come to an end, namely seventy years.

Of course, this is not a literal translation of Daniel's words, but an interpretaion of his thought. Of the word *chorbah* ("devastation") the *Interpreter's Bible* (Vol. 6, p. 485) gives this comment: "A word often employed to describe the state of a devastated land after the armies of an enemy have passed (Lev. 26:31, 33; Isa. 49:19; Jer. 44:22; Ezek. 36:34, Mal. 1:4; 1 Macc. 1:39)." (See also note 9.) It may be remembered that according to the Babylonian chronicle Nebuchadnezzar's armies passed through Palestine almost every year after the battle of Carchemish in 605 B.C.E., and in addition, because of Jehoiakim's rebellion, "Jehovah began to send against him marauder bands of Chaldeans and marauder bands of Syrians and marauder bands of Moabites and marauder bands of the sons of Ammon, and he kept sending them against Judah to destroy it." (2 Kings 24:2, NW. See also Jer. 35:11.) These armies and marauder bands gradually devastated the cities and the land, until Judah was laid completely desolate and depopulated after the destruction of Jerusalem in 587 B.C.E.

But it is not even necessary to suppose that Daniel had these successive devastations in mind. *Chorbah* often means "ruins," thus Daniel could simply have been talking of "Jerusalem's ruins." Raymond Hammer, in his *The Book of Daniel*,[20] translates: "I, Daniel, was reading the scriptures and reflecting on the seventy years which, according to the word of the LORD to the prophet Jeremiah, were to pass *while Jerusalem lay in ruins*." It would be wrong to interpret Daniel's words to mean that Jerusalem would lie in ruins *for seventy years*. What he discovered by reading Jeremiah's prophecy was not that Jerusalem's desolation would last for seventy years (this is nowhere stated in Jeremiah), but that *the desolations of Jerusalem would not cease until the seventy years "for Babylon" had been fulfilled.* This conclusion is the one that a reader of Jeremiah 29:10 (Daniel, for example), could easily arrive at.

This conclusion is also confirmed by other scholars, who have carefully examined Daniel's words. For example, the famous conservative scholar Edward J. Young, in his commentary on the book of Daniel, gives the following comment: "The thought may be paraphrased: 'With respect to the desolation of Jerusalem, 70 years must be completed.'"[21] Being mainly concerned with the desolated state of the holy city and its temple, Daniel discerned by books that the seventy years "for Babylon" had to be completed, before the devastations of Jerusalem could come to an end. This is the simplest meaning of Daniel's words in the light of what Jeremiah's prophecy actually said. As the Babylonian supremacy now suddenly had been replaced by the Medo-Persian rule, the seventy years "for Babylon" had been completed, and Daniel understood that the devastations of Jerusalem would soon come to an end. This was the reason for Daniel's excitement and strong feelings, as expressed in his prayer.

> *4. 2 Chronicles 36:20, 21*: Furthermore, he carried off those remaining from the sword captive to Babylon, and they came to be servants to him and his sons until the royalty of Persia began to reign; to fulfill Jehovah's word by the mouth of Jeremiah, until the land had paid off its sabbaths. All the days of lying desolated it kept sabbath, to fulfill seventy years. (NW)

A cursory reading of the text could give the impression that Ezra states that the land had enjoyed a sabbath rest of seventy years, and that this had been predicted by Jeremiah. But a thorough examination of the book of Jeremiah will show that he nowhere speaks of any sabbath rest. There is no reference at all to a sabbath rest in his book. Therefore Ezra's words, "until the land had paid off its sabbaths; all the days of lying desolated it kept sabbath," could not be a fulfillment of "Jehovah's word *by the mouth of Jeremiah.*" The two clauses about the sabbath rest are, as has been observed by most commentators, a reference to Leviticus 26:34, 35:

> At that time *the land will pay off its sabbaths* all the days of its lying desolated, *while YOU are in the land of YOUR enemies.* At that time the land will keep sabbath, as it must repay its sabbaths. All the days of its lying desolated it will keep sabbath, for the reason that it did not keep sabbath during YOUR sabbaths when YOU were dwelling upon it. (NW)

Like Daniel earlier, Ezra understood the desolation of Judah to be a fulfillment of this curse predicted in the law of Moses, and therefore he inserted these words from Leviticus 26 to show that they were fulfilled during the exile at Babylon, exactly as was predicted through Moses, "while you are in the land of your enemies." But Ezra did not mean to say that the land enjoyed a sabbath rest *of seventy years*, as this was not predicted, either by Moses or by Jeremiah. Actually, such an understanding of Ezra's words would be *in conflict with* Jeremiah's prophecy, as it depicted the seventy years as a period of *servitude* for many nations, a servitude that both the Bible and secular history show to have begun long before the desolation of Judah and Jerusalem. Some translators have put Ezra's quotation from Leviticus 26 within dashes or in parentheses, in order to emphasize that they do not refer to Jeremiah.[22]

What word, then, "by the mouth of Jeremiah," was fulfilled during the exile, according to Ezra? Not only his words about the seventy years "for Babylon." When Ezra states that "they came to be *servants to him and to his sons* until the royalty of Persia began to reign; to fulfill Jehovah's word by the mouth of Jeremiah," he evidently has in mind the prediction in Jeremiah 27:7: "And all the nations must *serve him and his son and his grandson* until the time even of his own land comes, and many nations and great kings must exploit him as a servant." (NW)

Ezra does not give an explanation of how this prophecy was fulfilled on "all the nations," but he does show how it was applicable to the Jewish exiles. These exiles had to stay in Babylonia until certain prophecies had been fulfilled, and this is exactly what Ezra points out. They had to stay there:

> (1) "until the royalty of Persia began to reign," (Jer. 27:7; 25:12; 29:10),
>
> (2) "until the land had paid off its sabbaths," (Lev. 26:34, 35), and
>
> (3) "until the seventy years were complete." (Jer. 25:11; 29:10 *Anchor Bible*)

It is important to observe that Ezra does not give any explanation of how to apply the seventy-year period. His purpose is another one, namely, to show that the Jewish exiles could not return to their homeland until certain prophecies had been fulfilled, among them the prophecy of the seventy years "for Babylon." As all knew that this period ended when "the royalty of Persia began to reign" in 539 B.C.E., in fulfillment of Jeremiah 25:12, it was not necessary for him to go into any details, and he does not explain when and how the period began. Further, when he says that the exiles were in Babylon and the land enjoyed a sabbath rest, "until the seventy years were complete," it would be wrong to conclude that Ezra held that the Jewish exile and the sabbath rest lasted for seventy years. If one goes to bed at midnight and sleeps "until the night is complete," he has not slept all night! Similarly, the land enjoyed a sabbath rest "until the seventy years were complete," but not from the beginning of the seventy years. The seventy-year period of Babylonian supremacy (and *servitude* for other nations) started many years before the destruction of Jerusalem and the depopulation of Judah as is proved both by the Bible and historical facts; and Ezra, of course, was well aware of this.

Many commentators hold that Ezra ended the seventy years in the first year of Cyrus (538-37 B.C.E.), because of what he says in the last two verses:

> And in the first year of Cyrus the king of Persia, *that Jehovah's word by the mouth of Jeremiah might be accomplished*, Jehovah roused up the spirit of Cyrus the king of Persia, so that he caused a cry to pass through all his kingdom, and also in writing,... (to the effect that the Jews would be allowed to return to Jerusalem and rebuild the temple). (2 Chron. 36:22,23, NW; See also Ezra 1:1–4)

If Jehovah's word "by the mouth of Jeremiah" is here taken to be another reference to the seventy years, it might prove that Ezra ended that period in 538-37 B.C.E. But in view of the fact that these verses actually deal with Cyrus' decree allowing the Jews to return to their homeland, it is more natural to understand his reference to Jeremiah's prophecy as a reference to what the prophet said immediately after his prediction of the seventy years "for Babylon" at Jeremiah 29:10: "For thus saith Jehovah, After seventy years are accomplished for Babylon, *I will visit you, and perform my good word toward you, causing you to return to this place*." (ASV)

Note that the prophet did not say that Jehovah *first* would visit the exiles, causing them to return to Jerusalem, and *after that* the seventy years would be accomplished. This is how the Watchtower Society applies this prophecy. But the prophet clearly states that the seventy years would be accomplished *first*, and *after that* he would visit the exiles and cause them to return to Jerusalem. So *the seventy years would be fulfilled while the Jewish exiles were still in Babylonia*! And so it happened: Babylon fell to Cyrus, the king of Persia, in October, 539 B.C.E., thus fulfilling the prophecy of the seventy years "for Babylon." The next year, or perhaps in 537, Cyrus issued his decree, allowing the Jewish exiles to return to Jerusalem. The end of the seventy years at the fall of Babylon, and the return of the Jews—one, two, or perhaps even three years later—are two separate events, and it is the last of these that Ezra is speaking of at 2 Chronicles 36:22,23. His reference to the word "by the mouth of Jeremiah" in these verses, then, must be a reference to the second half of verse 10 in chapter 29 of the book of Jeremiah.

Thus we find that 2 Chronicles 36:20, 21, like Daniel 9:2, may be brought into harmony with the prophecy of Jeremiah on the seventy years. Daniel ends the period while the Jewish exiles were still living in Babylonia, when "the royalty of Persia began to reign" in 539 B.C.E. Ezra lays stress upon the fact that the Jewish exiles could not return to Jerusalem until the seventy years had been fulfilled, or until the land had paid off its sabbaths. After that Jehovah caused them to return to their homeland, in fulfillment of Jeremiah 29:10b, in the first year of Cyrus. Ezra's words, correctly understood, cannot be taken to mean that the desolation of Judah after the destruction of Jerusalem and its temple lasted for seventy years.

The last two texts to be discussed, Zechariah 1:7,12 and 7:1-5, are sometimes thought to be two additional references to Jeremiah's prophecy about the seventy years, and the Watchtower Society holds them to be so. But the evidence for this conclusion is totally lacking. None of the texts contains any reference to Jeremiah (as do Dan. 9:2 and 2 Chron. 36:20, 21), and the *context* of these texts strongly indicates that the seventy years mentioned there must be given a different application. This is also the conclusion of many commentators. O. Plöger, for example, in the article referred to earlier (See note 22), says: "The two texts in the book of Jeremiah are not referred to here." This will also become apparent in the following discussion.

> 5. *Zechariah 1:7,12*: On the twenty-fourth [day] of the eleventh month, that is, the month Shebat, in the second year of Darius, the word of Jehovah occurred to Zechariah.... So the angel of Jehovah answered and said: "O Jehovah of armies, how long will you yourself not show mercy to Jerusalem and to the cities of Judah, whom you have denounced these seventy years?" (NW)

This statement about the seventy years of denouncement is dated to "the second year of Darius," "the twenty-fourth of the eleventh month." As Darius' second regnal year corresponded to 520-519 B.C.E.,[23] the twenty-fourth day of the eleventh month would be in February, 519 B.C.E.[24] According to the angel, Jehovah had then denounced Jerusalem and the cities of Judah for seventy years. The Watchtower Society applies these seventy years of denouncement ("indignation," KJV,ASV; "wrath," NEB) to the period 607-537 B.C.E., thus equating them with the seventy years of Jeremiah 25:10-12 and 29:10.[25] It seems evident, though, that the reason why the angel put this question about the denouncement was that Jehovah still, in 519 B.C.E., had not shown mercy to the cities of Judah. If the denouncement really had ended in 537, the angel would have known that, and his question would have been completely superfluous. Or did the angel mean to say that Jehovah had denounced Jerusalem and the cities of Judah for seventy years up to 537 B.C.E., and then continued to be hostile against them for about eighteen more years up to 519? This would make the period of hostility nearly ninety years, not seventy. But the "indignation" or "wrath" clearly refers to the devastated state of the cities of Judah, Jerusalem and its temple, which began after the destruction of Jerusalem in 587 B.C.E. This condition was still prevailing, as may be seen from Jehovah's answer to the angel's question: "Therefore this is what Jehovah has said, 'I shall certainly return to Jerusalem with mercies. My own house will be built in her.... Jehovah will yet certainly feel regrets over Zion and yet actually choose Jerusalem' " (Zech. 1:16, 17 NW) Counted from 587 B.C.E. the indignation had now, in 519, lasted for nearly seventy years, or sixty-eight years to be exact. And if counted from the *beginning* of the siege in January 589 B.C.E. (2 Kings 25:1; Ez. 24:1,2; Jer. 52:4), the indignation had lasted for almost exactly seventy years in February 519. But just two months earlier the rebuilding of the temple had been started and its foundation had been laid. (Hagg. 2:18) From that time onward Jehovah began to remove his indignation: "From this day I shall bestow blessing." (Hagg. 2:19)

It seems clear, therefore, that the seventy years mentioned

in this text do not refer to the prophecy of Jeremiah, but simply to the time that had elapsed by 519 B.C.E. since the siege and destruction of Jerusalem and its temple in 589-587 B.C.E.[26]

That seventy years elapsed from the destruction of the temple in 587 B.C.E. to its rebuilding in the years 520-515 is also confirmed by the next text in the book of Zechariah to be considered.

> 6. *Zechariah 7:1-5*: Furthermore, it came about that in the fourth year of Darius the king the word of Jehovah occurred to Zechariah, on the fourth [day] of the ninth month, [that is], in Chislev. And Bethel proceeded to send Sharezer and Regem-melech and his men to soften the face of Jehovah, saying to the priests who belonged to the house of Jehovah of armies, and to the prophets, even saying: "Shall I weep in the fifth month, practicing an abstinence, the way I have done these O how many years?"
>
> And the word of Jehovah of armies continued to occur to me, saying: "Say to all the people of the land and to the priests, 'When you fasted and there was a wailing in the fifth [month] and in the seventh [month], and this *for seventy years*, did you really fast to me, even me?' " (NW)

Again, this event is exactly dated to the fourth year of Darius, "on the fourth of the ninth month," corresponding to November, 518 B.C.E. Why did "all the people of the land" fast and wail in the fifth month and in the seventh month? Speaking of the fast in the fifth month the Watchtower Society admits: "It was observed evidently on the tenth day of that month (Ab), in order to commemorate how on that day Nebuzaradan, the chief of Nebuchadnezzar's bodyguard, after two days of inspection, burned down the city of Jerusalem and its temple. (Jer. 52:12, 13; 2 Kings 25:8,9)"[27] Further, the fast in the seventh month was "to commemorate the assassination of Governor Gedaliah, who was of the royal house of King David and whom Nebuchadnezzar made governor of the land for the poor Jews who were allowed to remain after the destruction of Jerusalem. (2 Kings 25:22-25; Jer. 40:13

to 41:10)''[28] For how long had the Jews been fasting during these months in memory of the destruction of Jerusalem and its temple and the assassination of Gedaliah? "For seventy years," according to the Bible. The year 518-517 was the seventieth year since 587 B.C.E.[29]

That the Jews still, in November 518 B.C.E., held these fasts in the fifth and seventh months is clear from the fact that the men from Bethel had come to ask if they, "now that the faithful remnant of Jews were rebuilding the temple of Jehovah at Jerusalem and were about half through, should ... continue to hold such a fast."[30] If now the destruction of Jerusalem and its temple is dated in 607 B.C.E. instead of 587, this would make the time these fasts had been observed ninety years rather than seventy. This is conceded by the Watchtower Society in the book quoted above,[31] but no satisfying explanation is given for this incompatibility. Thus Zechariah 1:7,12 and 7:1-5 both give very strong support for the year 587 B.C.E. as the correct date for the destruction of Jerusalem. As in the case of Jeremiah 25:10-12; 29:10; Daniel 1:1,2 and 2:1, the easiest and the most direct reading of Zechariah 1:7,12 and 7:1-7, too, is seen to be in open conflict with the interpretation the Watchtower Society gives to the seventy years.

HOW TO APPLY THE SEVENTY YEARS OF SERVITUDE

From a close examination of the texts dealing with the seventy years, certain facts have been established that cannot be ignored in any attempt to find an application of the seventy-year period that is in harmony with both the Bible and historical facts:

(1) The seventy years refer to *many nations*, not Judah only: Jeremiah 25:11.

(2) The seventy years refer to a period of *servitude* for these nations, that is, vassalage to Babylon: Jeremiah 25:11.

(3) The seventy years refer to the period of *Babylonian supremacy*, "seventy years *for* Babylon": Jeremiah 29:10.

(4) The seventy years were *accomplished when the Babylonian king and his nation were punished,* that is, in *539 B.C.E.:* Jeremiah 25:12.

(5) The seventy years of servitude *began many years before the destruction of Jerusalem* and its temple: Jeremiah chapters 27, 28, and 35; Daniel 1:1-4; 2:1; 2 Kings 24:1-7, the Babylonian chronicles and Berossus.

(6) *Zechariah 1:7-17 and 7:1-5 are not references to Jeremiah's prophecy*, but refer to the period from the siege and destruction of Jerusalem in the years 589-587 to the rebuilding of the temple in the years 520-515 B.C.E.

The application given by the Watchtower Society to the seventy-year prophecy, that it refers to Judah only, and to the period of complete desolation of the land, "without an inhabitant," following the destruction of Jerusalem and its temple, is seen to be in direct conflict with each of the above established biblical and historical facts. An application that is in clear conflict with both the Bible and such historical facts cannot have anything to do with reality. In a serious discussion of possible applications of the seventy years, this alternative is *the first which must be rejected*. It is held to by the Watchtower Society, not because it can be supported by the Bible and historical facts, but because it is a necessary prerequisite for their calculation of the supposed 2,520 years of Gentile times, 607 B.C.E.-1914 C.E. If their application of the seventy years is dropped, the Gentile times calculation immediately proves false, together with all the prophetic speculations that are tied to it.

The conclusion arrived at in the above discussion is that Judah and a number of the surrounding nations became vassals to the king of Babylon soon after the battle of Carchemish in 605 B.C.E. Does this mean that the seventy-year period "for Babylon" has to be applied to the period 605-539 B.C.E.? To this suggestion it might be objected that the length of this period is not seventy, but a little more than sixty six years. That, of course, is true. Many scholars argue, however, that the numeral "70" in the Bible often seems to be used as "a round number." It occurs fifty-two times independently in the Old Testament, and is used with a variety of different meanings—for weights, lengths of measurements, numbers of people, periods of time, etc. In a discussion of the biblical use of the numeral "70," which also includes extra-biblical occurrences, Dr. F.C. Fensham concludes: "It is quite probably used as a kind of symbolic figure, just like seven. With the usage of seven and seventy the ancient Semites tried to make a difference between a smaller symbolic figure and a larger one."[32] When used of periods of time it might have been used as a general term, as "an appropriate period of punishment." In an inscription of the Assyrian king Esarhaddon (680-667 B.C.E.), it is stated that the desolation of Babylon after its destruction by Sennacherib "should originally have lasted seventy years according to a decision of the god Marduk."[33] A few decades earlier Isaiah predicted that "Tyre must be forgotten seventy years, *the same as the days of one king*." (Isa. 23:15) The explanation that the seventy years should be understood as "the same as the days of one king" is often interpreted to mean a normal life-span of a king, or "the full span of human life," in accordance with Psalm 90:10, where the number seventy clearly is not meant to be an exact figure.

Thus it is quite probable that the seventy years of servitude predicted by Jeremiah were used as a round number. Such an understanding could also be supported by the fact that not all the nations surrounding Judah (some of which are obviously enumerated in Jer. 25:19-26) seem to have been made vassals to the king of Babylon at the same time, in 605 B.C.E. Some of them seem to have been brought into subjection somewhat later. The period of servitude, therefore, was not of exactly the same duration for all these nations, yet the prophet said that all of them were to serve the king of Babylon "seventy years."

On the other hand, the prophecy does not clearly imply that the seventy years should be reckoned from 605 B.C.E. Though it is true that Judah and a number of the surrounding nations were brought into vassalage shortly after the battle of Carchemish in 605 B.C.E., it must be remembered that *all* nations were predicted to become servants of Babylon: "And *all the nations* must serve him and his son and his grandson."[34] (Jer. 27:7 NW) Some nations had become subject to Babylon even *prior to* the battle of Carchemish in 605 B.C.E. If the seventy years "for Babylon" are counted from the time when Babylon crushed the Assyrian world empire, thus beginning to step forward as the dominant political power itself, even a more exact application of the seventy years is possible. A short review of the last years of Assyria, as recorded in the Babylonian Chronicle, will make this clear.

Up to 627 B.C.E. Assyria held hegemony over many countries, including Babylon and the Hatti-area (Syro-Palestine). But on the death of Ashurbanipal in that year, Assyria's power began to wane. Nabopolassar, a Chaldean, drove the Assyrians from Babylon in 626 and occupied the throne. In the following years he successfully established Babylonian independence. In 616, he attacked the Assyrians and defeated them, but an Egyptian army led by Psammetichus I came up to assist the Assyrian king (Sin-shar-ishkun), and Nabopolassar chose to withdraw to Babylon. By this time the Medes, too, began to attack Assyria, and in 614 they took Ashur, the ancient Assyrian capital. After the city had fallen, Nabopolassar, whose army arrived too late to help the Medes, made a treaty with the Median ruler, Cyaxares. In 612, the two allies attacked the Assyrian capital, Nineveh, captured it and destroyed it. The Assyrian king, Sin-shar-ishkun, perished in the flames. His successor, Ashur-uballit II, fled to the provincial capital of Harran, where he established his government, still claiming sovereignty over Assyria. During the subsequent years Nabopolassar successfully campaigned in Assyria, and by the end of 610, he marched against Harran, joined by the "Umman-manda" forces (a term which perhaps included both Medes and Scythians). Ashur-uballit fled, and the city was captured and plundered either late in 610 or early in 609 B.C.E. Late in the summer of 609 Ashur-uballit, supported by a large Egyptian force headed by Pharaoh Necho, made a last attempt to recapture Harran, but failed. This definitely put an end to the Assyrian world power.

Thus, the seventy years "for Babylon" may also be reckoned from 609 B.C.E. From that year the Babylonian king regarded himself as the legitimate successor of the king of Assyria, and in the following years he gradually took over the control of the latter's territories, beginning with a series of campaigns in the Armenian mountains north of Assyria. The Egyptian Pharaoh, Necho, after the failed attempt to recapture Harran in 609, took control over the areas in the west, Syria and Palestine, and made the nations in those areas, including Judah, his vassals for about four years. (See 2 Kings 23:29-34; 2 Chron. 35:20-36:4; Jer. 46:2.) But the battle at Carchemish in 605 B.C.E. put an end to this brief Egyptian rule in the west. After a series of successful campaigns to the "Hatti-country" (Syro-Palestine), Nebuchadnezzar made it clear to Necho that he was the real heir to the Assyrian Empire, "And never again did the king of Egypt come out from his land, for the king of Babylon had taken all that happened to belong to the king of Egypt up to the river of Euphrates." (2 Kings 24:7, NW)

If the Babylonian supremacy is reckoned from 609 B.C.E., the year that marked the definite end of the Assyrian Empire, exactly seventy years elapsed up to the fall of Babylon in 539 B.C.E. This period may be counted as the "seventy years for Babylon." (Jer. 29:10) In this way the seventy years, without strained interpretations and in full harmony both with the Bible and secular historical facts, may also be regarded as an exact number.[35]

It has been shown that the prophecy of the seventy years may be given an application that is in full agreement with a dating of the desolation of Jerusalem in 587 B.C.E. Does this mean that the 2,520 years of Gentile times started in 587 B.C.E. and ended in 1934 C.E.?

Ending the times of the Gentiles in 1934 would not be a new idea. As far back as 1886 Dr. Grattan Guinness pointed to 1934 in his book *Light for the Last Days*.[36] Dr. Guinness made use of three different calendars in his calculations and thus succeeded in giving the Gentile times three time periods of different lengths: 2,520, 2,484, and 2,445 years respectively. In addition, he also used several starting-points, the first in 747 and the last in 587 B.C.E.[37] This provided a series of terminal dates, extending from 1774 C.E. to 1934 C.E. With the 1934 date the Gentle times would *definitely* end, reckoned according to Dr. Guinness' longest scale and from his last starting-point. The four most important dates in his scheme were 1915, 1917, 1923 and 1934. His prophetic interpretations strongly influenced apocalyptic thinking during the subsequent decades, and several expositors picked up his ideas and calculations, especially in the years following the outbreak of the First World War in 1914 and up to the 1930s. Among these were some of the followers of Pastor Charles T. Russell.

At the climax of a crisis in the Watch Tower Bible and Tract Society of Pennsylvania following the death of Russell, many Bible students left the parent movement and formed the Associated Bible Students, in 1918 chartered as The Pastoral Bible Institute.[38] In the same year Paul S. L. Johnson broke away from this group and formed *The Layman's Home Missionary Movement*, today the strongest group to grow out of the Bible Student movement aside from the parent organization. Early in the 1920s the Pastoral Bible Institute changed Russell's application of the Gentile times, which caused an interesting debate between that movement, the Layman's Home Missionary

Movement, and the Watch Tower Bible and Tract Society.

An article entitled "Watchman What of the Night?" published in the Pastoral Bible Institute's periodical *The Herald of Christ's Kingdom,* April 15 (No. 8), 1921, marked a significant break with Pastor Russell's chronological system. Mainly responsible for this re-evaluation was R. E. Streeter, one of the five editors of the *Herald.* His views, accepted by the other editors, reflected a growing concern on the part of many Bible Students (as evidenced from letters received from nearly every part of the earth) who had experienced deep perplexity "as to the seeming failure of much that was hoped for and expected would be realized by the Lord's people by this time."[39] Some of the questions which had arisen were: "Why has not the Church realized her final deliverance and reward by this time? Why is not the time of trouble over with by now? Why has not the old order of things passed away? And why has not Christ's Kingdom been established in power before this? Is it possible that there may be an error in the chronology?"[40]

Assuming that Pastor Russell's predictions for 1914 had not been fulfilled, it was concluded that there was evidently an error in the former reckoning. This error was explained to be found in the calculation of the times of the Gentiles: "Careful investigation has resulted in our locating the point of difficulty or discrepancy in what we have considered our great chain of chronology. It is found to be in connection with the commencement of the 'times of the Gentiles'."[41] First, it was argued, the seventy years, formerly referred to as a period of desolation, more properly should be called "the seventy years of servitude." (Jer. 25:11) Then, referring to Daniel 2:1,37,38, it was pointed out that Nebuchadnezzar was the "head of gold" already in his second regnal year, and actually dominated the other nations including Judah, beginning from his very first year, according to Daniel 1:1. Consequently, the era of seventy years commenced eighteen to nineteen years *before* the destruction of Jerusalem. This destruction, therefore, had to be moved forward about nineteen years, from 606 to 587 B.C.E. But the 606 B.C.E. date could still be retained as a starting-point for the times of the Gentiles, as it was held that the *lease of power* to the Gentiles started with Nebuchadnezzar's rise to world dominion. Thus 1914 marked the end of the *lease of power*, but not necessarily *the full end of the exercise of power*, nor the complete fall of the Gentile governments, even as the kingdom of Judah did not fall and was not overthrown in the final and absolute sense until Zedekiah, a vassal king under Nebuchadnezzar, was taken captive nineteen years after the period of servitude began. "Accordingly it was 587 B.C. when Zekekiah was taken captive, and not 606 B.C., and hence while the 2520 years' lease of Gentile power starting in Nebuchadnezzar's first year, 606 B.C.,would run out in 1914; yet the full end of the Gentile times and the complete fall of Gentile governments is not indicated as taking place till nineteen years later, or in about 1934."[42]

So what could be expected to take place in 1934? *The Herald of Christ's Kingdom* indicated: "The reasonable deduction is that the great changes and events which we have heretofore expected to take place in 1914 would, in view of the foregoing, be logically expected to be in evidence somewhere around 1934."[43]

Other articles followed in the issues of May 15 and June 1 of the *Herald*, giving additional evidence for the necessity of these changes and answering questions from the readers. The changes evoked much interest among the Bible Students:

> Many have freely written to us that they have heartily accepted the conclusions reached.... It has been of special interest to us to receive advice from brethren in several different quarters telling of how for some months or years before receiving our present treatment of the subject, they have been led to make an exhaustive examination of the chronology and had arrived at exactly the same conclusions as those presented in the HERALD with regard to the 19 years difference in the starting of the Gentile Times, and found that all the evidences showed that Nebuchadnezzar's universal kingdom began in his first year instead of his nineteenth.[44]

However, most Bible Student groups rejected the conclusions of the Pastoral Bible Student editors. The first counter-attack came from P. S. L. Johnson, the founder of the Laymen's Home Missionary Movement and editor of its periodical *The Present Truth*. In the issue of June 1 (No. 6), 1921, he published a critical article entitled " 'Watchman, What of the Night?'—Examined" (pp. 87-93), in which he defended Pastor Russell's understanding of Daniel 1:1; 2:1, 37,38, and the seventy years of desolation, also adding some arguments of his own. This was followed by other articles in the issues of July 1 and September 1.[45]

In 1922, the Watch Tower Society, too, plunged into the debate. Evidently the chronological changes in the *Herald* rapidly came to the knowledge of many Bible Students from different quarters, and seem to have caused no little agitation among the readers of *The Watch Tower* magazine, too. This was openly admitted in the first article on the subject, "The Gentile Times," published in the May 1, 1922, issue of *The Watch Tower:*

> About a year ago there began some agitation concerning chronology, the crux of the argument being that Brother Russell was wrong concerning chronology and particularly in error with reference to the gentile times.... Agitation concerning the error in chronology has continued to increase throughout the year, and some have turned into positive opposition to that which has been written. This has resulted in some of the Lord's dear sheep becoming disturbed in mind and causing them to inquire, Why does not THE WATCH TOWER say something?[46]

Consequently, beginning with this article, the Society started a series in defense of Pastor Russell's chronology. The second article, entitled "Chronology," published in *The Watch Tower* of May 15, 1922, opened with a reaffirmation of belief in Russell's dates, and added the date 1925:

> We have no doubt whatever in regard to the chronology relating to the dates of 1874, 1914, 1918, and 1925. Some claim to have found new light in connection with the period of "seventy

> years of desolation" and Israel's captivity in Babylon, and are zealously seeking to make others believe that Brother Russell was in error.

The arguments put forth in this and subsequent articles were much the same as those earlier published by Paul S.L. Johnson. Johnson, who involuntarily had to side with the Watch Tower Society in this "battle," supported *The Watch Tower* with a series of new articles in the *Present Truth*, running parallel with the articles in *The Watch Tower.*[47]

These responses were not long left unanswered. The *Herald* of June 15, 1922, contained the article "The Validity of Our Chronological Deductions," which was a refutation of the arguments put forth in support of Pastor Russell's interpretation of Daniel 1:1 and 2:1. In the July 1 issue, a second article "Another Chronological Testimony" considered the evidence from Zechariah 7:5, and the July 15 issue contained a third on the desolation period, again signed by J.A.D. (See note 44.)

Gradually the debate subsided. The Pastoral Bible Institute editors summarized their arguments and published them in a special double number of the *Herald*, August 1-15 (No. 15, 16), 1925, and, again, in the May 15 (No. 10), 1926 issue. Then they waited to see what the 1934 date would bring.

As 1934 approached the Institute's editors assumed a very cautious attitude: "If the nineteen years was intended to indicate the exact length of time running out of the Gentile Times from 1915 onward, then that would carry us to approximately 1933-1934; but we do not *know* that this was so intended, nor do we have positive evidence as the exact length of the closing out of the Gentile Times beyond 1915."[48] This cautiousness proved to be wise, and when the 1934 date had passed, they could assert:

> Brethren who have perused carefully the pages of this journal, are well aware that much cautiousness and conservatism have been urged upon all in the direction of setting dates and fixing the

> time for various occurrences and events; and this continues to be the editorial policy of the 'Herald'.[49]

As to the question of why 1934 did not see the passing away of the Gentile nations, it was explained that 1934 should be looked upon as an *approximate* date, and that "we believe the progress of events and all the facts as we see them unfolding out of the present order more by degrees or stages rather than of the sudden crash and passing away of everything at one point of time, as the Apostle Paul suggests—'As travail upon a woman.' "[50] The worsening situation in the world leading to The Second World War seemed to give support to this way of looking at the matter.[51]

The years 1914 and 1934 have come and gone, and the Gentile nations still rule the earth. Some proper questions to ask now surely are: Is the 2,520-year period really a well-founded biblical calculation? And was Jesus' mention of the "Gentile times" at Luke 21:24 a reference to Nebuchadnezzar's "seven times" of madness?

ARE THE GENTILE TIMES "SEVEN TIMES" OF 2,520 YEARS?

When Jesus, at Luke 21:24, referred to the times of the Gentiles, did he then have in mind the "seven times" of madness that fell upon the Babylonian king Nebuchadnezzar as recorded in the book of Daniel, chapter four?[52] And were these "seven times" of madness meant to have a greater fulfillment beyond that upon Nebuchadnezzar, representing a period of 2,520 years of Gentile dominion? In spite of the many arguments put forth in support of these conjectures (See especially *Aid to Bible Understanding* pp. 94-96.), positive proof is missing, and some serious objections may be raised against them.

A. It is true that in his last great prophecy (Matt. 24,25: Luke 21: and Mark 13), Jesus referred at least twice to the book of Daniel. (*Aid to Bible Understanding* p. 95:4) Thus, when mentioning the "disgusting thing that causes desolation" he directly states that this was "spoken of through Daniel the prophet." (Matt. 24:15; Dan. 9:27; 11:31, and 12:11) And when speaking of the "great tribulation such as had not occurred since the world's beginning until now" (Matt. 24:21), he clearly quotes from Daniel 12:1: "and there will certainly occur a time of distress (the Greek Septuagint Version uses the word *thlipsis*, in the same way as in Matt. 24:21) such as has not been made to occur since there came to be a nation until that time." *But no such clear reference to the book of Daniel may be found at Luke 21:24.* The word "times"—*kairoi*, the plural form of *kairos*—is not, clearly, a reference to the "seven times" of Daniel 4, as this common word occurs many times in both its singular and plural forms in the Greek Scriptures, and about 250 times in the Greek Septuagint translation of the Hebrew Scriptures. Therefore, the supposed connection between the "times of the Gentiles" at Luke 21:24 and the "seven times" at Daniel 4:20, 29 appears to be no more than a conjecture. Evidently, as was observed by the well-known Bible commentator Dr. F. Godet, "This era of the Gentiles was a notion foreign to the O.T. [Old Testament]."[53] The phrase "times of the Gentiles" *kairoi ethnon* was evidently coined by Jesus himself as a designation of the period when Jerusalem was to be trampled upon by the Gentiles.

B. Two arguments have been proposed to support the conclusion that Nebuchadnezzar's "seven times" of madness prefigured the period of Gentile dominion up to the establishment of Christ's Kingdom.

1) "In the entire book of Daniel ... the element of time is everywhere prominent in the visions and prophecies it presents," and "the book repeatedly points forward toward the conclusion that forms the theme of its prophecies: the establishment of a universal and eternal Kingdom of God exercised through the rulership of the 'son of man.' "[54] Although this is true of most of the visions and prophecies in the book of Daniel, it is not true of

all of them. And as far as we know, no other vision or prophecy therein, with the exception of the vision of the handwriting on the wall, portending the impending conquest of Babylon by the Medes and the Persians (Dan. 5:28; See also Rev. 16:12.), and possibily also the prophecy of "the disgusting thing that is causing desolation" (Dan. 11:31; See Matt. 24:15.), has more than *one* fulfillment. There is nothing to indicate, either in the book of Daniel or elsewhere in the Bible, that the vision of the tree in Daniel 4 has more than one fulfillment. Daniel clearly says that the prophecy was fulfilled upon Nebuchadnezzar: "*All this befell Nebuchadnezzar the king*" (Dan. 4:28, NW). And further, in verse 33: "At that moment the word itself *was fulfilled upon Nebuchadnezzar.*" (NW) Dr. Edward J. Young comments: "lit., *was ended*, i.e., it came to an end in that it was completed or fulfilled with respect to Neb."[55] Other chapters, too, *do not* point forward toward "the establishment of a universal eternal kingdom of God through the rulership of the 'son of man,' ": chapter 1 (Daniel and his companions at the court of Babylon), chapter 3, (the three Hebrews in the fiery furnace), and chapter 6 (Daniel in the den of lions). Also, the prophecy of the seventy weeks (Dan. 9:24-27) points forward to Christ's *first*, not his second coming. So any precedent by which we have to give a greater application to Nebuchadnezzar's "seven times" of madness does not exist.

2) It is further stated that certain features in Daniel 4 point to a greater fulfillment, such as the *time* of the vision, the *person* to whom it was given, the tree symbolism, and especially the *theme* of the vision, namely, "that people living may know that the Most High is ruler in the kingdom of mankind and that to the one he wants to, he gives it and he sets up over it even the lowliest one of mankind." (Dan. 4:17)[56] "We know that this 'one' to whom the Most High chooses to give the 'kingdom' is Christ Jesus."[57]

Let us have a closer look at these arguments. If the *time* of this vision should indicate a greater fulfillment, pointing to a 2,520-year break in the royal dynasty of David, it should have been given close to, or preferably in the same year as the dethronement of Zedekiah. Often, *when the time* a prophecy is given is important and has a connection with its fulfillment, the prophecy is dated. This is, for example, the case of the prophecy of the seventy years. (Jer. 25:1, 11) The visions and prophecies in the book of Daniel are usually dated: the dream of the image in the *second year* of Nebuchadnezzar (Dan. 2:1), the vision of the four beasts in the *first year* of Belshazzar (Dan. 7:1), the vision of the ram and the he goat in the *third year* of Belshazzar (Dan. 8:1), the prophecy of the seventy weeks in the *first year* of Darius the Mede (Dan. 9:1), and the last vision in the *third year* of Cyrus (Dan. 10:1). *But no such date is given for the vision of the tree in Daniel 4*, which should have been done if this was important. The only information concerning time is given in verse 29, where the fulfillment of the dream is stated to have occurred twelve months later. Although no regnal years are given, it seems probable that Nebuchadnezzar's "seven years" of madness took place somewhere near the close of his long reign. After the destruction of Jerusalem, Nebuchadnezzar besieged Tyre for thirteen years (Josephus, *Against Apion*, I:21). He was also engaged in considerable building activity. The cuneiform inscriptions demonstrate that Nebuchadnezzar was primarily a builder, not a warrior. He renovated the two temples of Marduk and restored fifteen other temples in Babylon, completed the two great walls of the city, rebuilt the palace of Nabopolassar, constructed another palace and the famous hanging-gardens, among other architectural achievements.[58] It was evidently *at the close of* this building activity that the vision of the tree was given, as is indicated by Nebuchadnezzar's proud words in Daniel 4:30: "Is not this *Babylon the Great, that I myself have built* for the royal house with the strength of my might and for the dignity of my majesty?" This points towards the close of Nebuchadnezzar's forty-three-year-long reign, and consequently several years *after* the destruction of Jerusalem in his eighteenth regnal year. How then could the *time* at which the vision was given indicate anything about a greater fulfillment, beginning with the dethronement of Zedekiah many years earlier? Does not the fulfillment of a prophecy usually start, not before, but *after* the time at which the prophecy is given? The *time* of this dream, therefore, does not only seem to be unimportant, as the prophecy is not dated, but can actually be used as an argument *against* an application to a period starting with the destruction of Jerusalem, as the dream evidently was given some years *after* that event.

Does the *person* to whom this vision was given, that is Nebuchadnezzar, indicate it has to be applied to a supposed 2,520-year break in the royal dynasty of David? It is true that Nebuchadnezzar was instrumental in causing this break. But is it not improbable that Nebuchadnezzar's cruel and oppressive exercise of world sovereignty would be a symbol of Jehovah's sovereignty expressed through the Davidic dynasty, while during the "seven times" of madness his total powerlessness was a symbol of world dominion exercised by Gentile nations? Or did he play *two* roles during his "seven times" of madness—(1) his *powerlessness*, representing the dynasty of David during the 2,520-year period; and (2) his *beastlike state*, picturing the Gentile rule of the earth? As may be seen, the parallels between the literal fulfillment and the greater application are strained, and the greater application, therefore, becomes rather complicated and confusing. Would not this application have been easier if the vision had been given to one of the last kings of Judah instead of to Nebuchadnezzar? Would not a king of the royal dynasty of David be a more natural figure of that dynasty, and the "seven times" of loss of power experienced by such a king a more natural figure of the loss of sovereignty in the Davidic line? Of course, the Judean king, too, would still have to play a double role during the "seven times" of madness. Evidently, the *person* to whom the vision was given is no clear indication of another application beyond that one given directly through Daniel the prophet.

But does not the *theme* of the vision—"that people living may know that the Most High is ruler in the kingdom of mankind and that to the one he wants to, he gives it" —indicate that it points forward to the time for the establishment of God's kingdom by his Christ? To draw such a conclusion would be to read more into this statement (Dan. 4:17) than it actually says. Jehováh has always been the supreme ruler in the kingdom of mankind, although his supremacy has not always been recognized by everyone. But David did realize this: "Jehovah himself has firmly established his throne in the very heavens; and *over everything* his own kingship has held dominion." (Ps. 103:19) "Your kingship is a kingship *for all times indefinite*, And your dominion is throughout all successive generations." (Ps. 145:13) Thus Jehovah has always exercised control over the history of mankind and manuevered the events according to his own will: "And he is changing times and seasons, removing kings and setting up kings, giving wisdom to the wise ones and knowledge to those knowing discernment." (Dan. 2:21) This was a lesson that Nebuchadnezzar—as well as kings before and after him—had to learn. The 2,520-year period from 607 B.C.E. to 1914 C.E. represented no exception to Jehovah's supreme rule in spite of the break in the royal dynasty of David. The Gentile nations during this period did not rule supremely. Jehovah took action against the Babylonian empire by raising up Cyrus to capture Babylon in 539 B.C.E. (Isa. 45:1), and later Alexander the Great destroyed the Persian empire. Further, the expression "lowliest one of mankind" at Daniel 4:17 is no clear indication that Jesus Christ is intended, as Jehovah in his dealings with mankind many times has overthrown mighty and haughty kings and exalted lowly ones. This was stressed centuries later by Mary, the mother of Jesus: "He [Jehovah] has performed mightily with his arm, he has scattered abroad those who are haughty in the intention of their hearts. He has brought down men of power from thrones and *exalted lowly ones*." (Luke 1:51,52) Therefore, when the holy watcher in

Nebuchadnezzar's dream announced that "the Most High is ruler in the kingdom of mankind and that to the one he wants to, he gives it and he sets up over it the lowliest one of mankind," he simply seems to be stating a *universal principle* in Jehovah's dealing with mankind. There is no indication that he is giving a *prophecy* concerning the establishment of the Messianic kingdom with Jesus Christ on the throne. The *theme* of this vision—that the Most High is ruler in the kingdom of mankind—is demonstrated by Jehovah's dealing with the haughty Nebuchadnezzar who through his experience came to realize this universal principle. (Dan. 4:34-37) By reading about Nebuchadnezzar's humiliating experience, people living in every generation may come to realize this same truth.

C. The "seven times" have been calculated to represent a period of 2,520 years. As was clearly shown in Chapter I, this calculation is founded upon the so-called "year-day concept." As this concept is no longer accepted as a general principle by the Watchtower Bible and Tract Society, there is no need to deal with it here at any length. Although it was taken over by Pastor Russell from the Adventists, it was abandoned in the 1920s and early 1930s.[59] The 2,300 evenings and mornings (Dan. 8:14), the 1,260, 1,290, and 1,335 days (Dan. 12:7, 11, 12; Rev. 11:2, 3; 12:6, 14), earlier held to be as many *years*, have since then been interpreted to mean days only. The two texts in the Bible which earlier were quoted in proof of the year-day principle (Num. 14:34 and Ez. 4:6) are no longer understood as stating a universal principle of interpretation, although they are cited in support of the 2,520-year calculation. As was shown in Chapter I, note 2, it is not even necessary to apply the year-day principle to the prophecy of the seventy weeks in Daniel 9:24-27, as this prophecy does not mention days, just weeks.[60]

To apply the year-day principle to the "seven times" of Daniel 4 is evidently quite arbitrary, as it is no longer applied to other prophetic time periods (with the possible exception of the seventy weeks). The "seven times" are stated to be 2,520 days because "a time and times and a half time" (3½ times) are equated with 1,260 days at Revelation 12:6, 14. But while the 2,520 days are interpreted to mean a period of 2,520 *years*, the 1,260 days are understood to mean just 1,260 literal *days*, in spite of the fact that three-and-a-half times is half of seven times. As the interpretation of the seven times is derived from the three-and-a-half times (1,260 days), should not a consistent interpretation of these periods be given to both of them?[61] How do we know that the 2,520 days mean *years*, but not the 1,260 days? Obviously there is no real basis for the conclusion that "seven times" mean 2,520 *years*.

In the discussion above it has been shown that the Gentile times of Luke 21:24 cannot be proved to be an allusion to the "seven times" of Daniel 4. Nor is there any evidence to show that Nebuchadnezzar's "seven times" prefigured another period, amounting to 2,520 years of Gentile dominion. These identifications are obviously no more than a guesswork without foundation in the Bible itself—and should therefore be abandoned!

FAILED EXPECTATIONS— WRONG THINGS AT THE RIGHT TIME?

As was pointed out in Chapter I of this work, Pastor Russell's predictions for 1914 were not fulfilled. When the First World War ended, the Gentile nations still ruled the earth instead of Christ's Kingdom, and Jerusalem in Palestine was still trodden down by the Gentiles. Evidently, the *time* for these events could not be right. But to draw this simple conclusion was not an easy thing. Additionally, *something* had happened: the World War. So it was felt that the time was right after all. Russell's followers believed that they had been expecting the "wrong thing at the right time."

Gradually a new apocalyptic pattern emerged. The World War with the many crises following it came to be regarded merely as a *beginning* of the overthrow of the Gentile nations:

> God granted to the gentiles a lease of dominion for a term of 2,520 years, which term or lease ended about August, 1914. Then came forward the Landlord, the rightful Ruler (Ezekiel 21:27), and began ouster proceedings. It is not to be expected that he would suddenly wipe everything out of existence, for that is not the way the Lord does things; but that he would overrule the contending elements, causing these to destroy the present order; and that while this is going on he would have his faithful followers give a tremendous witness in the world....[62]

This reminds us of later explanations of the 1934 failure by Pastoral Bible Institute editors discussed above. The setting up of Christ's kingdom had earlier been seen as a process which began in 1878 and which would culminate in 1914 with the destruction of the Gentile nations.[63] But in 1922 the starting-point of this process was moved forward to 1914 and the overthrow of the Gentile nations was expected to take place in the near future. This new view was presented by J.F. Rutherford at the Cedar Point Convention of September 5-13, 1922 in his address, "The Kingdom of Heaven is at Hand." Three years later, in the article "Birth of the Nation" in *The Watch Tower*, March 1, 1925, a new interpretation of Revelation 12 was presented in accordance with the new understanding of the setting up of God's kingdom, to the effect that the kingdom had been "born" in heaven in 1914. Jesus Christ "took unto himself his great power and began his reign: the nations were angry, and the day of God's wrath began.—Ezekiel 21:27; Revelation 11:17, 18."[64]

But what about the trampling of Jerusalem by the Gentiles? In the autumn of 1914 the persecution of the Jews had practically stopped all around the world, and Pastor Russell saw in this fact a confirmation of his belief that the Gentile times had expired, although the city of Jerusalem at that time was still occupied by a Gentile nation, the Turkish Empire. But in December, 1917, more than one year after

Russell's death, a very interesting thing happened. On December 9, 1917, the British under General Allenby captured Jerusalem and thus made an end of the nearly seven-centuries-long Turkish occupation. This event was looked upon as a very important sign of the times.[65] The deliverance of Jerusalem from the Turks in 1917, together with the so-called Balfour declaration of November 2, 1917 which proclaimed that the British Government supported the establishment of Jewish National Home in Palestine, drastically accelerated Jewish immigration to Palestine. Thus, from October, 1922, to the spring of 1929 the Jewish population of Palestine increased from 83,794 to 165,000. Consequently, J.F. Rutherford's book *Life*, published in 1929, is simply one long argument in support of the idea that at Luke 21 Jesus predicted a return of the Jews to Palestine after the expiration of the Gentile times and that Jewish immigration to Palestine following 1914 was a fulfillment of this prophecy.

But shortly after the publication of *Life*, this whole idea was abandoned; the return of the Jews to the Promised Land was no longer seen as a fulfillment of Bible prophecies.[66] Since 1931 such prophecies have been applied to *spiritual* Israel. The logical consequence of this change could only be that the end of the treading down of Jerusalem was no longer applicable to the *literal* city of Jerusalem:

> The present-day city of Jerusalem over in Palestine is not the city of the Great King Jehovah God, even though Christendom calls certain places over there 'holy'. That city is doomed to destruction at the end of this world. But the true Jerusalem will live forever as the capital of Jehovah's universal organization.... Jesus Christ is the 'King of kings and Lord of lords' over that true Jerusalem. At the close of the Gentile times in 1914 he was enthroned as acting Ruler in the 'city of the great King', Jehovah. Thus, after an interruption of 2,520 years by Gentile powers, Theocratic Government over earth rose again to power in the New Jerusalem, never to be trodden down by the Gentile.[67]

What, exactly, was this "New Jerusalem"? The Watchtower

book *Your Will Be Done On Earth* (1958) explains on page 94:

> Back in 607 B.C.E. the Jerusalem that was overthrown stood for the kingdom of God because it had the typical throne of Jehovah on which the anointed one of Jehovah sat as his king. Likewise, the Jerusalem that is trampled upon by worldly nations stands for the kingdom of God .... So the end of the trampling down of Jerusalem at the complete fulfillment of the 'appointed times of the nations' would mean the rising again of the symbolic Jerusalem, namely, *the kingdom of God.*

Thus the end of the trampling down of Jerusalem was interpreted to mean the installation of Jesus Christ on Jehovah's throne in the heavenly Jerusalem in 1914.[68] But this change from the earthly to the heavenly Jerusalem created other questions, which never have been satisfactorily answered.

WHEN WAS JESUS CHRIST ENTHRONED?

In the publications of the Watchtower Society it is now constantly stressed Jesus Christ was "enthroned" and his Kingdom "set up" or "established" in heaven at the end of the Gentile times in 1914. However, several texts in the Bible clearly state that Jesus Christ was already enthroned after his resurrection in 33 C.E. For example, in his revelation to the Apostle John, perhaps about 96 C.E., Jesus says: "To the one that conquers I will grant to sit down with me on my throne, even as *I conquered and sat down with my Father on his throne.*" (Rev. 3:21)

With Jesus' resurrection, Psalm 110:1 began to be fulfilled according to Hebrews 10:12,13. Jesus' position of power since 33 C.E. is accentuated by Paul at Ephesians 1:20-23:

> ...he [Jehovah] raised him up from the dead and seated him at his right hand in the heavenly places, *far above every government and authority and power and lordship*, not only in this system of things, but also in that to come. *He also subjected all things under*

> *his feet*, and made him head over all things to the congregation, which is his body, the fullness of him who fills up all things in all.

This statement agrees with Jesus' own words to his disciples after his resurrection: "*All authority has been given me in heaven and on the earth*." (Matt. 28:18)

That the Kingdom rule has actually been in force since the year A.D.33 has also been emphasized in Watchtower publications in recent years. *Aid to Bible Understanding*, for example, explains:

> With Jesus' ascension to heaven, forty days after his resurrection, his disciples began to comprehend the heavenly nature of his kingdom. Ten days later, on Pentecost of the year A.D. 33, they had evidence that he had been "exalted to the right hand of God," as he poured out holy spirit upon them.... Since Jesus Christ was now sitting at his Father's right hand and was the head over his congregation, it is evident that *his kingly rule was in force toward them from Pentecost 33 C.E. onward*. (Eph. 5:23; Heb. 1:3; Phil. 2:9-11)[69] (*Italics mine*)

Consequently, from the year 33 C.E. and thereafter, Jesus Christ, as the legal heir to the throne of David has been sitting on the throne of Jehovah in *heavenly* Jerusalem and ruling over *spiritual* Israel just as the kings of the royal dynasty of David up to Zedekiah sat upon the "throne of Jehovah" in *earthy* Jerusalem, reigning over *fleshy* Israel. *How, then, can it be held that "Jerusalem," understood as being the Kingdom of God, was trodden down by the Gentiles right up to 1914?*

The Gentile nations, of course, could not "ascend into heaven" (John 3:13) in order to interfere with Christ's rule from Pentecost onward. Nor can the treading down of "Jerusalem" refer to the persecution of spiritual Israel, or the remnant of Christ's joint heirs to the kingdom still in the flesh, as this persecution did not stop in 1914. Those among Jehovah's Witnesses professedly being of this "heavenly" class have been the objects of much cruel persecution since 1914, especially during the two World

Wars. So what did the treading down of "Jerusalem" mean, and how did it stop in 1914? The official Watchtower explanation, briefly restated below, is far from satisfactory:

Christ's rule from 33 C.E. up to 1914 is regarded as a *passive* rule. Aside from his rule over his congregation he has been waiting "until his enemies should be placed as a stool for his feet." (Heb. 10:13; Ps. 110:1) But in 1914 "*the kingdom of the world* did become the Kingdom of our Lord and of his Christ." (Rev. 11:15) At that time Jesus began to take action against his enemies, starting with Satan and the demons, whom he "defeated and cast down to the earthly realm."[70] This event resulted in "woe for the earth and for the sea, because the Devil has come down to you, having great anger, knowing he has a short period of time." (Rev. 12:12) This "woe" is said to have begun with the First World War, followed by food shortages, earthquakes, lawlessness, and other things, understood as being part of the sign of Christ's "presence" (*parousia*) since 1914. (Matt. 24:3-22)

Could the ousting out of Satan and his demons from heaven be regarded as the end of the Gentile trampling of "Jerusalem"? This solution was tried in the November 1, 1949, issue of *The Watchtower* on page 331: "The Devil and his demons proved unable to tread down the heavenly New Jerusalem, but were themselves put under the King's feet.—Rev. 12:1-13." But this explanation would make Satan and his demons identical to the Gentiles, who were trampling on the "New Jerusaelem" until 1914. The main problem with this idea is that the word "gentile" (*ethne*) is used everywhere in the Bible to distinguish *the nations of the earth* from the Jews.[71] Obviously because of this fact, the Gentiles are not presently identified with Satan and his demons, and the question of how the Gentile trampling of Jerusalem stopped in 1914 *remains unanswered*.

Another problem is, how it can be said that the "kingdom of the world" (Rev. 11:15) became the kingdom of Christ in 1914, as no change took place in this regard from a human point of view. The Gentile nations have continued to rule the world since 1914 as much as they did before that date. Thus it seems obvious that "the kingdom of the world" did not become "the kingdom of our Lord, and of His Christ" in 1914. Rather, this statement in Revelation chapter eleven, verse 15, evidently refers to Christ's enthronement in 33 C.E., as shown by many other scriptures. Since then he has had the "authority over the nations" and the power to break them "to pieces like clay vessels." (Revelation 2:26, 27; compare Revelation 3:21, 22) As he himself stated following his resurrection, "All authority has been given me in heaven and on the earth." (Matthew 28:18) Since then he has been "the Ruler of the kings of the earth," and their rule up till now has been only with his permission (Revelation 1:5). No change in this respect took place in 1914.

But, the Watchtower Society insists, Jesus foretold that his future "invisible presence" would be accompanied by a period of "woes" (Revelation 12:12), consisting of wars, famines, pestilences, lawlessness, and so on. This "sign" of his "presence" is claimed to have appeared on earth since 1914. Is this a correct understanding of Matthew chapter 24? What are the facts regarding the claims made of an "invisible presence" and of a sign that supposedly enables Christ's followers to be aware of such "invisible presence"?

THE SIGN OF CHRIST'S "PAROUSIA"

When Jesus' disciples asked, "What will be the sign of your 'parousia'," they used a word which usually is translated "coming." (Matt. 24:3) The "sign," therefore, is usually understood to *precede* or *accompany* Christ's coming or arrival. This was also the way N.H. Barbour and his associates understood the matter—until 1874 had passed without Christ coming on the clouds. At that time one of the readers of Barbour's *Midnight Cry* discovered that the *Emphatic Diaglott* translation of the New Testament by

Benjamin Wilson translated the Greek word *parousia*, not "coming," but "presence." (See Chapter I of this work.) If this translation of *parousia* is correct, the disciples did not ask for the sign preceding or accompanying Christ's arrival, but for the sign which would *follow* his arrival and mark his (invisible) presence! This idea was accepted by Barbour and later, in 1876, by C.T. Russell. The "sign" was seen in the world events following the year 1874, and later in those following the year 1914. But does *parousia* really mean "presence"?

It is true that lexicons agree in giving the word *parousia* the literal meaning of "presence." But they also give "arrival" or "coming" as a second definition and the technical use of the word, especially as it applies to "the visit of a ruler."[72] The well-known *Theological Dictionary of the New Testament*, edited by G. Kittel and G. Friedrich, devotes fourteen pages to a discussion of the word *parousia*, thirteen of which are given to the "Technical Use of the Term." It presents very strong evidence for the conclusion that *parousia*, when used in connection with Christ's second coming, is used in its technical sense.

It cannot be denied that Christ's second coming is "the visit of a ruler." That the disciples of Jesus used the word *parousia* in its technical sense is clearly indicated by the context of Matthew 24. First it may be asked: When the disciples asked about Christ's *parousia*, did they then have in mind his "invisible presence" and want to know the sign thereof? *The Watchtower* of January 15, 1974, gives the answer on page 50:

> When they asked Jesus, "What will be the sign of your presence?" they did not know that his future presence would be invisible. (Matt. 24:3) Even after his resurrection they asked: "Lord, are you restoring the kingdom to Israel at this time?" (Acts 1:6) They looked for a visible restoring of it.

Now, if they did not know that Jesus' future presence would be invisible, why did they ask for a sign in proof that it would be? Would not his visible presence be sign enough? Evidently they wanted to know the sign *accompanying or preceding* his arrival as is confirmed by the way Jesus answered their question. After having mentioned wars, food shortages, earthquakes, the great tribulation, and his coming on clouds, he said "Now learn from the fig tree as an illustration this point: Just as soon as its young branch grows tender and it puts forth leaves, you know that *summer is near*." (Matt. 24:32) Note that he did not say: "as soon as its young branch grows tender and it puts forth leaves, you know that *summer is present*." Then he continues: "Likewise also you, when you see all these things, know that *he is near at the doors*." (Matt. 24:33)

"All these things," therefore, would prove that he "is near at the doors," not that he is invisibly present, just as the young branch of the fig tree growing tender and putting forth leaves proves that the "summer is near," not present. So the comparison is between the summer as *being near*, and Christ as *being near*. Evidently "all these things" mentioned by Jesus would *precede* his arrival, not *follow* it.

What, exactly, did Jesus point to as the sign of his *parousia*? When he said, "When you see *all these things*, know that he is near" (Matt. 24:33), did he then refer back to all things mentioned from verse 4 to verse 31—wars, food shortages, earthquakes, the great tribulation, his own coming on the clouds, etc.? Although this could be the immediate impression given to the reader, an examination of Jesus' prophecy seems to point to a special part of his answer as denoting the sign of his *parousia*. Jesus starts his answer with a warning: "Look out that nobody misleads you," after which he refers to false Christs and "wars and reports of wars." "For these things must take place, but the end is not yet." (vs. 4-6) Such things, therefore, would not be the sign of his *parousia*. As is shown in the book *God's Kingdom Of A Thousand Years Has Approached* (1973), pages 296-297, the events mentioned up to verse 22—wars, food shortages, eathquakes, etc.—marked the period up to the destruction of Jerusalem in 70 C.E.

Although these things most probably were meant also to mark the period up to his *parousia*, Jesus nowhere designates them as the "sign" of it. In fact, he does not deal with the question of his *parousia* until after his description of the great tribulation (in 70 C.E.). Then, in verses 23 f., he again starts with warnings of false Christs. From verse 29, for the first time in his answer, he gives a direct description of things related to his second coming: "The sun will be darkened, and the moon will not give its light, and the stars will fall from heaven, and the powers of heaven will be shaken. *And then the sign of the Son of man will appear in heaven*." (vs. 29, 30) Here Jesus directly refers to the "sign" of his coming, evidently in answer to the question of the disciples.[73] What could this "sign in heaven" be?

As the "sign" is said to appear "in heaven," is it possible that it could be identical to the events mentioned in the preceding verse, the darkening of the sun and the moon, and the falling of the stars from heaven? Most probably so, as Luke in his parallel account directly states that "there will be *signs* (*semeia*, the plural number of *semeion*) in sun and moon and stars" as portents of Christ's coming on the clouds. Exactly what these "signs in heaven" are cannot be know in advance, of course, but when they appear, their meaning will be apparent to everybody, and "all the tribes of the earth will beat themselves in lamentation." (Matt. 24:30) The world events from 1914 and on are frightening indeed. But "the tribes of the earth" do not recognize them as "the sign of the Son of man," causing them to "beat themselves in lamentation." What, then, do these events since 1914 mean?

1914—A BALANCED VIEW

If 1914 did not mark the end of the Gentile times, nor the beginning of Christ's invisible presence, why did the First World War break out at a date predicted thirty-nine years in advance? This seems very remarkable. But first it must be remembered that none of the things predicted to occur on that date actually happened. Secondly, an endless number of dates have been set for the second coming of Christ, and also the end of the Gentile times. A predicted date sometimes accidentally happens to coincide with some important historical event, although the event itself was not predicted. Of the dates fixed for the expiration of the Gentile times, some were put very near to the 1914 date: 1915 (Guinness, 1886), 1917 (J. A. Brown, 1823), 1918 (Bickersteth, before 1850), and 1923 (Guinness, 1886). It is even more remarkable when some event taking place at a predicted date happens to have some relation to the events foretold for the date in question. But this has happened, too. For example, 1917 would, according to Brown in 1823, see "the full glory of the kingdom of Israel ... perfected." Although this did not happen in 1917, an important step was taken that year toward the establishment of the state of Israel. (See note 65.) But more remarkable still were Robert Fleming's predictions of the French Revolution during the years 1789-1798, made *nearly a hundred years prior to that event*!

Fleming's book *The Rise and Fall of Papacy* was first published in 1701. Commenting upon the *fourth vial* at Revelation 16:8,9, he identifies the "sun" as the Papacy, and France as instrumental in pouring out the fourth vial. After that, France itself will be humbled:

> ...we may justly suppose that *the French monarchy*, after it has scorched others, will itself consume by doing so—its fire, and that which is the fuel that maintains it, wasting insensibly, till it be exhausted at last *towards the end of this century*.[74]

> I cannot but hope that some new mortification of the chief supporters of the Antichrist will then happen; and perhaps the French monarchy may begin to be considerably humbled about that time; that whereas the present French king takes the sun for his emblem, and this for his motto, 'Nec pluribus impar,' he may at length, or rather his successors, and *the monarchy itself (at least before the year 1794)*, be forced to acknowledge that, in respect to neighbouring potentates, he is even 'Singulis impar.'

> but as the expiration of this vial, I do fear it will not be until the year 1794.[75]

Shortly after the Republic had been proclaimed in 1792, when the horrors of the French Revolution were at their most extreme and Louis XVI was about to die on the scaffold, Fleming's incredible predictions were recalled to memory. Thus his book began to be reprinted both in England and America. The sensation his predictions produced was great and caused much excitement; and their fulfillment was a strong incentive to increased study of biblical prophecies after the French Revolution. Fleming's calculation of the 1,260 year-days was taken over by many others, although the termination date for them was soon changed by many from 1794 to 1798, the year when the Pope was deposed as ruler of the Papal States and banished by French troops. Thus the 1798 date came to be regarded as marking the beginning of the "time of the end" by Adventist groups. The calculation was later adopted also by C. T. Russell and his followers but changed slightly to the following year, 1799. That date is still held to by the Seventh-Day Adventists.

Should not "fulfilled" predictions of this kind help us to take a more sober view of the 1914 date? In Chapter II of this work a number of strong arguments were presented against the 607 B.C.E. date as the year of the destruction of Jerusalem and the starting-point of the 2,520 year Gentile times calculation. In this chapter it was first demonstrated that the seventy-year prophecy is in good agreement with the 587 B.C.E. date for the fall of Jerusalem to Nebuchadnezzar. Thus, the 2,520 years *could not have ended in 1914*. Then it was shown that a change of the expiration date of those times from 1914 to 1934 resulted in just another failed prophecy. Next, the question was raised, "Is the 2,520-year calculation really founded on a sound biblical basis?" The examination that followed demonstrated it is not. Finally, the re-evaluation of the meaning of the 1914 date in the Watchtower publications since 1922 was examined and found to be deficient. For all these reasons, should not the 1914 date be wholly and entirely discarded as the pivotal point in the application of Bible prophecies to our own century? The answer is clear.

EPILOGUE

A RECENT ATTEMPT TO CONCEAL FACTS

As told in the *Prologue*, this work was orginally presented to the Watchtower Bible and Tract Society in 1977. During the subsequent correspondence with the headquarters of that organization, additional lines of evidence were presented which are included in the present revised edition of it. In possession of all this information, it might be expected that the Governing Body of Jehovah's Witnesses or its Writing Committee at the Brooklyn headquarters would have been prepared to reevaluate their Gentile times calculations in accord with their stated interest in biblical truth and historical facts. On the contrary, they chose to retain the disproved 607 B.C.E. date and the antiquated theories founded upon it. Thus, in the summer of 1981 another presentation of these prophetic speculations was published in the book "*Let Your Kingdom Come.*" In an "Appendix to Chapter 14" of that book, some of the lines of evidence against the 607 B.C.E. date are briefly discussed and rejected. The discussion, however, is seriously lacking in objectivity and proves to be nothing more than a weak attempt to conceal facts.

MISREPRESENTATIONS OF HISTORICAL EVIDENCE

In the area of historical research an event is generally regarded as a "historical fact" if it is testified to by at least *two* independent witnesses. We recognize this rule from the Bible: "At the mouth of *two or three witnesses* every matter may be established." (Matt. 18:16) In Chapter II of the present work *seven witnesses* against the 607 B.C.E. date were presented, *at least four of which* are clearly independent of each other. Most of the records giving this *sevenfold testimony* are found on documents preserved from the Neo-Babylonian era itself. These include the royal inscriptions, business documents and the Apis stelae from the contemporary Egyptians Saite dynasty. Only the astronomical diaries and the king lists of Ptolemy and Berossus are found on later documents, but those records, too, were seen to be copied from earlier ones that—directly or indirectly—went back to the Neo-Babylonian era. The evidence against the 607 B.C.E. date, therefore, is overwhelming, and very few reigns in ancient history may be established with such conclusiveness as the reign of Nebuchadnezzar II (604-562 B.C.E.).

The Watchtower Bible and Tract Society in its "Appendix to Chapter 14" very briefly mentions *some* of the lines of evidence against the 607 B.C.E. date, including Ptolemy's canon and Berossus' king list, but *fails to mention* that both of these authors got their information from sources that had reached them from the Neo-Babylonian period itself, indicating instead that the origin of their dates is to be found in the Seleucid era. (p. 186) Further, for the first time it mentions the *Nabonidus Harran Stele* (Nabon. H 1, B), a *contemporary* document establishing the length of the whole Neo-Babylonian era up to the ninth year of Nabonidus. But it *fails to mention another contemporary stele* from the reign of Nabonidus, *the Hillah stele*, that also establishes the length of the whole Neo-Babylonian era, including the reign of Nabonidus! Thirdly, the astronomical diary VAT 4956 is mentioned. Referring to the fact that it is a copy of an original text from the reign of Nebuchadnezzar, made during the Seleucid era, the Society repeats the theory that "it is possible that its historical information is simply that which was accepted in the Seleucid period." (p. 186) This reasoning is completely fallacious, however, as it has been proven wrong by another astronomical diary, *B.M. 32312*, discussed in Chapter II of the present volume (see pp. 83-86 above), a fact the Society passes over in silence, although it is very well aware of it. Finally, the Society mentions the *business tablets*, admitting that these thousands of *contemporary* documents give the reigns of *all* the Neo-Babylonian kings, and that the lengths of reign given by these documents *agree with* all the other lines of evidence referred to—Ptolemy's canon, Berossus' king list, Nabonidus' royal inscriptions, and the astronomical diaries. (p. 187) It *fails to mention*, though, that such agreement refutes the notion that the information on VAT 4956 could have been concocted during the Seleucid period. Apart from the above-mentioned lines of evidence, another strong one against the 607 B.C.E. date is completely ignored, too, namely, *the synchronisms to the contemporary and independently established Egyptian chronology*.

By omitting nearly half of the lines of evidence (the Hillah stele, the diary B.M. 32312, and the contemporary Egyptian documents) and misrepresenting some of the others, the real facts about the strength of the established Neo-Babylonian chronology *are concealed*. From this basis Watchtower scholars proceed to a critical appraisal of the limited evidence presented. They state: "However, no historian can deny the possibility that the present picture of Babylonian history might be misleading or in error. It is known, for example, that ancient priests and kings sometimes altered records for their own purposes." (p. 187)

Again, the facts are concealed. Though it is true that ancient scribes sometimes distorted history in order to glorify their kings and gods, scholars agree that, though such distortion is found in *Assyrian* royal inscriptions and other documents, Neo-Babylonian scribes *did not* distort history in this way. This was also pointed out in Chapter II of the present work (see under the subheading "Chronicles and Other Historical Records"), where A.K. Grayson, a well-known authority on Babylonian historical records, was quoted as saying: "Unlike the Assyrian scribes the Babylonians neither fail to mention Babylonian defeats nor do they attempt to change them into victories." Of the Neo-Babylonian *chronicles* he says: "The chronicles contain a reasonably reliable and representative record of important events in the period with which they are concerned," and "Within the boundaries of their interest, the writers are quite objective and impartial." Of the Babylonian *royal inscriptions* (such as the Nabonidus' stelae) Grayson remarks: "Babylonian royal inscriptions are primarily records of building activity and on the whole seem to be reliable." (*Orientalia*, Vol. 49, Fasc. 2, 1980, pp. 170, 171, 175) The scribal distortion of history, then, refers to Assyrian, but not to Neo-Babylonian history, a fact which is *concealed* in the Watchtower Society's "Appendix" to *Let Your Kingdom Come.*

The next argument advanced by the Society in the "Appendix" is that, "even if the discovered evidence is accurate, it might be misinterpreted by modern scholars or be incomplete so that *yet undiscovered material could drastically alter the chronology* of the period." (p. 187) Evidently the Watchtower Society realizes that all the evidence discovered hitherto since the middle of the last century unanimously points to 587 B.C.E. instead of 607 as the eighteenth year of Nebuchadnezzar. Among the thousands of discovered documents from the Neo-Babylonian era they have not been able to find the slightest support for their 607 B.C.E. date—hence, the reference to "*yet undiscovered material.*" A chronology that has to be based on "yet *undiscovered* material," because it is demolished by the *discovered* material, is resting on a weak foundation indeed. If an idea, refuted by an overwhelming mass of *discovered* evidence, is to be retained because it is hoped that "yet undiscovered material" will support it, *all* ideas, however false, could be retained on the same principle. But it should be remembered that such a faith is not founded upon "the evident demonstration of realities though not beheld" (Hebr. 11:1); it is founded solely upon wishful thinking.

If it really were true that (1) "no historian can deny the possibility that the present picture of Babylonian history might be misleading or in error," that (2) "priests and kings sometimes altered" the Neo-Babylonian historial records, that (3) "even if the discovered evidence is accurate, it might be misinterpreted by modern scholars or be incomplete," and that (4) "yet undiscovered material could drastically alter the chronology of the period," what reason do we have for accepting *any* date from the Neo-Babylonian era established by historians—for example 539 B.C.E. as the date for the fall of Babylon? This date, too, has been established *solely* by the aid of secular documents of the same type as those which have established 587 B.C.E. as the eighteenth year of Nebuchadnezzar. Of the two dates, 587 has better support than 539 B.C.E.![1] If 587 is to be rejected for the above-mentioned reasons, the 539 B.C.E. date should also be rejected for the same, if not stronger, reasons! Yet the Watchtower Society not only accepts the 539 B.C.E. date as reliable, but even puts so much trust in it that it has made it *the very basis of its Bible chronology!*[2] If its reasons for rejecting the 587 B.C.E. date are valid, they are equally valid for the 539 B.C.E. date, too. To reject one date and retain the other is not only inconsistent; it is a sad example of scholastic dishonesty.

MISREPRESENTATION OF SCHOLARS

In support of their reasons for rejecting the Neo-

Babylonian chronology established by historians, a well-known authority on ancient Near Eastern history is referred to.

"Evidently realizing such facts,"—that the present picture of Babylonian history might be in error, that ancient priests and kings might have altered the ancient Neo-Babylonian records, and that the undiscovered material could drastically alter the chronology of the period:

> Professor Edward F. Campbell, Jr., introduced a chart, which included Neo-Babylonian chronology, with the caution: "It goes without saying that these lists are provisional. The more one studies the intricacies of the chronological problems in the ancient Near East, the less he is inclined to think of any presentation as final. For this reason, the term *circa* [about] could be used even more liberally than it is."

This quotation is taken from a chapter written by Edward F. Campbell, Jr., which first appeared in *The Bible and the Ancient Near East*, a work edited by G. Ernest Wright and published by Routledge and Kegan Paul of London, in 1961. The Watchtower Society *did not mention*, however, that the chart referred to in this work covers the chronologies of Egypt, Palestine, Syria, Asia Minor, Assyria and Babylon *from c. 3800 B.C.E. to the death of Alexander the Great in 323 B.C.E.*, and although the term *circa* is placed before many of the reigns given in the lists for this long period, *no circas are placed before any of the reigns given for the kings of the Neo-Babylonian period!* The question is: When Professor Campbell, in co-operation with Professor David N. Freedman, (who succeeded Professor Campbell in 1976 as editor of the well-known periodical *Biblical Archaeologist*) prepared the chronological lists in *The Bible and the Ancient Near East*, did he then feel that "the present picture of Babylonian history might be misleading or in error" when it comes to the *Neo-Babylonian* era? Did he think there was any possibility that "ancient priests and kings sometimes altered" the *Neo-Babylonian* records "for their own purposes"? Was he, for whatever reason, prepared to put the term *circa* before any of the reigns of the *Neo-Babylonian* kings? In other words, did the Watchtower Society give a correct presentation of the views of Dr. Campbell (and of Dr. Freedman)?

When these questions were put to Dr. Campbell, he answered:

> As perhaps you will have concluded, I am dismayed at the use made of Noel Freedman's and my chronological lists by the Watch Tower Society. I fear that some earnest folk will reach for any straw to support their already-arrived-at conclusions. This is most certainly a case of doing just that.
>
> Let me first explain that the division of responsibility for the chronological lists in *BANE* assigned the larger Near Eastern chronology to me and the Biblical data to Professor David Noel Freedman, now of the University of Michigan. We did indeed talk about the *caveats* we placed before our charts, but there was absolutely no intent to suggest that there was leeway of as much as twenty years for the dates relating to Babylonia and Judah. I am fairly confident that Dr. Freedman makes explicit somewhere in the apparatus of the *BANE* chapter that the 587-6 date can be off by no more than one year, while the 597 date is one of the very few *secure* dates in our whole chronological repertoire. I know that he remains convinced of this, as I do. There is not a shred of evidence that I know of to suggest even the possibility that the dates in The Babylonian Chronicle have been altered by priests or kings for pious reasons. I am in hearty agreement with Grayson.[3]

Dr. Campbell forwarded the questions put to him to Dr. Freedman, to give the latter an opportunity to express his views. Dr. Freedman had the following to say on the matter:

> ... I agree entirely with everything that Dr. Campbell has written to you. It is true that there are some uncertainties about biblical chronology for this period, but those uncertainties stem from confusing and perhaps conflicting data in the Bible, and have nothing to do with the chronological information and evidence for the Neo-Babylonian period from cuneiform inscriptions and other non-biblical sources. This is one of the best-known periods of the ancient world, and we can be very sure that

> the dates are correct to within a year or so, and many of the dates are accurate to the day and month. There is therefore absolutely no warrant for the comments or judgments made by the Watch Tower Society based on a statement about our uncertainty. What I had specifically in mind was the disagreement among scholars as to whether the fall of Jerusalem should be dated in 587 or 586. Eminent scholars disagree on this point, and unfortunately we do not have the Babylonian chronicle for this episode as we do for the capture of Jerusalem in 597 (that date is now fixed exactly). But it is only a debate about one year at most (587 or 586), so it would have no bearing upon the views of the Jehovah's Witnesses who apparently want to rewrite the whole history of the time and change the dates rather dramatically. There is no warrant whatever for that.[4]

Thus the Watchtower Society, in its attempt to find support for the 607 B.C.E. date, *misrepresented* the views of Dr. Campbell and Dr. Freedman. Neither of them believes that ancient priests or kings might have "altered records" from the Neo-Babylonian period, or "that yet undiscovered material could drastically alter the chronology of the period." And neither of them is prepared to put the term *circa* before any of the reigns given in their lists for the kings of the Neo-Babylonian era. The only uncertainty they point to is whether the date for the desolation of Jerusalem should be set at 587 or 586 B.C.E., and this uncertainty does not come from any errors or obscurities in the extra-biblical sources, but from the seemingly conflicting figures given in the Bible!

MISREPRESENTATION OF ANCIENT WRITERS

The last two pages of the "Appendix" to "*Let Your Kingdom Come*" are devoted to a discussion of Jeremiah's prophecy of the seventy years. (pp. 188, 189) All arguments in this section have been thoroughly refuted in Chapter III of the present work, in the subsection "the Seventy Years: Desolation or Servitude—Which?" to which the reader is directed. Only a few points will be made here.

Against Berossus' statement that Nebuchadnezzar took

Jewish captives in his accession-year, shortly after the battle at Carchemish (see Chapter III above), it is argued that "there are no cuneiform documents supporting this." (p. 188) But the Watchtower Society *fails to mention that Berossus' statement is clearly supported by the most direct reading of Daniel 1:1-6.* (See Appendix B.) Daniel reports that "in the third year of the kingship of Jehoiakim" (corresponding to the accession-year of Nebuchadnezzar; see Jer. 25:1) Nebuchadnezzar took a tribute from Judah, consisting of utensils from the temple and "some of the sons of Israel and of the royal offspring and of the nobles," and brought them to Babylonia. This was evidently a very small deportation, and it is true that the Babylonian Chronicle does not specifically mention these Jewish captives. It does mention, however, that Nebuchadnezzar, in his accession-year, "marched unopposed through the Hatti land" (Syro-Palestine), and that "*he took the heavy tribute of the Hatti terrritory to Babylon.*" Most probably captives from the Hatti territory were included in this "heavy tribute," as is also pointed out by Professor Gerhard Larsson: "It is certain that this 'heavy tribute' consisted not only of treasure but also of prisoners from the conquered countries. To refrain from doing so would have been altogether too alien from the customs of the kings of Babylon and Assyria."[5] Thus, although the cuneiform documents do not specifically mention the small Jewish deportation in the accession-year of Nebuchadnezzar, they strongly indicate this to have taken place, in agreement with the *direct* statements of Daniel and Berossus.

The Society finds another argument against this conclusion in Jeremiah 52:28-30: "More significantly, Jeremiah 52:28-30 carefully reports that Nebuchadnezzar took Jews captive in his seventh year, in his 18th year and his 23rd year, *not* his accession year." (Appendix, p. 188) But this argument presupposes that Jeremiah 52:28-30 contains a *complete* record of the deportations, which it clearly does not. The sum total of Jewish captives taken in the three deportations referred to in the passage is given in verse 30 as "four thousand and six hundred." However, 2 Kings 24:14-16 gives the number of those deported during only *one* of these deportations as 18,000 (10,000 in verse 14 and 8,000 more in verse 16)! Different theories have been proposed to explain this discrepancy, none of which may be regarded as more than a guess. *Aid to Bible Understanding*, for instance, claims that the figure at Jeremiah 52:28-30 "apparently refers to those of a certain rank, or to those who were family heads." (p. 297) *The New Bible Dictionary* (ed. J.D. Douglas, London: Inter-Varsity Press, 1962) holds that "the difference is doubtless due to different categories of captives being envisaged." (p. 669) All agree that Jeremiah 52:28-30 does not give a complete number of those deported, and some commentators also suggest that not all deportations are mentioned in the text.[6] At least the one in the accession-year of Nebuchadnezzar described by Daniel is not mentioned—which does not prove that it did not take place. The reason why it is not included among the deportations enumerated in Jeremiah 52:28-30 most probably is that it was a very small deportation only, consisting of Jews chosen from among "the royal offspring and of the nobles" with the intention of using them as servants at the royal palace. (Dan. 1:3,4) The important thing is that Daniel, *independently of Berossus*, mentions this deportation in the accession-year of Nebuchadnezzar. Against the clear statements of Daniel and Berossus, the Watchtower Society refers to Josephus, who claims that Nebuchadnezzar, in the year of the battle of Carchemish, conquered all of Syria-Palestine "excepting Judea." (*Ant.* X, vi, 1) Josephus wrote this more than 600 years after Daniel and almost 400 years after Berossus. Even if he were right, this would not contradict the claim that the seventy years of *servitude* began in the accession-year of Nebuchadnezzar, as Jeremiah's prophecy clearly applies the servitude to "these nations" (Jer. 25:11), that is, the nations surrounding Judah. In fact, Josephus even *supports* the conclusion that these nations became subservient to Nebuchadnezzar in his accession-year, as he states that "the king of Babylon *took all Syria, as far as Pelusium*, excepting Judah," at that time. Pelusium lay on the border of Egypt.

But there is no reason to believe that Josephus' statement is more trustworthy than the information given by Daniel and Berossus. Josephus here evidently presented a conclusion of his own, based on a misunderstanding of 2 Kings 24:1. Dr. Hengstenberg, in his thorough discussion of Daniel 1:1ff., gives the following comment on the expression "excepting Judah" in Josephus' *Antiquities*. X, vi, 1: "It should not be thought that Josephus got the *parex tes Ioudaias* [excepting Judah] from a source no longer available to us. What follows shows clearly that he just derived it from a misunderstanding of the passage at 2 Kings 24:1. As he erroneously understood the three years mentioned there as the interval between the two invasions, he thought that no invasion could be presumed before the 8th year of Jehoiakim."[7] Josephus' statement, then, weighs as nothing against the testimony of Berossus, who evidently, unlike Josephus, got his information from sources preserved from the Neo-Babylonian period, and Daniel's testimony, as one personally involved in the deportation he describes.

The Watchtower Society next quotes two passages from Josephus' works, where the seventy years are described as seventy years of *desolation*. (*Ant*. X, ix, 7, and *Against* Apion, I, 19) But they conceal the fact that Josephus, in his third and last reference to the period of Jerusalem's desolation, states that *the desolation lasted for fifty years, not seventy*! In *Against Apion* I, 21, he says:

> These accounts agree with the true history in our books [that is, the Holy Scriptures]; for in them it is written that Nebuchadnezzar, in the nineteenth year of his reign, laid our temple desolate, and so *it lay in that state for fifty years*; but that in the second year of the reign of Cyrus, its foundations were laid and it was finished again in the second year of Darius.

In support of this statement Josephus first quotes

Berossus and then the records of the Phoenicians. Thus in this passage Josephus contradicts his earlier statements on the length of the period of desolation. (See also Chapter III, note 10.) Is it really honest to quote Josephus in support of the idea that the desolation lasted for seventy years, but conceal the fact that he also gives fifty years for the same period later in his work? It is quite probable that he, in the last passage, *corrected* his earlier statements about the length of the period!

The translator of Josephus, William Whiston, wrote a special dissertation on Josephus' chronology, entitled "Upon the Chronology of Josephus," which he included in his publication of Josephus' complete works as *Appendix V.*[8] In this careful study Whiston points out that often in the later parts of his works, Josephus *corrected* his earlier figures. Thus he demonstates that Josephus first gives the length of the period from the Exodus to the building of the temple as 592 years, which figure he later changed to 612.[9] The next period, from the building of the temple to its destruction, he first gives as 466 years, which he later corrected to 470.[10] Of the seventy years, which Joesphus first reckons from the destruction of the temple to the return of the Jewish exiles in the first year of Cyrus, Whiston says that "it is certainly Josephus's own calculation," and that the 50 years for this period given in *Against Apion*, section 21, "May probably be his own correction in his old age."[11] If this is the case, Josephus might even be quoted as an argument *against* the application of the seventy years made by the Watchtower Society! In any case, it is very obvious that his statements on the seventy years cannot be used as an argument against Berossus in the way the Society does. His last figure for the length of the desolation period is in complete agreement with Berossus', and Josephus even emphasizes this agreement. (See *Against Apion*, I, 20, 21.)

In addition to Josephus, the Society also refers to Theophilus, bishop of Antioch, who wrote a defence of Christianity towards the end of the second century.[12] As the Society points out (p. 188), he commenced the seventy years with the destruction of the temple. But they conceal the important fact that Theophilus founded his chronology upon the Greek *Septuagint* version, which renders Jeremiah 25:11,12 quite differently from the Hebrew Massoretic Text. The chronology of the Septuagint version disagrees completely with that of the Hebrew text (see Chapter III, note 8),[13] and if the Society would follow it, their present chronology would collapse altogether. Theophilus' application of the seventy years was evidently his own calculation, as were those of other early writers. His contemporary, Clement of Alexandria (c. 150-216 C.E.), ended the seventy years in the second year of Darius Hystaspes (520-19 B.C.E.),[14] as did also Eusebius in his chronicle (published c. 303 C.E.), thus indicating that the desolation of Jerusalem took place c. 589 B.C.E. or later. Eusebius also tries another application, starting with the year in which Jeremiah began his activity, forty years prior to the desolation of Jerusalem, and ends the seventy years in the first year of Cyrus, which he sets at c. 560 B.C.E. Julius Africanus, in c. 221 C.E., applies the seventy years to the period of Jerusalem's desolation, the end of which he, like Eusebius later, erroneously dates to c. 560 B.C.E. It is very obvious that these early Christian writers did not have access to sources that could have helped them to establish an exact chronology for this ancient period.

The Society's use of ancient writers, then, is demonstrably very selective. They quote Josephus on the seventy years of desolation, at the same time concealing the fact that he later gives fifty years for the period. Their reference to Theophilus reflects the same methods: He is quoted, not because he really presents evidence that supports them, but because his calculation agrees to some extent with theirs. Other contemporary Christian writers, whose calculations differ from theirs, are ignored. This procedure is a clear misrepresentation of the full body of evidence from the various ancient writers who discussed the matter at hand.

MISREPRESENTATION OF THE BIBLICAL EVIDENCE

In its further discussion of the seventy years, the Watchtower Society attempts to show that, even if the historical evidence is against their application of the period, the Bible is on their side. First, at the top of page 188 of *"Let Your Kingdom Come,"* they state, categorically, that "we believe that the most direct reading of Jeremiah 25:11 and other texts is that the 70 years would date from when the Babylonians destroyed Jerusalem and left the land of Judah desolate." The simple truth is, however, that the Society bluntly refuses to accept the most natural understanding of Jeremiah 25:11,12 and a number of other texts related to this subject. (See Appendix B.) The most direct reading of Jeremiah 25:11, for example, shows the seventy years to be a period of *servitude, not desolation*: "... These nations will have to *serve* the king of Babylon seventy years." As Avigdor Orr points out in *Vetus Testamentum* Vol. VI, 1956, page 305, footnote 1, the Hebrew word for "serve" in this text is a political term, "recognized and accepted the rule of," and his conclusion is: "It follows from v. 11b that the seventy years begin from the imposition of the Babylonian yoke on Judah and its neighbours." Further, the other text in Jeremiah referring to the seventy years, Jeremiah 29:10, *confirms* this understanding. The most direct reading of the best and most literal translation of this text shows them to be a reference to the Babylonian rule: "When seventy years have been completed for *Babylon*." (*New American Standard Version*, 1973) If the seventy years refer to *the Babylonian rule*, as this verse clearly shows, this period ended with the fall of Babylon in 539 B.C.E.; and this is directly stated at Jeremiah 25:12: "And it must occur that *when seventy years have been fulfilled* I shall call to account against the king of Babylon." As Jehovah called to account the king of Babylon in 539 B.C.E., the end of the seventy years cannot be extended beyond that date, either to 537 B.C.E. or any other date, as that would be in conflict with a direct reading of Jeremiah 25:12. Orr, in the article quoted above, on page 305, logically concludes: "While the date of 605 may thus be postulated as extremely likely, to say the least, for the beginning of the seventy years in Jer., there is no doubt whatsoever as to their ending; v. 12 states that they are to end with the fall of the king of Babylonia and his land, in full accord with our findings in Jer. xxix 10, that is to say in 539."

There cannot be the slightest doubt about the matter: The most direct reading of Jeremiah's prophecy (Jer. 25:11,12; 29:10) is in clear conflict with the application that the Watchtower Society gives to the seventy years. In spite of this, it boldly declares: "But the Bible itself provides even more telling evidence against the claim that the 70 years began in 605 B.C.E. and that Jerusalem was destroyed in 587-6 B.C.E." (pp. 188:4f.) What "telling evidence"? This: "As mentioned, if we were to count from 605 B.C.E., the 70 years would reach down to 535 B.C.E. However, the inspired Bible writer Ezra reported that the 70 years ran until 'the first year of Cyrus the king of Persia,' who issued a decree allowing the Jews to return to their homeland" in 537 B.C.E. But did Ezra really report that? As was shown in the discussion of 2 Chronicles 36:21-23 in Chapter III, Ezra *does not* clearly indicate that the seventy years ended "in the first year of Cyrus," or in 537. On the contrary, such an understanding of his words would be in direct conflict with Jeremiah 25:12, where the seventy years are ended in 539 B.C.E.! This scripture provides the most telling evidence *against* the claim that the seventy years ended in 537 B.C.E. or in any other year after 539! It is true that in the original version of "The Gentile Times Reconsidered" (sent to the Society in 1977), one of the possible applications of the seventy years considered was that they could be counted from 605 to 535 B.C.E. But this application was presented as a less likely alternative. Thus in the present published edition, I have not included it as a suggestion because, like the application of the period advocated by the Watchtower Society, it was found to be in clear conflict with Jeremiah's prophecy. Very few (if any) commentators attempt to stretch Cyrus' "first year from 538 down to 535 B.C.E." as the Society claims that they do. (p. 189) Most evidently end the seventy years in 539 or 536. Curiously, these better alternatives are not even mentioned in the "Appendix" to *"Let Your Kingdom Come"*![15]

Finally, the Watch Tower Society claims,

> ... we are willing to be guided primarily by God's Word rather than by a chronology that is based principally on secular evidence or that disagrees with the Scriptures. It seems evident that the easiest and most direct understanding of the various Biblical statements is that the 70 years began with the complete desolation of Judah after Jerusalem was destroyed. (p. 189)

Again, these statements tend to give the impression that there is a conflict between the Bible and the secular evidence on the seventy years, and that the Society faithfully stands for the Bible against secular evidence. But nothing could be further from the truth. On the contrary, biblical and historical data are in good agreement on the period under discussion. Here, historical and archaeological discoveries, as in so many other cases, *uphold and confirm* biblical statements. On the other hand the interpretation of the seventy-year period given by the Society does conflict with facts established by secular evidence. As has been clearly demonstrated above and in Chapter III, it is also in flagrant conflict with the "easiest and most direct understanding of the various Biblical statements" on the seventy years, such as Jeremiah 25:11; 29:10; 25:12; Daniel 1:1-6; 2:1; and Zechariah 1:7,12, and 7:1-5. The *real* conflict, therefore, is not between the Bible and secular evidence, but between the Bible and secular evidence on the one hand, and the Watchtower Society on the other. As its application of the seventy years is in conflict both with the Bible and the historical facts, it has nothing to do with reality *and should be rejected by all sincere Christians*.

SUMMARY

It has been amply demonstrated above that the Watchtower Society in its "Appendix" to *"Let Your Kingdom Come"* does not give a fair presentation of the evidence against their 607 B.C.E. date. (1) Its writers misrepresent *historical evidence* by omitting from their discussion nearly half of the evidence (the Hillah stele, the diary BM 32312, and contemporary Egyptian documents) and by giving some of the other lines of evidence a biased and distorted presentation. They erroneously indicate that priests and kings might have altered historical documents (chronicles, royal inscriptions, etc.) from the Neo-Babylonian era, in spite of the fact that all available evidence shows the opposite to be true. (2) They misrepresent *authorities on ancient historiography* by quoting them out of context and attributing to them views and doubts they do not have. (3) They misrepresent *ancient writers* by concealing the fact that Berossus is supported by the most direct reading of Daniel 1:1-6, by quoting Josephus when he talks of seventy years of desolation without mentioning that in his last work he changed the length of the period to *fifty* years, and by referring to the opinion of the second century bishop, Theophilus, without mentioning that he follows the Septuagint and that other contemporary Christian writers disagreed with him. And finally, (4) they misrepresent *biblical evidence* by concealing the fact that the most direct understanding of the passages dealing with the seventy years shows them to be the period of Neo-Babylonian rule, not the period of Jerusalem's desolation. This understanding is in good agreement with the historical evidence, but in glaring conflict with the application given to it by the Watchtower Society. It is really distressing to discover that individuals, upon whose spiritual guidance millions rely, deal so carelessly and dishonestly with facts. Their "Appendix" to *"Let Your Kingdom Come"* in defence of their chronology is nothing but yet another clever exercise in the art of concealing truth.

APPENDIX A

METHODS OF RECKONING REGNAL YEARS

THE ACCESSION- AND NONACCESSION-YEAR SYSTEMS

Babylon, and later Medo-Persia, applied the *accession-year system*, in which the year during which a king came to power was reckoned as his accession-year, and the next year beginning on Nisan 1 (spring), was reckoned as his first year. In Egypt the opposite method was applied: the year in which a king came to power was counted as his first year. There is evidence to show that the latter method, the *nonaccession-year system*, was also applied in the Kingdom of Judah. The evidence is as follows:

1. The battle of Carchemish in 605 B.C.E. is stated at Jeremiah 46:2 as having occurred "in the *fourth* year of Jehoiakim," which year, according to Jeremiah 25:1, was "the *first* year of Nebuchadnezzar." But the Babylonian Chronicle (B.M. 21946) clearly states that this battle took place in Nebuchadnezzar's *accession-year*, not in his first

year. The reason why Jeremiah reckons Nebuchadnezzar's accession-year as his first year seems to be that Judah did not apply the accession-year system. Jeremiah, therefore, applied the Jewish nonaccession-year system not only to Jehoiakim, but also to Nebuchadnezzar.

2. In 2 Kings 24:12; 25:8, and Jeremiah 52:12 Jehoiachin's deportation and the destruction of Jerusalem are said to have taken place in Nebuchadnezzar's eighth and nineteenth regnal years, while the last verses of the book of Jeremiah (52:28-34) put these events in Nebuchadnezzar's seventh and eighteenth years, respectively. The difference in both cases is one year. The Babylonian Chronicle (B.M. 21946; see also *Aid to Bible Understanding* p. 326) is in agreement with Jeremiah 52:28 in stating that Nebuchadnezzar seized Jerusalem and captured Jehoiachin in his seventh year. As has been pointed out by C.F. Keil and others, the last chapter in the book of Jeremiah is probably an addition by another writer.[1] This is also supported by the last words of Jeremiah, chapter 51: "Down to this point are the words of Jeremiah." (v 64) As to the difference of one year in the reference to Nebuchadnezzar's regnal years in Jeremiah 52:28-30, Professor Albertus Pieters in all probability gives the correct explanation when he states: "This difference is perfectly explained if we assume that the section in question was added to the prophecies of Jeremiah by someone in Babylon who had access to an official report or record, in which the date would, of course, be set down *according to the Babylonian reckoning.*"[2] As a writer living in Babylon, he naturally applied the Babylonian accession-year system, while the writer of 2 Kings (Jeremiah) applied the Jewish nonaccession-year system.

This conclusion is further confirmed by the way the writer of Jeremiah 52:31 refers to the year of Evil merodach's reign, in which Jehoiachin was released from prison. He states that it was "in the year of his becoming king," not in his first year. According to Professor Pieters the clause "in the year of his becoming king" (see 2 Kings

25:27) "is the technically correct term for the year of the monarch's accession,"[3] the Babylonian documents using a similar expression when referring to the accession-year.

That the writer of Jeremiah 52:28-34 uses the accession-year system as distinguished from the writer of 2 Kings is the conclusion of many modern biblical scholars, for example Dr. Jack Finegan and Dr. J. Philip Hyatt.[4]

3. The accession-year system is most probably also employed by the prophet Daniel at Daniel 1:1, where he dates the first deportation of Jewish exiles to the "*third* year" of Jehoiakim, though this event must have followed the battle of Carchemish in the *fourth* year of Jehoiakim. (Jer. 46:2) It seems obvious, therefore, that Daniel, living in Babylon and occupying a high rank in its administration, applied the Babylonian calendar system, and even did so to Jehoiakim's reign, just as Jeremiah applied the Jewish nonaccession-year system in referring to Nebuchadnezzar's reign.[5]

4. Even as late as the Persian era, the Jews in the colony at Elephantine in Egypt continued to employ the nonaccession-year system. In the Aramaic papyri discovered on this island at the end of the nineteenth century, the accession-year of some Persian kings is referred to as their first year.[6]

Several difficult problems in biblical chronology are easily solved if the accession- and nonaccession-year systems are taken into consideration. A study of the chronological tables of Appendix C will make this clear.

NISAN AND TISCHRI YEARS

It is well known that the Babylonian and Persian calendar year started on Nisan 1, which was also the beginning of the regnal years. The Jews, in later times, had two beginnings of their calendar years: Nisan 1 and Tischri 1 — Tischri 1 being the older new-year day.[7] Although Nisan was the beginning of the *sacred* calendar year, and the months were always numbered from it,[8] Tischri was retained as the beginning of the *secular* calendar year. The problem is: Did the kings of Judah follow the custom of Babylon and other countries in reckoning the regnal years from Nisan 1 (spring), or did they reckon them from Tischri, the beginning of their secular year? Although *Aid to Bible Understanding* (p. 338) states that the regnal years ran from Nisan to Nisan, there is much evidence to show that the kings of Judah reckoned their regnal years on a Tischri-to-Tischri basis.

1. Jeremiah 1:3 states that Zedekiah "went into exile in the *fifth* month," (which is in agreement with the record in 2 Kings 25:8-12). Yet this fifth month is said to have been at "the *end* of ("completion of", NW) the eleventh year of Zedekiah." (ASV) If reckoned from Tischri (the seventh month), the fifth month was obviously at the end of the regnal year, which then ended with the next month, Elul, the sixth month.

2. According to 2 Kings 22:3f. King Josiah, in his eighteenth year, began repairs on the house of Jehovah. During these repairs High Priest Hilkiah found the book of Jehovah's law in the temple. This discovery resulted in an extensive campaign against idolatry throughout the whole land. After that Josiah reinstituted the passover on Nisan 14, two weeks after the beginning of the new year according to the sacred calendar. (2 Kings 23:23) Very interestingly, this passover is said to have been celebrated "In the *eighteenth* year of King Josiah." As the repairs of the temple, the cleansing of the land from idolatry and many other things recorded in 2 Kings 22:3-23:23 could not reasonably have occurred within just two weeks, it seems obvious that Josiah's eighteenth regnal year was not counted from Nisan 1, but from Tischri 1.

3. Another indication of a Tischri reckoning of regnal years in Judah is given in Jeremiah 36: "In the fourth year of Jehoiakim" (v. 1) Jehovah told Jeremiah to write in a book all the words he had spoken to him against Israel, Judah, and all the nations (v. 2). This Jeremiah did through Baruch, his secretary (v. 4.). When Baruch had

finished the work, Jeremiah asked him to "enter into the house of Jehovah" and "read aloud from the roll that you have written at my mouth the words of Jehovah in the ears of the people at the house of Jehovah in the day of fast." (vv. 5, 6) Which fast? It was evidently a special fast proclaimed for some unspecified reason. Most probably the reason was the battle of Carchemish "in the fourth year of Jehoiakim" (Jer. 46:2) and the subsequent events, including the siege laid against Jerusalem in that same year according to Daniel 1:1f. (See Appendix B.) Though Nebuchadnezzar by now, due to the death of his father, had returned to Babylon, the Jews had good reasons for fearing that he soon would return and continue his operations in Judah and the surrounding areas. Against this background, the proclamation of "a fast before Jehovah" is quite understandable. Very interestingly, this fast, at which Baruch was to read aloud from the roll he had written, took place "in the *fifth* year of Jehoiakim the son of Josiah, the king of Judah, *in the ninth month.*" (vv. 9, 10) If Jehoiakim's regnal years were counted from Nisan, the first month, Baruch began to write down Jeremiah's prophecies about a year prior to this fast. Besides, it seems to have been proclaimed already in the *fourth* year of Jehoiakim (vv. 1, 6), and thus at least about nine months before it was held. All this seems very improbable. But if Jehoiakim's regnal years were counted from Tischri, the seventh month, his fourth year ended with Elul, the sixth month (corresponding to August-September, 605 B.C.E.), and the fast in the ninth month (November-December, 605 B.C.E.) took place a little more than two months after the beginning of Jehoiakim's fifth year. Baruch's writing down of Jeremiah's prophecies, then, took only a few months, which is more probable, and the fast could have been proclaimed only two months before it was held, and not long after the battle of Carchemish and the subsequent Babylonian operations in Syria and Palestine in the summer and autumn of 605 B.C.E.

4. There is evidence, too, that Jewish writers, when

referring to foreign kings, at least sometimes reckoned their regnal years according to the Tischri year. This is done by Nehemiah for example. In Nehemiah 1:1 he refers to the month Chislev (November-December) in the *twentieth* year of Artaxerxes. But the month Nisan of the next year is still referred to as in Artaxerxes' *twentieth* year of rule. (Neh. 2:1) If Nehemiah reckoned Artaxerxes' regnal years from Nisan 1, he should have written *twenty-first* year at chapter 2, verse 1. Nehemiah, therefore, obviously reckoned the regnal years of the Persian king Artaxerxes according to the Jewish Tischri-to-Tischri calendar, not according to the Persian Nisan-to-Nisan count. This is also supported in *Aid to Bible Understanding* p. 1216.

That Judah followed a Tischri-to-Tischri reckoning of the regnal years is the conclusion of many of the best scholars and students of Bible chronology, e.g., S. Movinckel, Morgenstern, Kienitz, and Thiele.[9] Although this way of reckoning regnal years makes the synchronisms between Judah and Babylon somewhat more complicated, it clears up many problems when applied. In the chronological tables of Appendix C, both kinds of regnal years are parallelled with our modern calendar.

APPENDIX B

DANIEL 1:1,2 AND 2:1

Daniel 1:1f. dates the first deportation of Jewish prisoners by Nebuchadnezzar to the "third year of Jehoiakim." As was shown in Appendix A, in this passage Daniel seems to follow the Babylonian method of counting regnal years, employing an accession-year even for kings outside Babylon, including Jehoiakim. This makes Jehoiakim's fourth year (Jer. 46:2) his third year in the accession-year system, and this third year of Jehoiakim in turn corresponds to Nebuchadnezzar's accession-year. Thus it is seen that this first deportation took place in the same year as the famous battle at Carchemish, and evidently shortly after that battle, in the year 605 B.C.E. Daniel 1:1f., therefore, strongly supports the conclusion that Judah became a vassal to Babylon eighteen years before the destruction of Jerusalem in 587 B.C.E., in confirmation of the conclusion that the seventy years (Jer. 25:11; 29:10) should be understood as a period of *servitude*, not of desolation.

In order to undermine the strength of Daniel 1:1 several arguments have been advanced in the publications of the Watchtower Society against a natural reading of this text. As early as 1896 Pastor Charles T. Russell, in writing in *Zion's Watch Tower* of May 15, page 106 (Reprints p. 1976) argued against those who quoted Daniel 1:1 in support of the secular dates for Nebuchadnezzar's reign:

> For instance, they adopt the uncertain secular date for the beginning of Nebuchadnezzar's reign; and then referring to Dan. 1:1, they *thus* fix the date of Jehoiakim's reign and alter other matters to suit. Then again, they apply the "seventy years" as years of *captivity* and begin them in the third year of Jehoiakim; whereas the Scriptures unequivocally declare, repeatedly, that those were years of "desolation of the land," "without an inhabitant." (Jer. 25:11,12; 29:10; 2 Chron. 36:21; Dan. 9:2).

Several years later two prominent members of Russell's movement, John and Morton Edgar, published the two-volume *Great Pyramid Passages*.[1] On pages 31 and 32 of Volume II, they summarize their arguments against a natural reading of Daniel 1:1:

> 1) It cannot be admitted that the 70 years desolation of Jerusalem and the land began in the 3rd year of Jehoiakim, for according to the Scriptures "desolation" implies "without an inhabitant," and Jerusalem and the land were not without an inhabitant until after the dethronement of Zedekiah.
>
> 2) [A natural reading of Daniel 1:1] conflicts with Daniel 2:1. In reading over the 1st chapter of Daniel it would appear that the Hebrew children were taken captive by Nebuchadnezzar in the 3rd year of Jehoiakim. They were trained in the learning and tongue of the Chaldeans for three years (verses 4, 5), and yet, according to Dan. 2:1, 25 they were brought into the presence of Nebuchadnezzar in or before his *second* year, though verse 18 of the 1st chapter shows that the three years had completely expired.

How, then, is Daniel 1:1 to be understood? The Edgar brothers point out that "a number of commentators suggest that the 3rd year of Jehoiakim in Dan. 1:1 should be understood as meaning the 3rd year of his vassalage to Nebuchadnezzar," which in effect was his eleventh and last regnal year.[2] In this way the deportation of Daniel and other Hebrew captives was made identical with the deportation of Jehoiachin in the seventh year of Nebuchadnezzar.

But this explanation did not negate the seeming conflict with Daniel 2:1, which dates the image dream of Nebuchadnezzar to his second year; in fact, that conflict was exacerbated. If Daniel was not deported to Babylon until the seventh year of Nebuchadnezzar, how could he be at his court interpreting his dreams in his second year, five years earlier? This called for another interpretation of Daniel 2:1, as well. The Edgar brothers suggested that the number "2" is an error, which "has evidently risen out of the number 12."[3] Later these arguments were adopted by the Watchtower Society. They were, for example, incorporated into the 1922 edition of the booklet *The Bible on Our Lord's Return*, pages 84-88.

But the explanation that Daniel 1:1 refers to Jehoiakim's third year of *vassalage* to Nebuchadnezzar, corresponding to Nebuchadnezzar's seventh regnal year, creates another problem. If this vassalage ended in the seventh year of Nebuchadnezzar, it must have begun three years earlier according to 2 Kings 24:1, or in Nebuchadnezzar's *fourth* year, which was the eighth year of Jehoiakim. As is stated in 2 Kings 23:34-37, Jehoiakim was a tributary king *of Egypt* before he became a vassal to Babylon. This means that his vassalage to Egypt continued up to his eighth year, although both Jeremiah 46:2 and the Babylonian Chronicle (B.M. 21946) indicate that Jehoiakim's vassalage changed from Egypt to Babylon in the same year as the battle of Carchemish, or in the *fourth* year of Jehoiakim. In the book *Equipped for Every Good Work*, published in 1946, the arguments against a natural reading of Daniel 1:1 are repeated on pages 225-227. But interestingly, the Egyptian vassalage is now discussed:

> Jehoiakim was put on the throne by Egyptian decree and was tributary to Egypt for several years, but *when Babylon defeated*

> *Egypt Jehoiakim came under Babylonian control and so remained for three years*, after which three-year period as tributary to Babylon the Judean king rebelled.[4]

Here it is admitted that Jehoiakim's vassalage changed from Egypt to Babylon *when Babylon defeated Egypt*. But the real problem is concealed, as it is not mentioned that Egypt was defeated in the fourth year of Jehoiakim (Jer. 46:2), and not in his eighth year!

Another interesting change may also be noted in *Equipped for Every Good Work*. Instead of holding to the earlier guess that the "second year" in Daniel 2:1 originally read "twelfth year," the following interpretation is presented:

> The time of this dream and its interpretation is stated as the second year of Nebuchadnezzar's reign.... In the nineteenth year of his reign Nebuchadnezzar was used as God's executioner to destroy faithless Jerusalem and end Israel's history as an independent Theocratic nation. Then Nebuchadnezzar began reigning in a unique way, as the first of the world rulers. In the second year of his reign *in this special capacity* the dream showing the end of Satan's organization and rule and the taking over of power by Christ's kingdom came to Nebuchadnezzar, as recorded at chapter 2.[5]

Thus, according to this explanation, the "second year" of Daniel 2:1, or the second year of the Gentile times, reckoned from 607 B.C.E., was actually Nebuchadnezzar's *twentieth* regnal year! Why did Daniel use this curious way of reckoning regnal years only in this passage of his book? No other arguments are proposed for this new position except this statement: "Here again, as at Daniel 1:1, the peculiarity which the writer of this book has of making a secondary reckoning of the years of a king's reign is demonstrated. He reckons by counting from epochal events within the reign that put the king in a new relationship."[6]

The latest discussion of these problems is found in *Aid to Bible Understanding*, pages 879-880. Daniel 1:1 is still interpreted as meaning the third year of Jehoiakim's vassalage to Babylon, beginning at the end of his eighth year of reign and ending in his eleventh and last year. On page 1212 of the same work, an attempt is made to find support for this in the Babylonian Chronicle. (B.M. 21946) After recording the battle of Carchemish in Nebuchadnezzar's accession year, this Chronicle refers to several succeeding campaigns in Hatti-land (Syro-Palestine) by Nebuchadnezzar, in his first, second, third and fourth years. Mentioning these campaigns, *Aid to Bible Understanding* says: "...it may be that in the fourth year he made Judean King Jehoiakim his vassal. (2 Kings 24:1)"

But this conclusion is not supported by the Babylonian Chronicle. On the contrary, this chronicle very strongly indicates that Jehoiakim's vassalage to Babylon began in Nebuchadnezzar's accession-year, or his first year, and that the fourth year was the year in which he revolted against his Babylonian vassalage. To demonstrate this, it is necessary to quote important parts of the Babylonian Chronicle, from the first to the fourth year of Nebuchadnezzar:

605/04 B.C.E. Jan.-Feb. 604	In the 'accession year' Nebuchadnezzar went back again to the Hatti-land and until the month of Sebat marched unopposed through the Hatti-land; in the month of Sebat he took *the heavy tribute of the Hatti-territory* to Babylon.
May-June 604 Nov.-Dec. 604	In *the first year* of Nebuchadnezzar in the month of Sivan he mustered his army and went to the Hatti-territory, he marched unopposed in the Hatti-territory until the month of Kislev. *All the kings of the Hatti-land* came before him and *he received their heavy tribute.*
April-May 603	In *the second [year]* in the month of Iyyar the king of Akkad gathered together a powerful army and [marched to the land Hatti]. [.........] he threw down, great siege-towers he [.........] [.........] from the month of Iyyar until the mon[th of ... he marched about unopposed in the land of Hatti.]
602 B.C.E.	In *the third year* [... he.] eft and [.........] [in the month of .... on the] thirteenth day, Nabu-suma-lisir . . . .

.... the king of Akkad mustered his troops and [marched] to the Hatti-land and brought (back) much (spoil) from the Hatti-land into Akkad.

601 In *the fourth year* the king of Akkad mustered his army and
B.C.E. marched to the Hatti-land. In the Hatti-land they marched
Nov.- unopposed. In the month of Kislev he took the lead of his
Dec. 601 army and *marched to Egypt*. The king of Egypt heard (it) and mustered his army. *In open battle they* smote the breast (of) each other and *inflicted great havoc on each other*. The king of Akkad and his troops turned back and returned to Babylon.[7]

From this chronicle it is seen that the *whole* Hatti-territory (Syro-Palestine) became tributary to Nebuchadnezzar from his accession year. And in Nebuchadnezzar's first year it is explicitly stated that *all the kings* of the Hatti-territory were tributary to him, which reasonably cannot have excepted Jehoiakim. The fourth year, in which *Aid to Bible Understanding* supposes the Jehoiakim's Babylonian vassalage *began*, was most probably the year in which Jehoiakim *revolted* against Nebuchadnezzar, because in that year Nebuchadnezzar battled with Egypt, and both seem to have suffered great losses. Nebuchadnezzar had to return to Babylon, where he remained in the fifth year "and gathered together his chariots and horses in great numbers."[8] This unsuccessful battle with Egypt probably encouraged Jehoiakim to throw off the Babylonian yoke, thus *ending* his three years of vassalage to Babylon.[9]

2 Kings 24:1-7 seems to support the above conclusion. Verse 1 states that "in his (Jehoiakim's) days Nebuchadnezzar the king of Babylon came up, and so Jehoiakim became his servant for three years. However, he turned back and rebelled against him." As a result, Jehovah (through Nebuchadnezzar) "began to send against him marauder bands of Chaldeans and marauder bands of Syrians and marauder bands of Moabites and marauder bands of the sons of Ammon, and he kept

sending them against Judah to destroy it, according to Jehovah's word that he had spoken by means of his servants the prophets." (Verse 2) The wording of this passage indicates that these marauder bands kept on raiding the territory of Judah for quite a time, evidently for some years. Jehovah "began" to send them, and "he *kept* sending them" against Judah. This was not one attack only, like that mentioned in Daniel 1:1, but it came upon Judah in waves, time and again. Consequently, they could not have begun these attacks in the last year of Jehoiakim's reign, and this also calls for an earlier beginning of Jehoiakim's rebellion.

Another line of evidence supporting a natural reading of Daniel 1:1, is that according to 2 Chronicles 36:7, 10 and 18 the vessels of the temple were brought to Babylon in *three* successive installments:

1. The first time, during *Jehoiakim's* reign, "*some* of," or "*a part* of" the vessels were brought to Babylon. (v. 7, NW, By., Je)

2. The second time, together with *Jehoiachin*, the "*desirable* articles," or "the *precious* furnishings," "the *choice* vessels," were brought to Babylon. (v. 10, NW, Je., By)

3. The third time, together with *Zedekiah*, "*all*" the vessels were brought to Babylon. (v. 18 , NW)

From these texts we learn that *some* of the vessels were brought to Babylon *during Jehoiakim's reign*, the *desirable* vessels were brought *at the deportation of Jehoiachin*, and *all the rest* of the vessels were taken to Babylon *at the end of Zedekiah's reign*. Of the three deportations of vessels, the first is clearly referred to at Daniel 1:1,2, as this text states that during the "third year of ... Jehoiakim" "a *part* of" ("*some* of," By, Je) the vessels were brought to Babylon. Again, this indicates that Daniel 1:1,2 refers to a deportation *different from and earlier than* that which took place at the end of Jehoiachin's short reign. This gives additional support to the conclusion that the phrase "the third year of the kingship of Jehoiakim'' means what it says—Jehoiakim's third regnal year, not his eleventh.

Finally, if the deportation mentioned at Daniel 1:1f, is equated with the one that took place at the end of Jehoiachin's three months reign, why does Daniel state that ''Jehovah gave into his hand *Jehoiakim*,'' instead of *Jehoiachin*? (Dan. 1:2)When Jehoiachin was taken captive, Jehoiakim had been dead for over three months. (2 Kings 24:8-17; 2 Chron. 36:9, 10) There is even evidence to show that Jehoiakim was already dead when Nebuchadnezzar, in his seventh year, left Babylon for the siege of Jerusalem that ended up in Jehoiachin's deportation. The evidence is as follows:

Nebuchadnezzar's siege of Jerusalem during the reign of Jehoiachin is also described in the Babylonian chronicle BM 21946. For the seventh year of Nebuchadnezzar this chronicle says:

> The seventh year: In the month Kislev the king of Akkad mustered his army and marched to Hattu. He encamped against the city of Judah and on the second day of the month Adar he captured the city (and) seized (its) king. A king of his own choice he appointed in the city (and) taking the vast tribute he brought it into Babylon.[10]

Nebuchadnezzar's army left Babylon ''in the month of Kislev,'' which was the ninth month, and seized Jehoiachin ''on the second day of the month Adar,'' that is, the twelfth month.[11] This means that even if the army left Babylon in the *beginning* of the ninth month (Kislev), the interval between the day it left Babylon until the city was captured and its king (Jehoiachin) seized, in the beginning of the twelfth month (Adar), was *three months at the most*.[12] As Jehoiachin ruled for ''three months and ten days'' (2 Chron. 36:9), he evidently had been ruling for some time *already when Nebuchadnezzar left Babylon in the month of Kislev!* If the seige of Jerusalem described at Daniel 1:1f. referred to this siege during the reign of Jehoiachin, how could it be said that it took place *during the reign of Jehoiakim* (Dan. 1:1), that Nebuchadnezzar came up "against *him*" (2 Chron. 36:6), and that "Jehovah gave into his hand *Jehoiakim*" (Dan. 1:2), when Jehoiakim was already dead when Nebuchadnezzar left Babylon? Equating the siege described at Daniel 1:1f. with the one that took place during the reign of Jehoiachin (2 Kings 24:10-12; 2 Chron. 36:10) is clearly impossible! Daniel obviously describes an *earlier* siege and an *earlier* deportation, during the reign of *Jehoiakim*. There is no reason to believe that the "third year" of Daniel 1:1 means anything else but his third year of reign. There is no evidence at all, either in the book of Daniel, in the other books in the Bible or in the contemporary Neo-Babylonian historical texts, that regnal years were reckoned from a king's vassalage, or from Nebuchadnezzar's rise to world dominion. Such theories are nothing more than unfounded guesses, adopted only in an attempt to defend an erroneous application of the seventy years of servitude predicted by Jeremiah.

But what about the three years of training referred to in Daniel 1:5,18, which seem to conflict with a natural reading of Daniel 1:1 and 2:1? Is there no simpler way to solve this seeming conflict than to suppose that the prophet in Daniel 1:1 reckoned Jehoiakim's regnal years from the beginning of his *vassalage* to Babylon, and Nebuchadnezzar's regnal years in Daniel 2:2 from the year of his *rise to world dominion*? Why should Daniel reckon the regnal years of these two kings in such a confusing manner when he knew that his readers no doubt would misunderstand him? And why does he not reckon the regnal years in this peculiar way elsewhere in his book, for instance in 7:1, 8:1, 9:1; and 10:1, where he follows the ordinary method of reckoning regnal years? Before such strained explanations are adopted, should not a simpler and more natural solution be sought?

It has already been demonstrated in Appendix A that there is no real discrepancy between the *third* year of

Jehoiakim in Daniel 1:1, and his *fourth* year in Jeremiah 25:1 and 46:2. When the accession- and nonaccession-year systems are taken into consideration, this difference of one year is easily understood.[13] This solution also has bearing upon the seeming conflict between the three years of training and Daniel 2:1. If Daniel 1:1 refers to Nebuchadnezzar's accession-year (in agreement with the Babylonian Chronicle), his "second year" at Daniel 2:1 may be regarded as the third year of the training of the Jewish captives. According to the Hebrew way of reckoning time periods, whereby fractions of time were reckoned as full units, this would make three years.[14] The three years are not necessarily three *full* years. Dr. Young presents the following table:[15]

Years of training	*Nebuchadnezzar*
First year	Year of accession
Second year	First year
Third year	Second year

Applying this simple and biblical method to the problem solves the seeming conflict without unfounded theories and strained explanations. Many modern Biblical scholars, who regard the book of Daniel as authentic, have adopted this simple solution. Gerhard F. Hasel, for one, says:

> It is no longer necessary to explain the difficulty between Dan. 2:1 and 1:1,18 through textual emendation (H. Ewald, A. Kamphausen, J.D. Prince, K. Marti, and J. Jahn) or double reckoning (C.B. Michaelis, G. Behrmann). The practice of inclusive reckoning, together with the recognition of the Babylonian usage of the king's accession year as not being counted, removes all difficulties.[16]

APPENDIX C

CHRONOLOGICAL TABLES COVERING THE SEVENTY YEARS

The subsequent tables have been developed in order to facilitate an examination of the arguments set forth in this work. The Babylonian and Persian Nisan-to-Nisan regnal years and the Judean Tischri-to-Tischri regnal years have been paralleled with our modern calendar. Also, the Babylonian accession-years and the Judean nonaccession-years have been duly considered. The guiding principle has been to take the biblical dates as they stand, if nothing else is indicated by the context. A thorough study of the tables will show that the different biblical dates are brought into a natural harmony with each other, and also with the Babylonian chronicles. A few points require special comments:

1. JOSIAH'S DEATH AT MEGIDDO, SUMMER 609 (2 KINGS 23:29)

It has been debated whether Josiah's death took place in

609 or 608 B.C.E.,[1] partly because the Judean nonaccession-year system has not been applied to this period by some chronologers. This question is now settled, since the new chronicle B.M. 22047 (published by Wiseman, 1956) shows that the battle at Megiddo must have taken place in the summer of 609, during Pharaoh Necho's march up to the Euphrates to help Ashur-uballit recapture Harran. This unsuccessful attempt took place between Tammuz and Elul (c. July-September) in Nabopolassar's seventeenth regnal year (609-08), according to the chronicle.[2] As the Egyptian army needed almost a month to travel from Megiddo up to the Euphrates, the battle at Megiddo and Josiah's death took place early in the summer of 609 B.C.E.[3] As may be seen from the tables, this date is in good agreement with a Judean Tischri-to-Tischri reckoning of regnal years.

2. JEHOAHAZ' THREE MONTHS OF REIGN AND JEHOIAKIM'S SUCCESSION

After the death of Josiah, the Jews made Jehoahaz the son of Josiah king in Jerusalem. (2 Chron. 36:1) After only three months reign, Pharaoh Necho, on his return from the Euphrates, removed Jehoahaz and put his brother Jehoiakim on the throne in Jerusalem. From then on Judah was a vassal to Egypt. As the Egyptian-Assyrian attempt to recapture Harran ended in Elul (Aug.-Sept.), and the Egyptian retreat from Harran to Jerusalem took almost a month, the removal of Jehoahaz and installation of Jehoiakim must have occurred in the next month, Tischri (Sept.-Oct.). According to the Judean nonaccession-year system, Jehoiakim's first regnal year, then, should be counted from Tischri 1, 609 B.C.E. Jehoahaz' three months of reign were evidently included in Josiah's reign of thirty one years, instead of being counted as a separate regnal year (Jehoiachin's three months were evidently treated in a similar way, being a part of Zedekiah's first regnal year).

3. ZEDEKIAH'S FIRST YEAR, 598-97

As was shown in Appendix B, The Babylonian chronicle B.M. 21946 dates Jehoiachin's removal from the throne to the second Adar of Nebuchadnezzar's seventh regnal year, corresponding to March 16, 597, Julian calendar, after which Zedekiah was appointed king. Following the nonaccession-year system, Zedekiah's first year, then, was reckoned from Tischri, 598, to Tischri, 597 B.C.E. Zedekiah's first regnal year was the same as Jehoiachin's first year *of exile*, which is seen from a comparison of Ezekiel 24:1,2 with 2 Kings 24:20 and 25:1. This is quite natural, as Jehoiachin's three months of reign began after Tischri 598. His first regnal year, therefore, would have been reckoned from Tischri 1, 598, had he not been removed from the throne. Now his three months had to be included in Zedekiah's first regnal year.

4. HANANIAH'S PROPHECY, JULY-AUGUST 594 (JER. 28:1)

In Nebuchadnezzar's tenth year a rebellion broke out in his army from the month of Kislev to the month of Tebet (c. Nov. 595-Jan. 594 B.C.E.), according to the Babylonian Chronicle.[4] If this rebellion caused the revolt plans among the Jewish exiles, which also spread to Judah as reflected in Jeremiah, chapters 27-29, these plans must have developed soon after the Babylonian rebellion. The prophecy of Hananiah is dated to the *fifth* month of the *fourth* year of Zedekiah. This fifth month (Ab, corresponding to July-August), therefore, must have fallen in July-August, 594 B.C.E., a few months after Nebuchadnezzar had crushed the rebellion. A look at the table shows that the fifth month of Zedekiah's fourth year actually fell in July-August, 594 B.C.E., thus indicating that the chronological system presented in the tables is correct.

5. THE SIEGE OF JERUSALEM, 589-587 B.C.E.

It has been debated whether the siege lasted for eighteen months, or for about two-and-a-half years.[5] According to a Nisan-to-Nisan regnal year the siege lasted for eighteen months (compare 2 Kings 24:20; 25:1; Jer. 52:3,4 and Ez. 24:1,2 with 2 Kings 25:2-4; Jer. 39:1-3 and Ez 33:21), but this conflicts with the statement in Ezekiel 33:21, which says that an escapee from the destruction of Jerusalem reached Ezekiel "in the *twelfth year*, in the tenth month, on the fifth day of the month." This would mean that the escapee reached Ezekiel with the message that the city had been taken about *one-and-a-half years after* the destruction of Jerusalem. This seems incredible. Therefore, it is often argued that Ezekiel 33:21 originally read "*eleventh* year," which is supported by the Syriac Version, the Greek Septuagint Version, and a few Hebrew manuscripts.[6] But if a Tischri-to-Tischri regnal year is applied, the well-attested reading of "twelfth year" may be retained, with the escapee reaching Ezekiel about six months after the capture of Jerusalem, which seems more natural. Further, it is shown by this reckoning that the siege lasted for about two- and a-half years, instead of eighteen months.

6. JEHOIACHIN'S THIRTY-SEVENTH YEAR OF EXILE, 562-561 B.C.E.

In Jeremiah 52:31 and 2 Kings 25:27, Jehoiachin's thirty-seventh year is equated with the accession-year of Evil-Merodach. Here we have an excellent confirmation of the conclusion that the Judean kings applied a Tischri-to-Tischri regnal year. Evil-Merodach ascended to the throne in the autumn of 562 B.C.E., and his accession-year ran to Nisan, 561 B.C.E. Jehoiachin's release from prison took place in the *twelfth* month of Evil-Merodach's accession-year (Jer. 52:31), on the twenty-fourth day. This corresponded to March, 561 B.C.E. If Nisan-to-Nisan regnal years are applied to Jehoiachin's exile, his thirty-seventh year cannot be counted from Nisan, 561 B.C.E., as this month fell *after* his release from prison. But if his thirty-seventh year of exile is reckoned from Nisan, 562 B.C.E., in order to retain the synchronism to Evil-Merodach's accession-year, his *first* year of exile has to be reckoned from Nisan, 598, to Nisan, 597 B.C.E. As his deportation took place around Nisan 1, 597 B.C.E. (2 Kings 24:10-17; 2 Chron. 36:10, and B.M. 21946:11-13), this would mean that his first year of exile fell nearly exactly one year before he was deported! As this is impossible, his years of exile must have been reckoned according to Tischri-to-Tischri years.

THE CHRONOLOGY OF THE SEVENTY YEARS

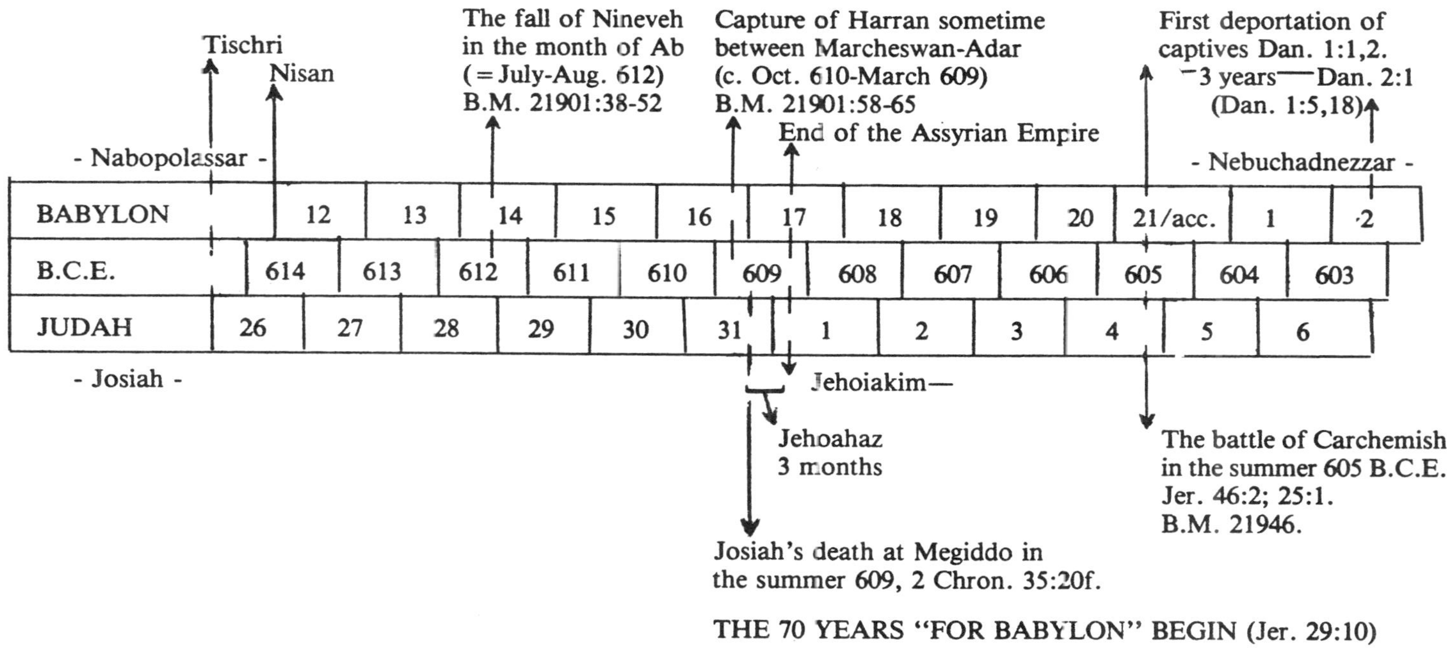

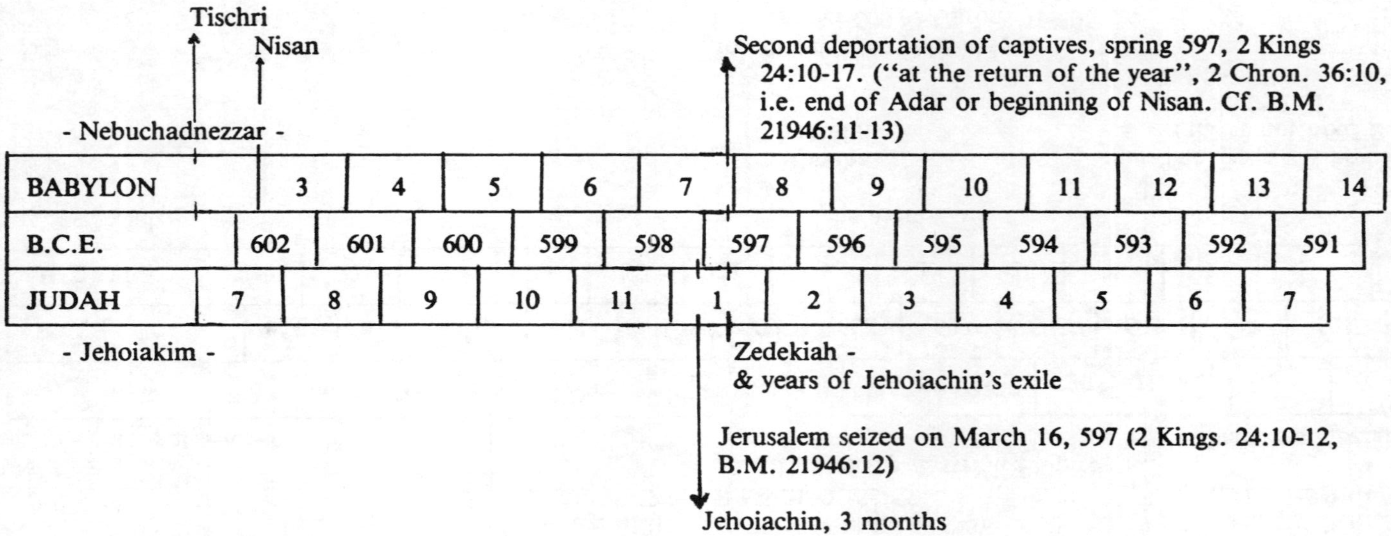
Tischri
Nisan
- Nebuchadnezzar -
Second deportation of captives, spring 597, 2 Kings 24:10-17. ("at the return of the year", 2 Chron. 36:10, i.e. end of Adar or beginning of Nisan. Cf. B.M. 21946:11-13)
BABYLON
3
4
5
6
7
8
9
10
11
12
13
14
B.C.E.
602
601
600
599
598
597
596
595
594
593
592
591
JUDAH
7
8
9
10
11
1
2
3
4
5
6
7
- Jehoiakim -
Zedekiah -
& years of Jehoiachin's exile
Jerusalem seized on March 16, 597 (2 Kings. 24:10-12, B.M. 21946:12)
Jehoiachin, 3 months

Tischri

Nisan

- Nebuchadnezzar -

An escaped one reaches Ezekiel "in the twelfth year", i.e. in January, 586 BCE. Ez. 33:21.

Fourth deportation of captives, Jer. 52:30.

BABYLON	15	16	17	18	19	20	21	22	23	24	25	26
B.C.E.	590	589	588	587	586	585	584	583	582	581	580	579
JUDAH	8	9	10	11	12	13	14	15	16	17	18	19

- Zedekiah -
- Jehoiachin's exile -

- Jehoiachin's exile -

Jerusalem besieged in January, 589 BCE 2 Kings 25:1; Ez. 24:1,2; Jer. 52:4.

Jerusalem captured in July, 587 BCE Jer. 39:2; 52:6,7; 2 Kings 25:2-4.

Temple burned and Jerusalem destroyed in August, 587 BCE; 2 Kings 25:8f. and Jer. 52:12f. Third deportation of captives.

Nebuchadnezzar's 37th year astronomically fixed (VAT 4956)

Tischri

Nisan

- Nebuchadnezzar -

BABYLON	27	28	29	30	31	32	33	34	35	36	37	38
B.C.E.	578	577	576	575	574	573	572	571	570	569	568	567
JUDAH	20	21	22	23	24	25	26	27	28	29	30	31

- year of Jehoiachin's exile -

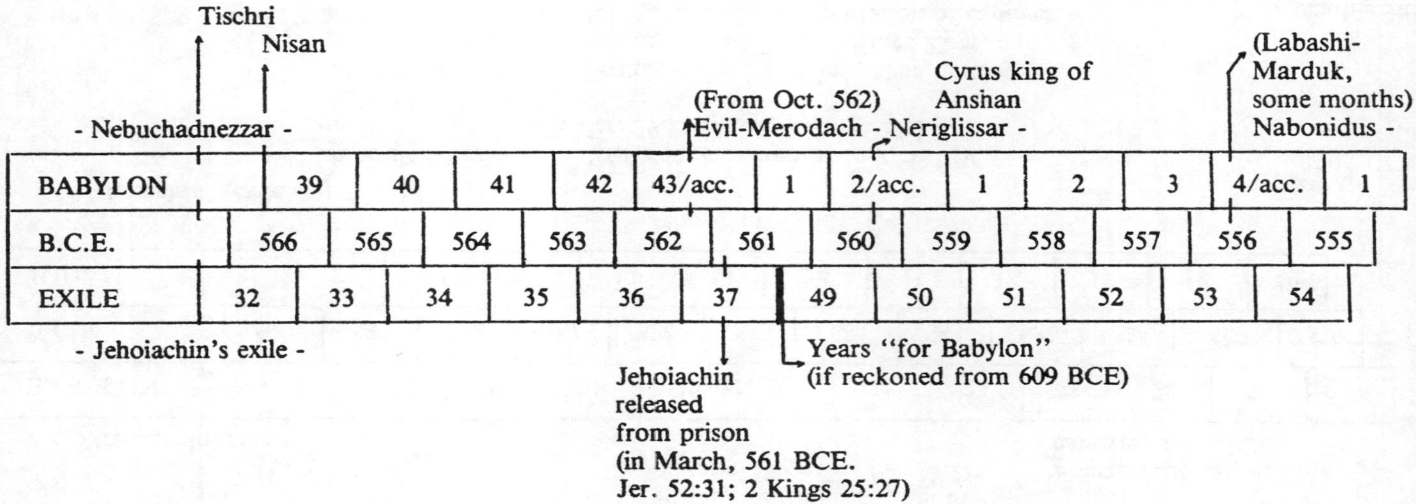
Tischri
Nisan
- Nebuchadnezzar -
(From Oct. 562)
Evil-Merodach - Neriglissar -
Cyrus king of Anshan
(Labashi-Marduk, some months)
Nabonidus -
BABYLON
39
40
41
42
43/acc.
1
2/acc.
1
2
3
4/acc.
1
B.C.E.
566
565
564
563
562
561
560
559
558
557
556
555
EXILE
32
33
34
35
36
37
49
50
51
52
53
54
- Jehoiachin's exile -
Jehoiachin released from prison (in March, 561 BCE. Jer. 52:31; 2 Kings 25:27)
Years "for Babylon" (if reckoned from 609 BCE)

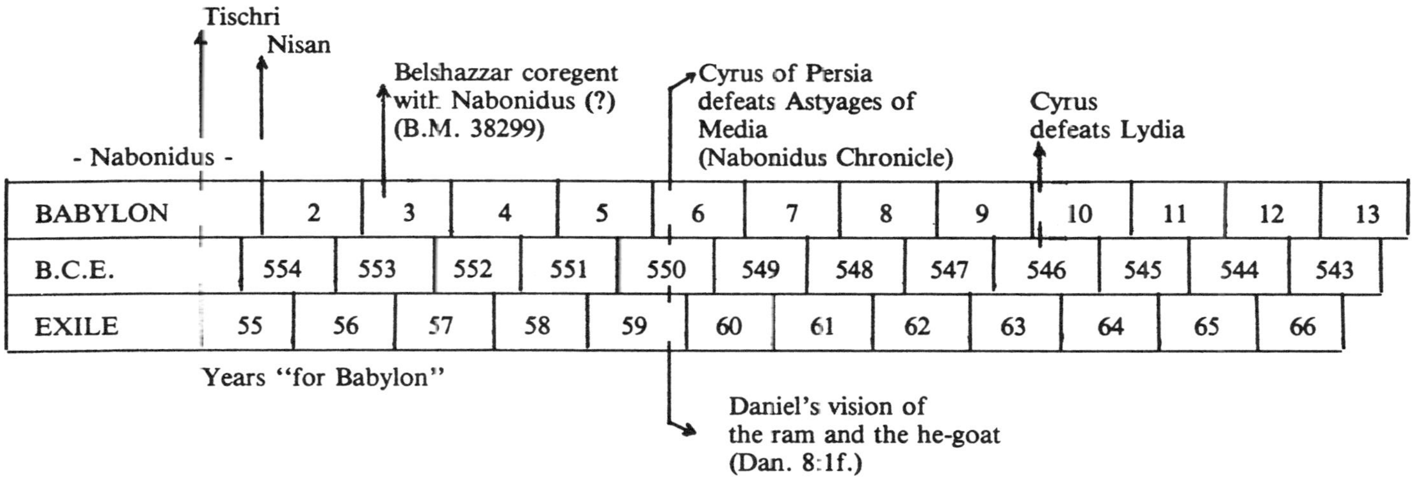
Tischri
Nisan
- Nabonidus -
Belshazzar coregent with Nabonidus (?) (B.M. 38299)
Cyrus of Persia defeats Astyages of Media (Nabonidus Chronicle)
Cyrus defeats Lydia
BABYLON
2
3
4
5
6
7
8
9
10
11
12
13
B.C.E.
554
553
552
551
550
549
548
547
546
545
544
543
EXILE
55
56
57
58
59
60
61
62
63
64
65
66
Years "for Babylon"
Daniel's vision of the ram and the he-goat (Dan. 8:1f.)

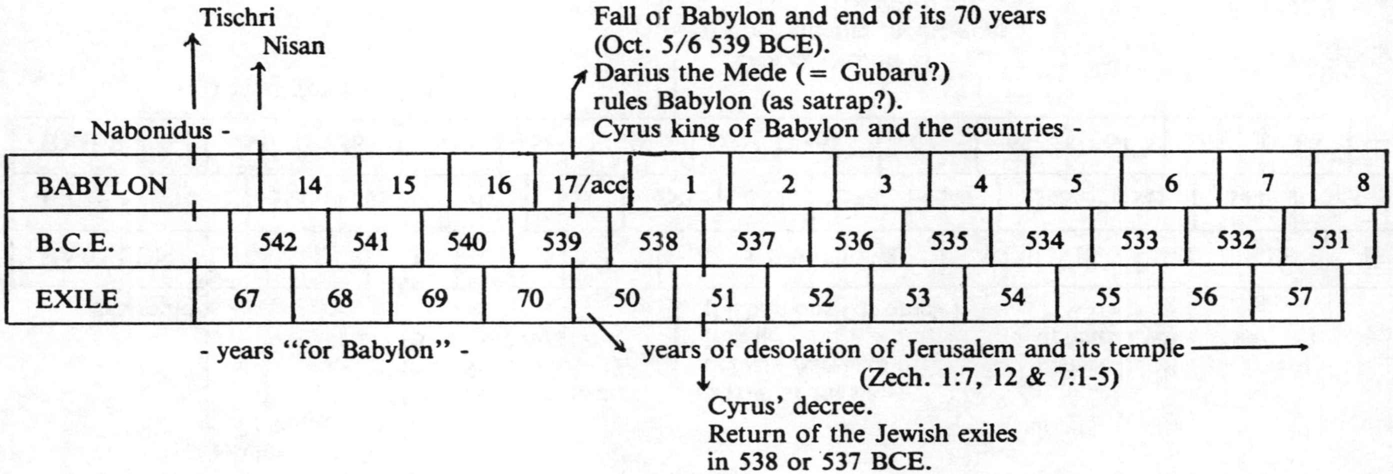
Tischri
Nisan
- Nabonidus -
Fall of Babylon and end of its 70 years
(Oct. 5/6 539 BCE).
Darius the Mede (= Gubaru?)
rules Babylon (as satrap?).
Cyrus king of Babylon and the countries -
BABYLON
14
15
16
17/acc
1
2
3
4
5
6
7
8
B.C.E.
542
541
540
539
538
537
536
535
534
533
532
531
EXILE
67
68
69
70
50
51
52
53
54
55
56
57
- years "for Babylon" -
years of desolation of Jerusalem and its temple
(Zech. 1:7, 12 & 7:1-5)
Cyrus' decree.
Return of the Jewish exiles
in 538 or 537 BCE.

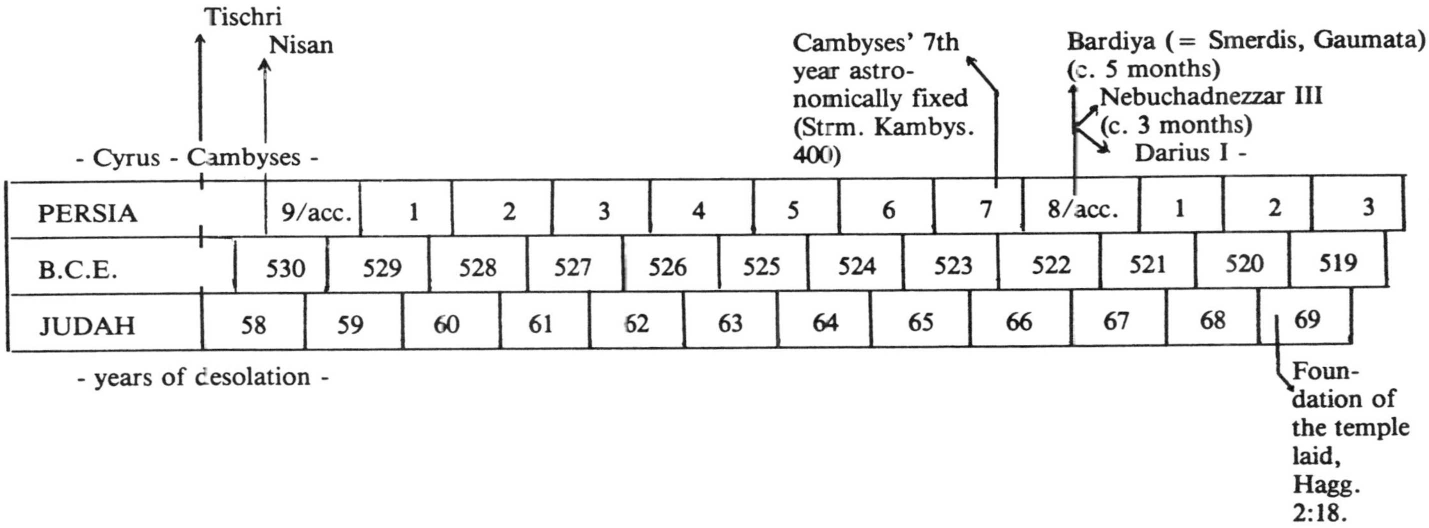
Tischri
Nisan
- Cyrus - Cambyses -
Cambyses' 7th year astronomically fixed (Strm. Kambys. 400)
Bardiya (= Smerdis, Gaumata) (c. 5 months)
Nebuchadnezzar III (c. 3 months)
Darius I -
PERSIA
9/acc.
1
2
3
4
5
6
7
8/acc.
1
2
3
B.C.E.
530
529
528
527
526
525
524
523
522
521
520
519
JUDAH
58
59
60
61
62
63
64
65
66
67
68
69
- years of desolation -
Foundation of the temple laid, Hagg. 2:18.

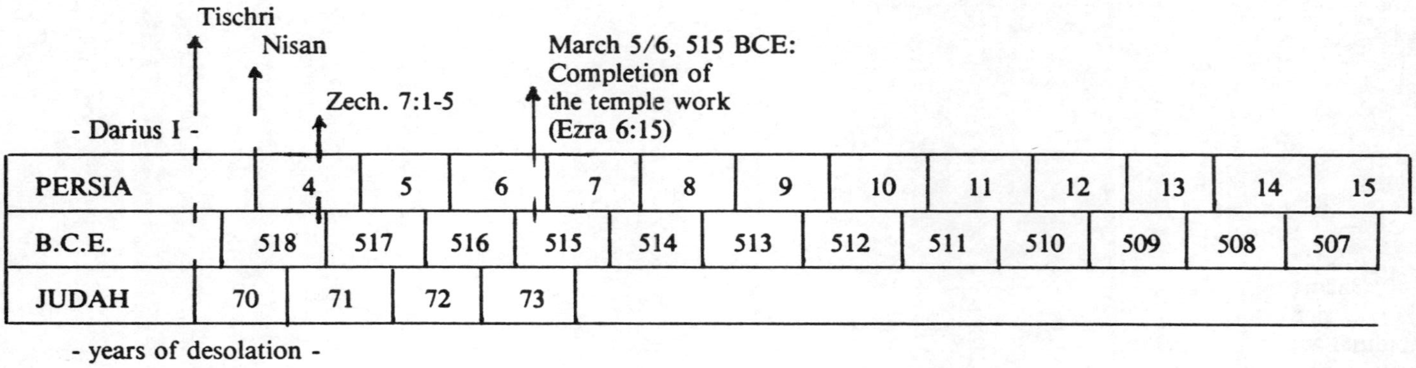
Tischri
Nisan
Zech. 7:1-5
March 5/6, 515 BCE:
Completion of
the temple work
(Ezra 6:15)
- Darius I -
PERSIA
4
5
6
7
8
9
10
11
12
13
14
15
B.C.E.
518
517
516
515
514
513
512
511
510
509
508
507
JUDAH
70
71
72
73
- years of desolation -

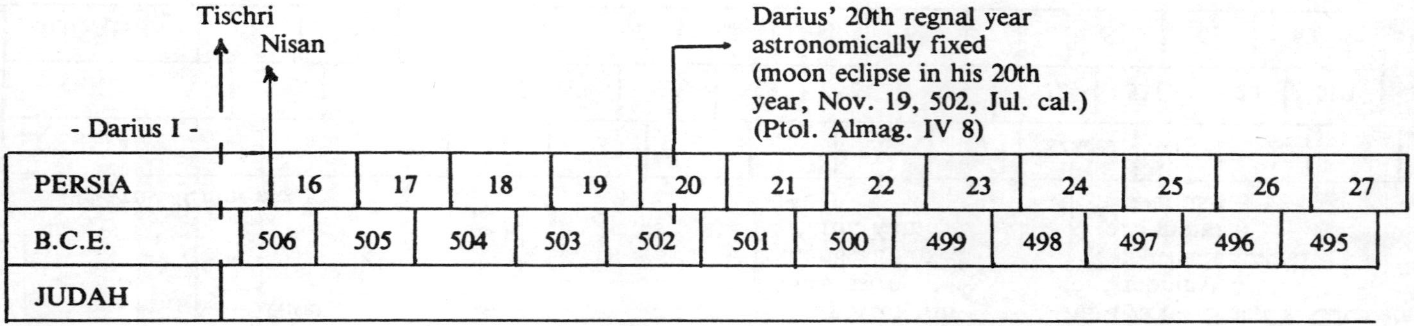
Tischri
Nisan
Darius' 20th regnal year
astronomically fixed
(moon eclipse in his 20th
year, Nov. 19, 502, Jul. cal.)
(Ptol. Almag. IV 8)
- Darius I -
PERSIA
16
17
18
19
20
21
22
23
24
25
26
27
B.C.E.
506
505
504
503
502
501
500
499
498
497
496
495
JUDAH

APPENDIX D

SOME OBSERVATIONS ON NEBUCHADNEZZAR'S "SEVEN TIMES" OF MADNESS AND ON LUKE 21:24

Nebuchadnezzar's "seven times" of madness are often understood as a period of seven *years*. Anyone acquainted with the reign of Nebuchadnezzar knows there are great problems with this understanding. It is difficult to find a period of seven years within his reign of 43 years when he was absent from his throne or inactive as ruler.

That Nebuchadnezzar ruled for 43 years is known not only from secular sources but also from the Bible. Jehoiachin's exile began toward the end of Nebuchadnezzar's 7th regnal year, according to 2 Kings 24:10-17 and 2 Chronicles 36:10. This would mean that Nebuchadnezzar's 43rd year and the accession-year of his successor, Evil-Merodach, would correspond (partly) to Jehoiachin's 37th year of exile (7 + 36 = 43). And this is exactly what we are told in Jeremiah 52:31:

> ''But in the thirty-seventh year of the exile of Jehoiachin king of Judah, in the twelfth month, on the twenty-fifth day of the month, Evil-merodach king of Babylon, in the year he came to the throne, pardoned Jehoiachin king of Judah and released him from prison.''—*Jerusalem Bible*. (Compare 2 Kings 25:27.)

Where, then, during Nebuchadnezzar's 43 years of rule, can we find a period of seven years when he was absent from the throne and not involved in royal activities of any kind? The table on the following page shows the years when the Biblical and extra-Biblical sources show Nebuchadnezzar still actively ruling on his throne.

As can be seen, the documented activities of Nebuchadnezzar appear to exclude an absence from the throne for any period of seven years. Even if we ignore the secular documents and ''just stick to the Bible,'' we still have practically the same problem. The longest period for which we have no evidence of his activity is from his 37th to his 43rd and last year, a period of about six years. This period ended with his death. It should be remembered, however, that Nebuchadnezzar, after his ''seven times'' of madness, was re-established on his throne and evidently ruled for some time afterward. (Daniel 4:26, 36) So what about the ''seven times''? Do they necessarily refers to *years*, as is often held?

Actually, the word for ''times'' in the original Aramaic text of Daniel (*iddan*) commonly means ''time, period, season.'' Admittedly, the view that at Daniel chapter four, verses 16, 23, 25, 32 it refers to years is not restricted to the Watch Tower Society. This understanding can be found in ancient sources. Thus, the *Septuagint* (LXX) version of Daniel translated the word as ''years,'' and so does Josephus in *Antiquities* X:x,6. But the LXX text of Daniel, which is preserved only in a copy from the 9th century A.D., was rejected by early Christians in preference of the Greek version of Theodotion (2nd century A.D.) which says ''times'' (Greek *kairoi*), not ''years'' in Daniel

DOCUMENTED ACTIVITY OF NEBUCHADNEZZAR'S RULE

Events	*References*	*N. on the throne*	*Years B.C.E.*
Battle at Carchemish & 1st invasion of Judah. 1st deportation	Jer. 46:2; Dan. 1:1f.; Jer. 25:1; 35:1,11; 2 Chron. 36:6; 2 Ki. 24:1,7; BM 21946	accession-year accession-year	605 605/04
Campaign to Hattu	BM 21946	1st year	604/03
N's dream of the image	Dan. 2:1f.	2nd year	603/02
Campaigns to Hattu	BM 21946	2nd-6th years	603/02-599/98
Building activity of N.	Royal inscription (Berger, AOAT 4:1, p. 108)	7th year	598/97
2nd deportation. Jehoiachin brought to Babylon	2 Ki. 24:11,12; 2 Chron. 36:10; Jer. 52:28; BM 21946	7th year	597
Campaigns to Hattu & Tigris	BM 21946	8th-9th years	597/96-596/95
Rebellion in N's army. Revolt plans among exiles spread to Judah; Zedekiah sends envoys to N. Jeremiah's letter to exiles. N. marches to Hattu	BM 21946; Jer. 28:1f. 29:1-3, 4-30	10th year	595/94
Campaign to Hattu	BM 21946	11th year	594/93
Building activity of N.	Royal inscription (Berger, AOAT 4:1, p. 108)	12th year	593/92
Jerusalem besieged for 2½ yrs, desolated. 3rd deportation	2 Ki. 25:1f., Jer. 32:1,2; 39:1,2; 52:4-16	15th-18th years	589-587
Ezekiel predicts siege of Tyre	Ez. 26:1,7	18th year	587
N. besieges Tyre for 13 years	Josephus' *Ant.* X:x,1	19th-32nd years	586/85-573/72
Ezekiel confirms siege ended	Ez. 29:17,18	33rd year	572/71
N. attacks Egypt as predicted	BM 33041 (Jer. 43:10f. Ez. 29:1-16,19,20)	37th year	568/67
N. dies. Evil-Merodach's accession-year	Jer. 52:31-34; 2 Ki. 25:27-30	43rd year	562/61

chapter four. That some Jews at an early stage interpreted the "times" of Daniel chapter four as "years" can also be seen in the so-called "Prayer of Nabonidus," a fragmentary Aramaic document found three decades ago at Qmran dating from the end of the first century BCE. This document, which is probably a late, distorted version of Daniel's narrative, says that Nabonidus was stricken with an evil disease "for seven years" in the Teman oasis. (The most recent reconstruction and translation of the fragments is that by F. M. Cross in the *Israel Exploration Journal*, Vol. 34, No. 4, 1984.)

What are the other alternatives? Realizing that the literal meaning of the Aramaic word *iddan* is not "year" but "period" or "season," Hippolytus of the 3rd century says that some viewed a "time" as one of the four seasons of the year. Hence "seven seasons" would be less than two years. Bishop Theodoret of the 5th century, however, noted that people of ancient times, such as the Babylonians and Persians, spoke of only *two* seasons a year, winter and summer, the rainy and the rainless seasons. This was also the custom among the Hebrews. In the Bible there are no references to spring and autumn, only to the summer and winter seasons. According to this line of reasoning, the "seven seasons" of Nebuchadnezzar's madness meant three and one-half years.

Some of the most highly regarded of conservative Bible scholars of recent times, such as Carl F. Keil and E. J. Young, either reject or feel strong doubts about the theory that the "seven times" of Daniel chapter four refer to seven *years*. The great Assyriologist Donald J. Wiseman even concluded that the "seven times" should be understood as "seven months." (See *The New Bible Dictionary*, ed. J. D. Douglas, London, 1962, p. 873.) Any of these last-mentioned viewpoints would be in acceptable agreement with the information we have on the rule of Nebuchadnezzar.

Some, of course, will point to Revelation chapter twelve, arguing that since the 3½ "times" in verse 14 correspond to the 1260 days (=3½ years) of verse 6, seven times must mean 2520 days, or seven years. There is, however, no reason to conclude that the way "times" is used in Revelation chapter twelve must automatically apply also in other contexts. The fact remains that, since the Aramaic word *iddan* simply means "time, period, season," it could refer to periods of different lengths. It does not refer to the same, fixed period everywhere it is used. The context must always decide its meaning. And even if it could be shown that the "time, and times and half a time" at Daniel chapter seven, verse 25, mean three and a half *years* (which is doubtful!), this still would not prove that the "seven times" or "seasons" (*Rotherham*), or "periods" (*New American Standard Bible*), at Daniel chapter four, verses 16, 23, 25 and 32, mean "seven *years*." The two chapters deal with two very different events and periods and therefore should not be confused.

OBSERVATIONS ON LUKE 21:24

In trying to understand the phrase "times of the Gentiles," or "appointed times of the nations" at Luke 21:24, it is important to consider the context of this prophecy. Does the context really indicate that by the word "Jerusalem" Jesus did not refer to the literal city of Jerusalem, but to "the kingdom of God," "the kingdom of the dynasty of King David" (*Aid to Bible Understanding* p. 95:1), or as some other expositors have concluded, "the spiritual promises of Israel"?[1] And further, what evidence is there to show that the "times of the Gentiles" started with Nebuchadnezzar's overthrow of Jerusalem, or as some other expositors hold, "with the Babylonian captivity of Judah" eighteen or nineteen years earlier?[2]

A careful examination of the context of Luke 21:24 does not seem to give any support to the views above. The terms used in the context ("Jerusalem," "Gentiles" or "nations," etc.) are clearly meant to be understood *literally*. For example, the term "gentiles" (*ethne*) evidently refers to non-Jewish nations.[3] The Jews were to be "led captive into all the *nations* (*ethne*), i.e., the non-Jewish nations, and after that Jerusalem would be "trampled on by the *nations*," which still could not mean other than *literal* non-Jewish nations. Thus, during the absence of literal Jews, Jerusalem would be trampled on or controlled by literal non-Jewish nations. Does not this indicate that the word "Jerusalem," too, refers to the *literal* city of Jerusalem? Actually, this was what took place after the destruction of Jerusalem in the year 70 C.E.: The literal city of Jerusalem began to be trampled on by literal non-Jewish nations: Rome (up to 615 C.E.), Persia (up to 629 C.E.), the Byzantine Empire (up to 637 C.E.), the Saracen Empire (up to 1099 C.E.), the Christian Crusader Kingdom (up to 1187 C.E.), Egypt (up to 1229 C.E.), the Holy Roman Empire (up to 1243 C.E.), Turkey (up to 1917 C.E.), Great Britain (up to 1948 C.E.), and Jordan (up to 1967). It cannot be denied that Jesus' prophecy has been fulfilled *literally*. If this simple application is made and the literal fulfillment fits every detail of the prophecy, why should it not be accepted as the correct one?

When in Luke 21:20 Jesus speaks of "encamped armies" which were to surround Jerusalem, did he think of Jerusalem as a representation of "the kingdom of God," "the kingdom of the dynasty of King David"? Obviously not, as "the kingdom of the dynasty of King David" could not reasonably have been surrounded by the (Roman) armies in the year 66 C.E. By the term "Jerusalem" Jesus evidently meant the literal city of Jerusalem that was destroyed by Roman armies in 70 C.E. If he thought of the kingdom of David, he could not have said that the "desolating of *her*" would "draw near" (in 70 C.E.), or that "those in the country places should not "enter into *her*." (in 66-70 C.E., Luke 21:20, 21) The "Jerusalem" of verse 24 that would be "trampled on by the nations" could scarcely be any other than the Jerusalem that would be surrounded by encamped armies, namely, the *literal* city of

Jerusalem. If so, it could not have been "the kingdom of the dynasty of King David."

When did the "trampling on" of this literal city of Jerusalem begin? Although it is true that since the destruction of Jerusalem in 587 B.C.E., the city has been controlled by Gentile nations most of the time (with the exception of the independent Maccabean rule 135-63 B.C.E.), Jesus seems to be referring to the period of "trampling" following the destruction of Jerusalem in 70 C.E. Note that he does not state that "Jerusalem shall *continue* to be trampled on by the nations," as if this "trampling" was going on at the time he uttered this prophecy. He speaks of the "trampling" as something in the future, using the future tense: *estai patoumene/"will be* being trampled."[4] The situation described as preceding the destruction of Jerusalem presupposes that the Gentiles *did not* trample Jerusalem *before* its destruction. When Jesus said that Jerusalem would be surrounded by encamped armies (v. 20), this implies, of course, that those armies would not be "trampling" or controlling Jerusalem at that time. If they did, why should they surround Jerusalem in order to try to capture it? The actual situation in the years 66-70 was that the Jews were in control of Jerusalem, not the Gentiles. But after the destruction of Jerusalem in 70 C.E., the Jews were "led captive into all the nations," and the city, now ruined, was "trampled on" by Gentile nations from that time on. Thus the conclusion that the "times of the Gentiles" began in the time of Nebuchadnezzar seems to be unfounded.

Another assumption made is, that the expiration of the Gentile times coincides with Christ's second coming or *parousia*.[5] But Jesus did not state that. Although it is true that the Gentile dominion *of the earth* will end at Christ's coming, the end of the Gentile dominion *of Jerusalem* could well end *before* that time. In our own century the literal trampling on the literal city of Jerusalem has gradually ceased, step by step: On December 9, 1917, the British army delivered Jerusalem fom the Turks, and in the same year the "Balfour Declaration" was issued. On Friday,

May 14, 1948, David Ben-Gurion declared the State of Israel at Tel Aviv, and on June 7, 1967, the Jews took possession of the old city of Jerusalem. Since that day the Jews have been in control of the city of Jerusalem with the exception of the most important part of the city, the temple site. Thus Jesus' prophecy, taken in its most literal sense, has almost been fulfilled, *literally*. But does this mean that the Jews will again become God's chosen people, that the temple will be rebuilt on its old site, that Jerusalem will become the capital from which Jesus Christ will rule the world during his 1,000-year reign, etc.? Again, Jesus did not say that. He simply prophesied that the trampling on Jerusalem by the Gentile nations would come to an end some time in the future, either by a Jewish reoccupation of the city, or by the final destruction of these Gentile nations. It is not necessary to add more to Jesus' prophecy than that. He could merely have meant that Jerusalem would again be occupied by the Jews, just as Tyre would regain its prominence after having been forgotten for seventy years (Isaiah 23:15-18), or as the Egyptians were to be recollected and brought back to Egypt after having been scattered among the nations for forty years. (Ez. 29:12-14) In either case, the context of Luke 21:24 points to a *literal* meaning of the terms used, and therefore the fulfillment of this prophecy must be sought in relation to the *literal* city of Jerusalem.[6]

NOTES

PROLOGUE

1. *The Watchtower*, June 15, 1981, p. 28.

2. Schroeder may have had two non-Witness publications which attack the Society's chronology in mind: Edmund C. Gruss, *The Jehovah's Witnesses and Prophetic Speculation* (Nutley, N.J.: Presbyterian and Reformed Publishing Co., 1972), and William MacCarty, *1914 and Christ's Second Coming* (Washington, D.C., Review and Herald Publishing Association, 1975).

3. Abandoning the 607 B.C.E.-1914 C.E. calculation also implies abandoning those interpretations founded upon it such as the idea that God's kingdom was established in 1914 and that Christ's "invisible presence" began in that year. Of Jehovah's Witnesses who cannot embrace such views, *The Watchtower* of July 15, 1979, stated on page 13: "*Lawless persons* have even tried to penetrate the true Christian congregation, arguing that the 'promised presence' of our Lord is not in this day.... Persons of this kind are included in Jesus' warning recorded at Matthew 7:15-23: "Be on the watch for the *false prophets* that come to you in sheep's covering, but inside they are ravenous wolves.... In that day I will confess to them: I never knew you! Get away from me, you *workers of* lawlessness." Further, *The Watchtower* of August 1, 1980, page 19, said:

"Peter was also speaking of the danger of being 'led away' by some within the Christian congregation who would become '*ridiculers*,' making light of the fulfillment of prophecies concerning Christ's 'presence' and adopting a *law-defying* attitude toward 'the faithful and discreet slave,' the Governing Body of the Christian congregation and the appointed elders." See also paragraph 11 on the same page and paragraph 14 on page 20 of the same issue.

4. *Spectrum*, Vol. 11, No. 4, 1981, p. 63. This journal is published by the Association of Adventist Forums, Box 4330, Takoma Park, Maryland, U.S.A.

5. Even aside from the chronology, this claim has become difficult to defend since the Society's own re-interpretation of Matthew 24:42-51 in 1973. Originally it was held that verses 45-51 were an expansion of verses 42-44 and related to the same event, namely to Christ's "coming to the temple" in 1918. *Vindication* (Brooklyn, N.Y.: Watchtower Bible and Tract Society, 1932) Vol. 3, pp. 121, 122. Then in 1973, the Society, while retaining its position regarding verses 45-51, *postponed the 'coming' mentioned at verses 42-44 to the future "great tribulation."* (See *God's Kingdom of a Thousand Years Has Approached*, pp. 336, 337.) Contextually, however, there is no way to separate the "coming" of verses 42-44 from that of verses 45-51. Hence, if the "coming" of verses 42-44 is future, the "coming" of the master described in verses 45-51 is future also, as well as is his appointing of "the faithful and discreet slave over all his belongings."

6. Raymond Franz, former Governing Body member, wrote this letter.

CHAPTER I

1. LeRoy Edwin Froom, *The Prophetic Faith of Our Fathers* (Washington, D.C.: Review and Herald Publishing Co., 1948), Vol. II, p. 124.

2. It does not seem necessary to apply the "year-day principle" to this prophecy simply because it does not mention days, just *weeks*. To a Jew the Hebrew word for "week," *shabua*, did not always refer to a period of *seven days* as in English. *Shabua* literally means a "seven." The Jews also had a "seven" or *shabua* of *years*. (Lev. 25:3,4,8,9). When "weeks of years" were meant, the word for "years" was usually added, but not always: "In post-biblical Hebrew the meaning of 'weeks' in the sense of 'weeks of years' occurs hundreds of time for this term in Jubilees (c. 150 B.C.E.), the Mishna and the Talmud." See G. F. Hasel, *The Seventy Weeks of Daniel 9:24–27* (Washington, D.C.: Biblical Research Institute, 1976). When "weeks of days" were meant, the word for "days" was often added as in the other passage in Daniel where *shabua* is found. (10:2,3) Daniel 9:24 simply asserts that "seventy *sevens* are determined," and from the context it is apparent that "seventy sevens *of years*" are intended. That is why some translations read "seventy weeks of

years'' (AT, Mo, RS) See *Aid to Bible Understanding* (Brooklyn, N.Y.: Watchtower Bible and Tract Society, 1971), p. 1473 and Chapter III, note 60.

3. Froom, Vol. II, pp. 195, 196.

4. *Ibid.*, p. 196.

5. Charles Maitland, *The Apostles' School of Prophetic Interpretation* (London, 1849), pp. 37, 38.

6. E.B. Elliott, *Horae Apocalypticae*, 3rd ed. (London, 1847), Vol. III, p. 233.

7. *Ibid.*, pp. 233-240.

8. *Ibid.*, p. 240. The late Dr. LeRoy Edwin Froom, who was a modern defender of the year-day theory, arrived at a similar conclusion in his massive work, *The Prophetic Faith of Our Fathers.* In Volume I on page 700, he states: "Heretofore, for thirteen centuries the seventy weeks had been recognized generally as weeks of years. But the first thousand years of the Christian era did not produce any further applications of the principle, among Christian writers, save one or two glimpses of the 'ten days' of Revelation 2:10 as ten years of persecutions, and the three and a half days of Revelation 11 as three and a half years. But now Joachim for the first time applied the year-day principle to the 1260-day prophecy.''

9. Froom, Vol. I, p. 716.

10. *Ibid.*, pp. 717, 723, 727. The information here is based on the work *De Seminibus Scripturarum*, fol. 13v, col. 2 (as discussed in Froom) which was written in 1205 C.E. The manuscript is known as Vat. Latin 3813.

11. *Tractatus*, part 2, 1300 C.E. See also Heinrich Finke, *Aus den Tagen Bonifaz VIII* (Munster, 1902), pp. CXLVIII-CLI, CXLII and Froom, Vol. I, p. 756.

12. *Registrum* as translated in John Foxe, Acts and Monuments, 9th ed. (London, 1684), Vol. I, p. 547. See also Froom, Vol. II, p. 80.

13. Froom, Vol. II, p. 80.

14. John Napier, *A Plaine Discovery of the Whole Revelation of Saint John* (1593), pp. 64, 65. Froom, Vol. II, p. 458.

15. Bell's article is entitled "Downfall of Antichrist'' which was written July 24, 1795.

16. *Ibid.*, p. 57. Froom, Vol. II, p. 742.

17. For additional notes on this prediction, see Chapter III.

18. The second advent was expected to occur during the Jewish year 1843/44, reckoned from spring to spring. It has been maintained that expositors in the United States arrived at the 1843 date as the end of the 2,300 years independently. Although that *may* be true, it cannot be proved, and interestingly, the London, England, *Christian Observer*, a periodical founded in 1802 which frequently dealt with prophecy, also had an American edition published at Boston which ran article for article with the British edition. So Brown's article on the 2,300 years could have been read by many in the United States as early as 1810. Soon afterwards, the 1843 date began to appear in American prophetic expositions.

19. Perhaps some may be inclined to object to this statement on account of the table on pages 404 and 405 of Froom's *The Prophetic Faith of Our Fathers*, Volume IV. It is true that this table *seems* to show *James Hatley Frere* as the first to write on the 2,520 years in 1813. But the part of the table farthest to the right on page 405 entitled, "Dating of other time periods," does not have any close connection with the "Publication date" date column on page 404. It simply states the author's general position on other time periods. Besides, Frere never held the times of the Gentiles (or the "seven times") to be a period of 2,520 years. In his first book on prophecy, *A Combined View of the Prophecies of Daniel, Esdras, and St. John* (London, 1815), he does not comment on Daniel 4 or Luke 21:24. The "holy city" of Revelation 11:2, he explains to be "the visible church of Christ," and "during the period of 1260 years, the whole of this city is trodden under foot of the Gentiles, excepting the interior courts of its temple." (p. 87) Later Frere calculated the Gentile times to be a period of 2,450 years from 603 B.C.E. to 1847 C.E. See, for example, his book, *The Great Continental Revolution, Marking the Expiration of the Times of the Gentiles A.D. 1847-8* (London, 1848). Note especially pages 66-78.

John A. Brown, of course, was well acquainted with the many contemporary writings on prophecy, and Frere was one of the best known expositors in England. So there seems to be no reason to doubt Brown's own statement of priority.

20. John A. Brown, *The Even-Tide* (London: various publishers, 1823), Vol. II, pp. 134, 135: Vol. I, p. XLIII.

21. Henry Drummond, *Dialogues on Prophecy* (London, 1827), Vol. I, pp. 33, 34. "Sophron" (a pseudonym for the well-known expositor William Cuninghame) is quoted as saying that Mede "considers the times of the Gentiles under a two-fold aspect, political and spiritual. Book IV. 8," after which he (Cuninghame) dates the 2,520 years from the year when the ten tribes were carried into captivity by Shalmaneser, which he dates to 728 B.C.E., thus arriving at 1792 C.E. as their last year or termination date. Cuninghame arrives at the 2,520 years by doubling the 1,260 years, not by referring to the "seven times" of Daniel 4 or Leviticus 26. That was done by an "Anastasius" (Henry Drummond) in a later conversation. (pp. 324, 325)

Joseph Mede, who was referred to by Cuninghame, may have been the expositor who came *closest* to the period of 2,520 years before the nineteenth century. In his comments on the times of the Gentiles, he says: "I make no questions but that these *Times of the Gentiles*, with which the Jews Tribulation shall end, are either the Times of the Four Monarchies in general, (that is, the Times of that prophesied Dominion of the Gentiles), or, which is all one event, these last Times of the Fourth Kingdom of *A Time, Times* and a half Time...." Joseph Mede, *The Works* (London, 1664), Book 4, p. 920. Mede, however, does not fix the length of the Four Monarchies.

22. Found on page 48. Quoted in Froom, Vol. III, p. 576.

23. Edward Bickersteth, *A Scripture Help*, first edited in 1815. After 1832 Bickersteth began to preach and write on the prophecies, which also influenced later editions of *A Scripture Help*. The quotation is taken from the twentieth edition (London, 1850), p. 235.

24. William Miller, "A Dissertation on Prophetic Chronology" in *The First Report of the General Conference of Christians Expecting the Advent of the Lord Jesus Christ* (Boston, 1842), p. 5.

25. Froom, Vol. IV, pp. 699-701, 726-737.

26. "That I have been mistaken in the time, I freely confess; and I have no desire to defend my course any further than I have been actuated by pure motives, and it has resulted in God's glory. My mistakes and errors God, I trust, will forgive...." *Wm. Miller's Apology and Defence* (Boston, 1845), pp. 33, 34. This was a humble and honest confession, rare indeed among self-appointed prophets throughout the centuries.

27. In 1964 the Life and Advent Union merged with the Advent Christian Church.

28. Nelson H. Barbour, *Evidences for the Coming of the Lord in 1873; or the Midnight Cry*, 2nd. ed. (Rochester 1871), p. 32.

29. *Ibid.*

30. *Ibid.*, p. 33.

31. E.B. Elliott, *Horae Apocalypticae*, 4th ed. (London, 1851), Vol. IV, p. 236

32. *Herald of the Morning*, August 1879, p. 28 and September 1879, p. 36.

33. *Zion's Watch Tower*, October and November 1881, p. 3.

34. *Ibid.*

35. *Ibid.* Also *Zion's Watch Tower*, February 1881, p. 3.

36. *Zion's Watch Tower*, April 1880, p. 7.

37. As Barbour was acquainted with John A. Brown's works, it is possible that he ''corrected'' his starting-point for the Gentile times from 604 to 606 B.C.E., thus ending them in 1914. But Barbour could also have got the 606 B.C.E. date from E. B. Elliott. Although Elliott chose 707 B.C.E. for the beginning of the Gentile times, he added that ''they might be calculated, yet more naturally, from Nebuchadnezzar's own accession and invasion of Judah, B.C. 606.'' Elliott, Vol. IV, p. 238.

38. *Zion's Watch Tower*, July 15, 1906, pp. 230, 231.

39. *Ibid.*

40. This is also indicated by Russell himself who states: "...when we first met...I had much to learn from him concerning *time.*" *Zion's Watch Tower*, Reprints p. 3822. See also the extra edition of *Zion's Watch Tower*, April 25, 1894, entitled "A Conspiracy Exposed," p. 100.

41. *Zion's Watch Tower*, July 1894, Reprints p. 1677.

42. *Ibid.*, Reprints p. 2876.

43. *Ibid.*, Reprints p. 3389.

44. *Ibid.*, Reprints pp. 3436-3438.

45. *Ibid.*, Reprints p. 3415.

46. *Ibid.*, Reprints. pp. 3459, 3460, 3574-3579.

47. C.T. Russell, *The Time is at Hand* (Pittsburgh: Watch Tower Bible and Tract Society, 1889), p. 169.

48. *The Watch Tower*, Reprints p. 4067.

49. *Ibid.*

50. *The Watch Tower*, December 1, 1912, Reprints p. 5141. As the First World War broke out in 1914 and that year was retained as *the end* of the Gentile times, the starting point of those times had to be moved back one year from 606 to 607 B.C.E. in order to maintain a total of 2,520 years. Although some of the Society's adherents had pointed this fact out very early (see, for example the footnote on page 32 of John and Morton Edgar's *Great Pyramid Passages*, 2nd. ed., 1924) this necessary adjustment was not made by the Watchtower Society until 1943 when it was presented in the book, *The Truth Shall Make You Free*, on page 239. See also *The Kingdom Is at Hand*, p. 184.

51. *The Watch Tower*, Reprints p. 5249.

52. *Ibid.*, Reprints p. 5328.

53. *Ibid.*, Reprints p. 5373.

54. *Ibid.*, Reprints pp. 5373, 5374.

55. *Ibid.*, Reprints p. 5450.

56. *Ibid.*, July 1, 1914, Reprints p. 5496.

57. *Ibid.*, August 15, 1914, Reprints p. 5516.

58. *Ibid.*, November 1, 1914, p. 327.

59. *Ibid.*, Reprints p. 5568.

60. *Ibid.*, Reprints p. 5601.

61. *Ibid.*, Reprints p.5769, para. 8.

62. *Ibid.*, Reprints p. 5852.

63. *Ibid.*, Reprints., p. 5888, para. 13.

64. *Ibid.*, Reprints., p. 5950, para. 5.

65. See pages 28, 29. For a long time after 1914 it was held that the "time of trouble" (Matt. 24:21,22) really began in that year, but this view was abandoned by Jehovah's Witnesses some time ago.

66. A.H. MacMillian, *Faith on the March* (New York: Prentice Hall, Inc., 1957), p. 48.

67. *New Heavens and a New Earth* (Brooklyn, N.Y.: Watchtower Bible and Tract Society, 1953), p. 225.

68. "Birth of a Nation" in *The Watch Tower* of March 1, 1925.

69. *The Watch Tower*, October 1, 1922, p. 298; November 1, 1922, p. 334.

70. *From Paradise Lost to Paradise Regained* (Brooklyn, N.Y.: Watchtower Bible and Tract Society, 1958), p. 192. para. 30.

71. *The Golden Age*, 1930, p. 503; 1934, pp. 379-380. See also J.F. Rutherford, *Prophecy* (Brooklyn, N.Y.: International Bible Students Association, 1929), p. 65.

CHAPTER II

1. The year 539 B.C.E. has been termed an "absolute date." See, for example, *All Scripture Is Inspired of God and Beneficial* (Brooklyn, N.Y.: Watchtower Bible and Tract Society, 1963), p. 282, and *Aid to Bible Understanding* (Brooklyn, N.Y.: Watchtower Bible and Tract Society, 1971), p. 333. This, however, is not quite correct. The date has been arrived at in an indirect way. The astronomical tablet *Strm. Kambys.400*, which contains a large number of astronomical observations from the seventh year of Cambyses, the son and successor of Cyrus, has enabled modern astronomers to fix Cambyses' seventh regnal year to 523-522 B.C.E. This, therefore, may be termed an "absolute date." If Cambyses' seventh year was 523-522, his first regnal year was 529-528 B.C.E. His father, Cyrus, reigned in Babylon for nine years before Cambyses' sole reign, according to cuneiform tablets. This fixes Cyrus' first year as king of Babylon as 538-537 B.C.E. and, consequently, the fall of Babylon occurred some months earlier, or in the autumn of 539 B.C.E. Thus 539 is not in itself an "absolute date," but it has been *derived from* an absolute date, 523 B.C.E. Without an "astronomically fixed date," the year of the fall of Babylon would have been just a *relative* date. As Otto Neugebauer puts it: "An absolute chronology [is] a chronology which is based on astronomically fixed dates in contrast to a 'relative chronology' which tells us only the length of certain intervals, e.g., the total of regnal years in a dynasty." *A History of Ancient Mathematical Astronomy* (Berlin-Heidelberg-New York: Springer-Verlag, 1975), Book IV, p. 1071. If 539 B.C.E. may be termed an "absolute date" this is also true of a number of other dates, which likewise have been derived from astronomically fixed dates, e.g., 587-586 B.C.E. as the date of Nebuchadnezzar's eighteenth regnal year which has been derived from the astronomically fixed date 568-567 B.C.E. This will be discussed later.

2. The validity of this date will be dealt with in Chapter III.

3. Erich Ebeling and Bruno Meissner, eds., *Reallexikon der Assyriologie*, (Berlin and Leipzig: Walter de Gruyter and Co., 1938), Vol. II, p. 2, 3.

4. A translation with an extensive discussion of these fragments was published by Paul Schnabel in *Berossos und die Babylonisch-Hellenistische Literatur* (Leipzig-Berlin: B. G. Teubner, 1923). The first complete English translation of the surviving fragments of Berossus' work has been published by Stanley Mayer Burstein in *The Babyloniaca of Berossus* as Vol. I, fascicle 5 in *Sources from the Ancient Near East* (Malibu, Calif.: Undena Publications, 1978).

5. Eusebius' Chronicle is preserved only in an Armenian translation. A German translation of this version may be found in Joseph Karst, *Die Chronik, Eusebius Werke* 5 (Leipzig, 1911). Eusebius revised his work twice after 303 C.E.

6. *Against Apion*, Book I: 19-21; *Antiquities*, Book X:XI, para. 1. The earliest and most reliable of the quotations are those by Josephus (see Burstein, p. 11)

which is important as he gives the longest quotation of Berossus from the Neo-Babylonian period, including all the lengths of reign of the Neo-Babylonian kings.

7. Burstein, p. 13.

8. *Ibid.*, p. 8. Robert Drews, in his article "The Babylonian Chronicles and Berossus" in *Iraq*, Vol. XXXVII, part 1, Spring 1975, arrives at the same conclusion: "That the chronicles were among these records cannot be doubted." (p. 54) This has been demonstrated by a careful comparison of Berossus' statements with the Babylonian chronicles. Paul Schnabel, too, concludes: "*Dass er überall Keilschriftsberichte, vor allem Chroniken, benutzt hat, merkt man auf Schritt und Tritt.*" Schnabel, p. 184.

9. For a recent publication of Ptolemy's canon, see E. J. Bickerman, *Chronology of the Ancient World* (Ithaca, N.Y.: Cornell University Press, 1968), pp. 107-109.

10. *Aid to Bible Understanding*, p. 328, para. 1. See also footnote 1.

11. Burstein, p. 38.

12. Friedrich Schmidtke, *Der Aufbau der Babylonischen Chronologie* in *Orbis Antiquus*, Heft 7, Schriften der Altertumswissenschaftlichen Gesellschaft Münster, Westf., 1952), p. 41. Translated from the German.

13. Labashi-Marduk probably ruled for only two to three months. See R.A. Parker and W.H. Dubberstein *Babylonian Chronology 626 B.C.-A.D. 75* (Providence: Brown University Press, 1956), p. 13. The Uruk King List, (see below) indicates a rule of three months for Labashi-Marduk.

14. Edwin R. Thiele, *The Mysterious Numbers of the Hebrew Kings* (Chicago: University of Chicago Press, 1951), p. 46.

15. That is, Merodach baladan. See Isaiah 39:1.

16. Claudius Ptolemy, *Almagest*, IV, 5. The quotation is translated from F K. Ginzel, *Spezieller Kanon der Sonnen- und Mondfinsternisse* (Berlin: Mayer und Müller, 1899), p. 229.

17. Ginzel, pp. 229, 230.

18. *Ibid.*, pp. 130, 232, 233. See Th. R. v. Oppolzer, *Canon der Finsternisse* (Vienna, 1887), p. 332.

19. For example, the *Babylonian Chronicle* (B. M. 84-211, 356 and 92,502) and the *Babylonian King List A* (B.M. 33332) both give the lengths of reign of Babylonian kings from Nabonassar (747-733) to Esarhaddon (680-667), and

other ancient cuneiform texts span the rest of the period up to the Neo-Babylonian era. The lengths of reign given by these ancient documents agree with those given by Ptolemy's canon.

20. J. B. J. Delambre, *Histoire de l'Astronomie Ancienne* (Paris, 1817), Vol. II, p. XXV. Quoted by Robert R. Newton in *The Moon's Acceleration and Its Physical Origins* (Baltimore and London: The Johns Hopkins University Press, 1979), Vol. I, p. 43.

21. Newton, *The Moon's Acceleration*, p. 44.

22. Robert R. Newton, *The Crime of Claudius Ptolemy* (Baltimore and London: The Johns Hopkins University Press, 1977).

23. *Ibid.*, p. 373, Table XIII, 4.

24. B.R. Goldstein in *Science*, February 24, 1978, p. 872.

25. *Scientific American*, March 1979, (p. 93, American edition).

26. See for example Noel M. Swerdlow, "Ptolemy on Trial," in *The American Scholar*, Autumn 1979, pp. 523-531 and Julia Neuffer, " 'Ptolemy's Canon' Debunked?" in *Andrews University Studies*, Vol. XVII, No. 1, 1979, pp. 39-46.

27. K. P. Moesgaard, "Ptolemy's Failings" in *Journal for the History of Astonomy*, Vol. XI, 1980, pp. 133-135. See also Rolf Brahde's review in *Astronomisk Tidskrift*, 1979, No. 1, pp. 42, 43. An article by Owen J. Gingerich of Harvard University with a rebuttal by R.R. Newton is found in the *Quarterly Journal of the Royal Astronomical Society*, 21, 1980, pp. 253-266 and 388-399.

28. *The Watchtower*, December 15, 1977, p. 747.

29. Newton, *The Crime of Claudius Ptolemy*, p. 375.

30. *Ibid.*

31. *Ibid.*, p. XIV: "I thank Mr. Philip G. Couture of Santee, California for correspondence which led me to understand some of the relations between chronology and the work of Ptolemy." According to *Witness* (a magazine edited by E.B. Price of Hawthorn, Victoria, Australia) Vol. 5, No. 1, p. 14, Mr. Couture is a Jehovah's Witness, which he has been since 1947. He evidently based his information on chronology on material in *Aid to Bible Understanding*.

32. On page 189 of *The Moon's Acceleration and Its Physical Origins*, Newton says that Couture pointed out to him that "the accuracy of the epynom list is not beyond question. For example, the king, Sargon II, is believed from other evidence to have reigned only 17 years, but the number of *limmu* (eponyms) listed for his reign is 32, according to Couture (private communication); I have not

verified this number independently." This argument which is evidently taken from *Aid to Bible Understanding*, p. 326, is founded upon a gross error. Contemporary cuneiform texts, as well as the eponym canon itself, clearly show that a king did not always hold the eponym in his first regnal year as the *Aid* book indicates. Sargon's successor, Sennacherib, for example, held the eponym in his eighteenth regnal year! A king's reign, therefore, cannot be fixed by counting *limmus* in the list.

33. Newton, *The Crime of Claudius Ptolemy*, p. 375.

34. *Ibid*. See Also Newton, *The Moon's Acceleration*, p. 49.

35. A.K. Grayson, *Assyrian and Babylonian Chronicles* (New York: J.J. Augustin Publisher, 1975),, pp. 99, 100.

36. *Ibid*., p. 109.

37. *Ibid*., pp. 106, 107. "The sixth year," too, is missing, but as the record for each year is separated from the next year by a horizontal line, and as the account of Astyages' defeat immediately precedes the record for the seventh year, it is quite evident that it refers to the sixth year.

38. *Aid to Bible Understanding*, p. 328, agrees on this dating: "Historians such as Diodorus, Africanus and Eusebius show that Cyrus' first year as king of Persia corresponded to Olympiad 55, year 1 (560-59 B.C.E.), while Cyrus' last year is placed at Olympiad 62, year 2 (531-30 B.C.E.)."

39. P. 190. This work was published by the Watchtower Society in 1963. See also *Aid to Bible Understanding*, p. 408.

40. A.K. Grayson, "Assyria and Babylonia' in *Orientalia*, Vol. 49, Fasc. 2, 1980, p. 171.

41. *Ibid.*

42. *Ibid*., p. 175.

43. P. 10. Grayson's *Assyrian and Babylonian Chronicles* is the most comprehensive work published on those chronicles. It contains a new translation of all chronicles available.

44. Of the Old Testament historical books, Dr. Grayson gives the following appraisal: "In the books of the Old Testament historiography reaches an unprecedented height. The clarity and beauty of style found in the ancient Hebrew narratives is unique among historical documents from the ancient Near East." Grayson, *Assyrian and Babylonian Chronicles*, p. 1.

45. UVB = Vorläufiger Bericht über die von dem Deutschen Archaäologischen

Institut und der Deutschen Orient-Gesellschaft aus Mitteln der Deutschen Forschungsgemeinschaft unternommenen Ausgrabungen in Uruk-Warka. Two other translations have appeared: Oppenheim's in J. B. Pritchard's *The Ancient Near East* (Princeton University Press, 1969), p. 566, and Grayson's in Weidner von Soden, *Reallexikon der Assyriologie*, (Berlin and New York: Walter de Gruyter and Co., 1980). Vol. VI, page 97.

46. J. van Dijk, *UVB 18* (See note 45.), p. 57.

47. See Appendix A.

48. Stephen Langdon, *die Neubabylonischen Konigsinschriften* (Leipzig: J. C. Hinriches'sche Buchhandlung, 1912). This is Vol. IV in *Vorderasiatische Bibliothek*.

49. The first of the three planned volumes were published in 1973 as *Die neubabylonischen Königsinschriften* (Neukirchen-Vluyn: Neukirchener Verlag). This is Vol. 4: 1 in *Alter Orient und Altes Testament*.

50. H. Lewy, "The Babylonian Background of the Kay Kâûs Legend" in *Archiv Orientální* (ed. by B. Hrozný, Prague, 1949), pp. 50, 51. Lewy gives the following reasons for his choice: "During his (Nabonidus') reign, two lunar eclipses, visible in Babylonia, fell on the 13th day of Ululu; the first, occuring on September 26, 554 B.C., reached a degree of 10.3 inches, which means it was nearly total. In the second eclipse, taking place on September 16, 545 B.C., only a small segment of the moon was darkened. According to the tables of Neugebauer...the first eclipse began in Babylon at 3:00 a.m.; the time of the moon's setting was probably invisible in Babylon. The second eclipse, on the contrary, could be observed in Babylon between 1:18 a.m. and 3:12 a.m. As Nabunaid specially mentions the moon's setting in her obscuration, it is clear that he describes the eclipse of September 26, 554 B.C., which is Ululu 13 of his second full year." (p. 51, ftn. 105)

51. W. G. Lambert, "A New Source for the Reign of Nabonidus" in Ernst Weidner, ed., *Archive für Orientforschung*, (Graz, 1968-69), Vol. 22, pp. 1-8.

52. If anyone thinks it is possible to find another lunar eclipse on Elul 13 a number of years earlier that fits the description given by Nabonidus, perhaps about twenty years ealier, in order to adapt the observation to the chronology of the Watchtower Society, he should keep in mind the previous discussion of the Nabonidus Chronicle, which we saw connected Nabonidus' reign to that of the Persian king Cyrus. The information given in the chronicle limits the possible date for Nabonidus' second year to a period of a few years, in which the lunar eclipse of Elul 13 has to be sought. Of these few years only one year is, in fact, left for our choice: 554 B.C.E.

In this connection a few words should perhaps be added about lunar eclipses. *Aid to Bible Understanding*, quoting *The Encyclopaedia Brittanica*, points out that a particular town or city would, on the average, experience about forty lunar eclipses in fifty years. (*Aid*, p. 330:5) Although it is true that there is about one eclipse for every eight full moons (*circa*, 1.5 lunar eclipses per year), the frequency of the eclipses falling on a certain date, like Elul 13, is much lower. Other factors. too, affect the frequency. Even if a lunar eclipse occurs on the same date in the calendar after a number of years, the elipse will not occur *at the same time* of the day, or be of *the same magnitude*. If it occurs during daylight hours it will, of course, be invisible. If it occurs in the evening, or around midnight, it will not fit the eclipse described by Nabonidus, as he saw it in the morning before sunrise. *The Watchtower* of March 15, 1969, pp. 184ff., refers to another factor, which, it is held, makes it difficult to indentify ancient eclipses. It is pointed out that astronomers for a long time have been aware of the fact that the tides produced by the moon and the sun in the oceans and body of the earth create a retardation of the earth's rotation, causing a gradual lengthening of the day. This, it is said in the article, affects the ancient records. As astronomers for a long time have been aware of these effects, they have tried to calculate the degree of deviation between the ancient observations and modern calculations. Today they take this deviation into account in their study of ancient eclipses. *The Watchtower* article discussed *solar* eclipses, and as I wanted to know how ancient records of *lunar* eclipses are affected by this increasing of the solar day, I wrote to Professor Robert R. Newton, who is the leading authority on this problem. He has, for many years, examined the secular accelerations of the moon and the earth and has published a series of works on the subject. His book, *The Moon's Acceleration and Its Physical Origins*, is the best work currently available on the subject. I wanted to know how much the lengthening of the solar day has affected ancient records of lunar eclipses and if we can still rely upon the older tables of calculations of solar and lunar eclipses published by Oppolzer in 1887 and Ginzel in 1899. Newton, in his answer (dated May, 11, 1981) said: "I have not used Ginzel's canon much, and cannot speak specifically of the errors in it. However, I expect that his errors are about the same as those in Oppolzer's *Canon der Finsternisse*, which I have used extensively. The earliest lunar eclipse in his canon, for example, is that of -1206 April 21, which came at 20H 17M, Greenwhich Mean Time, with a magnitude of 2.6 digits, according to his calculations. According to my calculations, it came on that date at 20H 32M, with a magnitude of 2.4 digits. *Thus it is perfectly safe to use Oppolzer's Canon in indentifying ancient eclipses; his greatest errors are probably something like half an hour*." Thus the argument that the lenthening of the solar day caused by tides makes it more difficult to identify ancient eclipses is completely irrelevant. The effects are too small to cause any problems for astronomers, and Oppolzer's canon of eclipses may be safely used in identifying ancient eclipses.

53. Langdon, pp. 53-57, 270-289. For an English translation, see Pritchard's *Ancient Near Eastern Texts* (Princeton, N.J.: Princeton University Press, 1950), pp. 308-312.

54. Lewy, pp. 53-55.

55. Col. X. The Quotation is from J.B. Pritchard's *Ancient Near Eastern Texts* (commonly referred to as ANET), p. 11.

56. Grayson, p. 95.

57. C.J. Gadd, "The Harran Inscriptions of Nabonidus" in *Anatolian Studies*, Vol. VIII, 1958, pp. 47, 72, 73.

58. Owing to some vagueness in the inscriptions, it is not quite clear whether the Harran temple was completed early in Nabonidus' reign or after his ten-year stay at Teima in Arabia. Anyway, the work seems to have been started in the early years of his reign, and all agree that he reckons the fifty-four years from the sixteenth year of Nabopolassar to his own accession-year when "Sin's wrath calmed," according to Nabon. H1, B. The period had elapsed when the stele under discussion (Nabon. No. 8) was inscribed in the second year of Nabonidus. Berger, p. 110.

59. *Aid to Bible Understanding*, pp. 326, 327.

60. Gadd, p. 47, col. I:29-33.

61. *Ibid.*, pp. 49, 51, col. II:26-29. The 104 years should be corrected to 101 years. The scribe who made the inscription simply summed up the regnal years without taking into account that Assur-etillu-ili's three years covered a part of Nabopolassar's reign. See note 63 below.

62. Pritchard, p. 306.

63. The inscription seems to give the Assyrian king Assur-etillu-ili a reign of three years. This has been regarded as a problem as there is a contract tablet dated to the fourth year of this king. (See Gadd, p. 70ff.) Since Gadd published his translation of the text, other scholars have examined this and other problems related to the last Assyrian kings. Joan Oates (*Iraq*, Vol. 28, 1965, pp. 135-159) offers a solution which has been accepted by others as most probably the correct one: As is evident from the inscription, Adda-Guppi lived in Harran serving under Assyrian kings until the third year of Assur-etillu-ili, when she moved to Babylon because of internal Assyrian problems. There she served under Babylonian kings from that time on. As Oates explains, this does not mean that Assur-etillu-ili's third year was his last or that Adda Guppi came to Babylon in the accession-year of Nabopolassar. (See also Julian Reade, *Journal of Cuneiform Studies*, Vol. 23, 1970, p. 1-9.) Anyway, this problem does not affect the reigns of the Neo-Babylonian kings as given in the inscription. Our discussion concerns Neo-Babylonian chronology, and to establish this chronology, we need not, of course, solve the problems of Assyrian chronology.

64. R.P. Dougherty, *Archives from Erech, Neo-Babylonian and Persian Periods* (London: Yale University Press, 1933), p. 20.

65. R.P. Dougherty, *Nabonidus and Belshazzar* (London: Yale University Press, 1929), p. 1. Yet only a fraction of all the cuneiform texts have been published.

66. R.A. Parker and W.H. Dubberstein, *Babylonian Chronology: 626 B.C.-A.D. 75* (Providence: Brown University Press, 1956), pp. 10-14.

67. *Ibid.*, p. 13. One text from the last year of Nabonidus, published by G. Contenau in *Textes Cuneiformes, Tome XII, Contrats Neó-Babyloniens, I* (Paris: Librarie Orientaliste, 1927), Pl. LVIII, No. 121, evidently contains an error by the scribe or by Contenau. Line 1 gives the date as "VI-6-17," but when it is repeated in line 19 in the text it is given as "VI-6-18." One of them, obviously the latter, is in error. (See Parker and Dubberstein, p. 13.)

68. Ronald Herbert Sack, *Amel-Marduk: 562-560 B.C.* (Neukirchen-Vluyn: Verlag Butzon und Bercker Kevelaer, 1972), pp. 62, 63.

69. Ronald J. Sack, "Nergal-šarra-usur, King of Babylon as seen in the Cuneiform, Greek, Latin and Hebrew Sources" in *Zeitschrift fur Assyriologie* (ed. W. von Soden), Vol. 68, Berlin, August 1978, p. 132.

70. Bruno Meissner, *Babylonien und Assyrien* (Heidelberg, 1925), Vol. II, p. 331. The quotation is translated from the German.

71. W. St. Chad Boscawen, "Babylonian Dated Tablets, and the Canon of Ptolemy" in *Transactions of the Society of Biblical Archeology* (London, January 1878), Vol. VI, pp. 1-78.

72. *Ibid.*, p. 6.

73. Nabu-ahi-idina evidently died in the thirteenth year of Nahonidus. See Aurthur Ungnad, "Das Haus Egibi" in *Archiv für Orientforschung* (1941), Vol. XIV, 1941, p. 60.

74. Boscawen, pp. 9, 10, 24.

75. *Ibid.*, p. 24.

76. *Ibid.*, p. 11.

77. During excavations at Uruk in 1959-60, for example, an archive belonging to members of the Egibi family was unearthed. It contained 205 datable tablets from the sixth year of Nabonidus to the thirty-third year of Darius I. Most of the tablets were dated as from the reign of Darius. See Van Dijk, pp. 39-41. The latest discussion of the Egibi family is one by Hugo Lanz which appears in *Die neubabylonischen harranu-Geschäftsunternehmen* (Berlin: J. Schweitzer Verlag, 1976), pp. 148-165.

78. A complete bibliography of published Neo-Babylonian economic texts can be found (through 1974) in M. Dandamaev, *Rabstvo v Vavilonii VII-IV vv. do n.e. (626-331 gg.)*, (Moscow, 1974), pp. 7-12.

79. Dougherty, *Nabonidus and Belshazzar*, p. 10.

80. *Ibid.*, p. 7.

81. Paul V. Neugebauer and Ernst F. Weidner, ''Ein astronomischer Beobachtungstext aus dem 37. Jahre Nebukadnezars II. (– 567/66),'' in *Berichte über die Verhandlungen der Königl. Sächsischen Gesellschaft der Wissenschaften zu Leipzig: Philologisch-Historische Klasse*, Vol. 67, No. 2, May 1915, pp. 29-89.

82. The diary clearly states that the observations were made during Nebuchadnezzar's thirty-seventh year. The text opens with the words: "37th year of Nebuchadnezzar, the king of Babylon. On Nisan 1 the moon became visible behind the Hyades; visibility lasted for 64m...." It ends with Nisan 1 of the "38th year of Nebuchadnezzar," Neugebauer and Weidner, pp. 34, 38.

83. *Aid to Bible Understanding*, p. 1212 under the subheading "TAKES TYRE."

84. Neugebauer and Weidner, p. 34: ''*Saturn gegenüber dem südlischen Fishe des Tierkreises.*''

85. See also *Awake!*, May 8, 1972, p. 28.

86. *Aid to Bible Understanding*, p. 331.

87. B. L. van der Waerden, *Die Anfänge der Astronomie, Band 2: Erwachende Wissenschaft* (Basel und Stuttgart: Birkhäuser Verlag, 1968), p. 97. See also Otto Neugebauer, *A History of Ancient Mathematical Astronomy* (Berlin, Heideberg, New York: Sprimger-Verlag, 1975), Part Three, p. 1073.

88. Neugebauer and Weidner, pp. 35, 50, 69.

89. *Ibid.*, p. 69. Oppolzer, p. 334, No. 984.

90. See for example his prefatory words in Bryant Tuckerman, *Planetary, Lunar, and Solar Positions: 601 B.C. to A.D. 1 at Five-day and Ten-day Intervals* (Philadelphia: The American Philosophical Society, 1962).

91. *Aid to Bible Understanding*, p. 331.

92. Neugebauer and Weidner, p. 39. This is also the conclusion of other modern authorities. Waerden says: ''Es ist zwar nur einer Kopie aus viel späterer Zeit erhalten, stellt aber eine anscheinend getreue, lediglich orthographisch etwas modernisierte Abschrift eines Originals aus der Zeit NEBUKADNEZARS dar.'' (p. 98)

93. *Aid to Bible Understanding*, p. 331.

94. *Awake!*, May 8, 1972, p. 28.

95. A.J. Sachs, "Babylonian Observational Astronomy" in *Philos. Trans. Royal Soc. London*, ser. A. 276, 1974, pp. 43-50.

96. *Ibid.*, p. 48.

97. Grayson, pp. 131, 132.

98. As the first month, Nisan, began in the spring of 652 B.C.E., Adar, the twelfth month, fell in February-March, 651 B.C.E.

99. Cuneiform texts show that Kandalanu evidently died in his twenty-first regnal year, after which several pretenders to the throne fought for power, until Nabopolassar succeeded in ascending the throne. Business documents span the period of interregnum by artificially carrying on Kandalanu's reign into his twenty-second year. Other documents span the period differently. The "Uruk King List" gives Kandalanu twenty-one years, and gives the year of interregnum to two of the combatants: Sin-shum-lishir and Sin-shar-ishkun. Another document, B.M. 25127, states that "for one year there was no king in the land." All documents agree, however, to the total length of the period from Shamashshumukin to Nabopolassar.

100. B.M. 33041 was first published by T.G. Pinches in *Transactions of the Society of Biblical Archeology* (London, 1882), Vol. VII, pp. 210-225.

101. Friedrich Karl Kienitz, *Die politische Geschichte Ägyptens von 7. bis zum 4. Jahrhundert vor der Zeitwende* (Berlin: Akademie-Verlag, 1953), pp. 154, 155.

102. *Ibid.*, pp. 155, 156.

103. Lines 5/6 of the Ank-nes-nefer-ib-Re Stele. See G. Maspero, *Ann. Serv.* 5 (1904), pp. 85, 86, and the translation by James Henry Breasted, *Ancient Records of Egypt* (Chicago: The University of Chicago Press, 1906), Vol. IV, p. 505, para. 988E.

104. Manetho's *Egyptian History* is preserved only in extracts by Josephus and Christian chronographers, especially by Africanus in his *Chronicle* (c. 221 C.E.) and by Eusebius in his *Chronicon* (c. 303 C.E.). Africanus, who transmits Manetho's data in a more accurate form, gives forty-four years to Amasis and six months to Psammetichus III. This agrees with Herodotus' figures. Syncellus (8th century C.E.) quotes Manetho's figure for Amasis as forty-two years, which is evidently a late distortion. Diodorus of Sicily (I, 68) attributes fifty-five years to Amasis, but as he lived more than 500 years after Psammetichus III, his statements cannot be trusted.

105. Kienitz, p. 156 and R.A. Parker, "The Length of Reign of Amasis and the Beginning of the Twenty-Sixth Dynasty" in *Mitteilungen des Deutschen*

Archäologischen Instituts, Kairo Abteilung, XV, 1957, p. 210.

106. For accession-year and nonaccession-year reckoning, see Appendix A.

107. Parker, Mitteilungen..., pp. 208, 212.

108. *Aid to Bible Understanding*, p. 499. See also note 1 above.

109. In the last century E. Revillout, one of the founders of *Revue Egyptologique* in the 1870's, claimed that Psammetichus III ruled for at least two years, as one document dated to the fourth year of a king Psammetichus seemed to be written at the end of the Twenty-Sixth Dynasty. But since then many new documents have been discovered that make Revillout's theory impossible. The document evidently refers to one of the earlier kings known by the name of Psammetichus.

110. Parker, Mitteilungen..., pp. 210, 211. The Egyptian civil calendar was comprised of three seasons, with four months each. As *Šmw* was the third season, ''I Šmw'' refers to the first month of the third season, that is, the ninth month (named Pachons), and ''II Šmw'' refers to the second month of the third season, or the tenth month (Payni). See Richard A. Parker, *The Calendars of Ancient Egypt* (Chicago: The University of Chicago Press, 1950), p. 8.

111. The period from full moon to the next full moon is on the average 29.53059 days. The Egyptian lunar months therefore consisted alternately of 29 or 30 days. The lunar year was therefore a total of c. 354 days or more exactly $23 \times 29.53059 = 354.3671$ days.

112. The civil calendar: 25 x 365 days = 9,125 days; The lunar calendar: 309 x 29.53059 days = 9,124.95 days.

113. As was pointed out above, a lunar date, such as day 1 of lunar I Šmw, fell on a certain date in the civil calendar, such as I Šmw 29, at intervals of twenty-five years. It is possible, however, to find two or three years within this period when lunar I Šmw 1 came as close as one to two days from I Šmw 29 of the civil calendar. The Watchtower Society, in order to uphold its chronology, is forced to place Amasis' twelfth regnal year c. twenty years prior to 559 B.C.E., that is in c. 579 B.C.E. But neither in this year nor in any year near it did lunar I Šmw 1 even come close to I Šmw 29 of the civil calendar.

114. Erik Hornung, ''Die Sonnenfinsternis nach dem Tode Psammetichus I'' in *Zeitschrift für Ägyptische Sprache und Altertumskunde*, Berlin 1966, Vol. 92, pp. 38, 39.

115. See Appendix C.

116. His name in the Egyptian inscriptions is transcribed as Wahibrē´, which is close to the spelling of his name in the Septuagint: Ouaphré.

117. Pritchard, p. 308.

118. Grayson, *"Assyria and Babylonia,"* in *Orientalia* 49 (1980), p. 164.

119. *Ibid.*, p. 174. The astronomical observations recorded in these diaries, on the other hand, must be treated as a separate and independent line of evidence.

CHAPTER III

1. *Aid to Bible Understanding* (Brooklyn, N.Y.: Watchtower Bible and Tract Society, 1971), p. 339.

2. See for example Edward J. Young, *The Prophecy of Daniel* (Grand Rapids: Wm.B. Eerdman's Publishing Co., 1949), pp. 192-195.

3. Jewish rabbis made a similar application of this prophecy in the Talmud (Seder Olam), counting 490 years from the destruction of the first temple by the Babylonians to the destruction of the second temple by the Romans.

4. Republished in 1973 by Kregel Publications under the title *Chronology of the Old Testament*. See p. 20 on the 490 years.

5. *Bible Examiner*, 1863, p. 120.

6. During the years 1931-1940 the royal tombs of kings thought never to have existed were excavated in Persia. See *Collier's Encyclopedia*, Vol. 15, pp. 567, 568. That Ptolemy put these kings in the right order is also demonstrated by the inscription discovered on the walls of a palace of Artaxerxes III, which reads: "Says Artaxerxes the great king, king of kings, king of countries, king of this earth: I (am) the son of Artaxerxes (II) the king: Artaxerxes (was) the son of Darius (II) the king; Darius (was) the son of Artaxerxes (I) the king; Artaxerxes (was) the son of Xerxes the king; Xerxes (was) the son of Darius (I) the king; Darius was the son of Hystaspes by name." (E.F. Schmidt, *Persepolis I*, p. 224.)

7. The seventy years for Tyre at Isaiah 23:15-18 will not be discussed here, as it cannot be proved that they refer to the period of Neo-Babylonian supremacy. In fact, some of the best conservative scholars apply it to circa 700-630 B.C.E., when Tyre was controlled by Assyria. See, for example, W. Rudolph's article, "Jesaja 23, 1-14," in *Festschrift Freidrich Baumgartel (Erlangen: Erlanger Forschungen*, 1959), Vol. 10, pp. 166-174.

8. The quotation is from *The New World Translation*, which is based on the Hebrew Masoretic Text (MT). The Greek Septuagint Version (LXX) says: "and they will serve among the nations," instead of: "and these nations will have to serve the king of Babylon." There are many differences between MT and LXX with respect to the text of the book of Jeremiah. The LXX text is about one-

eighth shorter than the MT text. In Jeremiah 25:1-14 of the LXX, for some unknown reason, all references to the king of Babylon are omitted. (See verses 1, 9, 11 and 12.) It is well known that LXX adds about 1,500 years to the chronology from Adam to Christ, that period becoming c. 5,500 years instead of c. 4,000 years (MT). As the chronology of the Watchtower Society is based on the MT, the following discussion of the seventy years will follow that text, as represented by The New World Translation. It is true that the LXX was translated from a Hebrew text that was earlier than the MT, and that the writers of the New Testament often quote the LXX. This was quite natural since they wrote in Greek, but often they also supply a version of their own that agrees with the MT but contradicts the LXX, which shows that they did not regard the LXX as a version superior to the Hebrew text. It should be kept in mind that the LXX is a translation, not the original text; and as the editors of Bagster's *The Septuagint Version of the Old Testament* point out in the "Introduction," some of the translators of the LXX were not competent to their task and often inserted their own interpretations and traditions. The *oldest* witness to the Hebrew text is not the LXX, but the *Samaritan Pentateuch*, a form of the Hebrew text of the Pentateuch preserved by the Samaritans. Although in some cases it agrees with the LXX, it is *on the whole* in more substantial accord with MT (but not with its chronology, where it disagrees with both LXX and MT).

9. The Hebrew word for "devastation," *chorbáh*, is also used in verse 18 in this chapter where it is stated that Jerusalem and the cities of Judah would become "*a devastated place (*chorbáh), an object of astonishment, something to whistle at and a malediction, just as at this day." This prophecy was uttered "in the fourth year of Jehoiakim,...that is, the first year of Nebuchadnezzar" (v.1), the phrase "just as at this day" seems to indicate that the devastation, the *chorbáh*, to a certain degree had begun at this time, eighteen years prior to the destruction of Jerusalem.

That the word *chorbáh* does not in itself mean a state of desolation "without an inhabitant" can be seen from other texts which use the word, for example Ezekekiel 33:24,27 ("the *inhabitants* of these *devastated places*") and at Nehemiah 2:17. During Nehemiah's time Jerusalem was inhabited, yet the city is said to be "devastated." The phrase "desolate waste, without inhabitant," is found at Jeremiah 9:11 and 34:22. Although it refers to Jerusalem and the cities of Judah, it is nowhere equated with the period of seventy years. The word *chorbáh* is often used to describe the state of devastated lands and cities after the armies of an enemy have passed, and it would not be inaccurate, therefore, to talk of Judah as *chorbáh* eighteen years prior to its depopulation, *if the land had been ravaged by the army of an enemy at that time*! See also the comments on Daniel 9:2 below.

10. Flavius Josephus, who obviously was confused as to the actual length of the desolation, twice states that it lasted for seventy years (*Antiquities* X, vi, 1 and *Against Apion* I, 19). But, in his last work he says that it lasted for fifty years: "...Nebuchadnezzar, in the nineteenth year of his reign, laid our temple desolate, and so it lay in that state of obscurity for *fifty years*." (*Against Apion*, I, 21)

11. D.J. Wiseman, *Chronicles of the Chaldean Kings*, (London: *The Trustees of The British Museum*, 1961), pp. 66-75.

12. The quotations in the following are taken from A.K. Grayson's more recent translation of the Chronicle in his *Assyrian and Babylonian Chronicles* (New York: J.J. Augustin Publisher, 1975), pp. 99ff.

13. *Hamath* was a district in the area of *Hatti*, a geographical term which at that time included "the whole of Syria and Palestine." *Wiseman*, p. 25.

14. Nabopolassar's death occurred on 8 Ab, corresponding to August 16, 605 of the Julian calendar. Nebuchadnezzar took over the throne on Elul 1, which corresponded to September 7, 605. The battle of Carchemish was fought in May or June, 605, in the accession-year of Nebuchadnezzar. The reason why the Bible dates the battle to the first year of Nebuchadnezzar (compare Jer. 46:2 and 25:1) instead of his accession-year seems to be that the Jewish kings applied the nonaccession-year system, in which the accession-year was counted as the first year. See Appendix A.

15. Reasonably, Jehoiakim must have been one of "all of the kings of Hattu" paying tribute to Nebuchadnezzar at this time. Of this, J.P. Hyatt says: "It was probably in 605, or in the following year, that Jehoiakim submitted to the Babylonian king, as recorded in II Kings 24:1;...and II Kings 24:7 says that 'the king of Babylon took all that belonged to the king of Egypt from the Brook of Egypt to the River Euphrates.' " "New Light on Nebuchadnezzar and Judean History" in *Journal of Biblical Literature*, 75 (1956), p. 280.

16. For a thorough discussion of Daniel 1:1,2 and 2:1, see Appendix B.

17. Stanley Mayer Burstein, *The Babyloniaca of Berossus* (Malibu: Undena Publications, 1978), pp. 26, 27. Berossus' account of these events has been the subject of much criticism, but was accepted by historians such as H. Wincler, Edgar Goodspeed, James H. Breasted and Friedrich Delitzsch. See "The Third Year of Jehoiakim," by Albertus Pieters, in *From the Pyramids to Paul*, edited by Lewis Gaston Leary (New York: Thomas Nelson and Sons, 1935), p. 191. The later discovery of the Babylonian Chronicle B.M. 21946 has given additional support to Berossus' description of Nebuchadnezzar's conquests after the battle at Carchemish. It must be admitted, though, that his presentation is biased, as he intended to influence Greek ideas about Babylon. The most flagrant example is his presentation of Pharaoh Nechoh as a *rebellious satrap* in charge of Egypt, Coelesyria and Pheonicia.

"According to him the legitimate successor of Assyrian rule in the West was Babylonia and not Egypt" notes B. Porten in "The Identity of King Adon" in *Biblical Archeologist*, Vol. 44, No. 1, 1981, p. 49. See *Burstein*, p. 8.

18. Chapters 27 and 28 refer to the same year, the fourth year of Zedekiah according to Chapter 28:1. The reason for the widespread revolt plans in this year could have been the rebellion in Nebuchadnezzar's own army in Babylonia, in the

tenth year of his reign according to the Babylonian Chronicle B.M. 21946. (Grayson, p. 102) Nebuchadnezzar's tenth year partly overlapped Zedekiah's fourth year. See Appendix C (the chronological tables).

19. This conclusion is confirmed by other scholars. Avigdor Orr, in his article "The Seventy Years of Babylon," *Vetus Testamentum* Vol. VI, 1956, p. 305, says: "The sense of the Hebrew original might even be rendered thus: 'After seventy years of (the rule of) Babylon are accomplished, etc.' The seventy years counted here evidently refer to Babylon and *not* to the Judeans or to their captivity. They mean seventy years of Babylonian rule, the end of which will see the redemption of the exiles."

20. Raymond Hammer, *The Book of Daniel* in *The Cambridge Bible Commentary* (Cambridge: Cambridge University Press, 1976), p. 91.

21. Young, pp. 183, 184.

22. See O. Ploger's article "Siebzig Jahre" in *Festschrift Friedrich Baumgartel* (Erlangen, 1959), p. 126.

23. *Aid to Bible Understanding*, p. 422.

24. See *Paradise Restored to Mankind—By Theocracy!* (Brooklyn, N.Y.: Watchtower Bible and Tract Society, 1972), p. 127.

25. *Ibid.*, pp. 131-133.

26. This is also the conclusion of many modern commentators. J.A. Thompson, for example, says: "In Zech. 1:12 it seems to denote the interval between the destruction of the temple in 587 B.C. and its rebuilding in 520-515 B.C." *The Book of Jeremiah* (Grand Rapids: Wm.B. Eerdmans Publishing Co., 1980), p. 514.

27. *Paradise Restored to Mankind*, p. 235.

28. *Ibid.*

29. From August 587 B.C.E., when the temple was burned down, to November 518 it was sixty-nine years and four months. From September or October 587, when the remaining Jews fled to Egypt and left Judah desolated, to November 518 was sixty-nine years and about two months.

30. *Paradise Restored to Mankind*, p. 235.

31. *Ibid.*, p. 237.

32. F.C. Fensham, "The Numeral Seventy in the Old Testament and the Family of Jerubbaal, Ahab, Panammuwa and Athirat" in *Palestine Exploration*

Quarterly, July-December 1977, pp. 113-115.

33. Rykle Borger, "An Additional Remark on P.R. Ackroyd, JNES, XVII, 23-27" in *Journal of Near Eastern Studies*, Vol. XVII, January-October 1958, p. 74.

34. Nebuchadnezzar's son and successor was Evil-Merodach. His *grandson* was evidently Belshazzar, the son of Nabonidus who, according to R.P. Dougherty was married to Nitocris, a daughter of Nebuchadnezzar. R.P. Dougherty, *Nabonidus and Belshazzar* (New Haven: Yale University Press, 1929), p. 79.

35. Several historians and biblical scholars have been amazed at the exactness with which Jeremiah's prediction was fulfilled. Professor John Bright, for example, commenting on Jeremiah 29:10, says: "One cannot explain rationally why it was that Jeremiah was assured that Babylon's rule would be so relatively brief. But there is no reason to regard the verse as a *vaticinium ex eventu* (a "prophecy" made after the event); we can only record the fact that the prediction turned out to be approximately correct....From the fall of Nineveh (612) to the fall of Babylon (539) was seventy-three years; from Nebuchadnezzar's accession (605) to the fall of Babylon was sixty-six years." *The Anchor Bible: Jeremiah* (New York: Doubleday and Company, Inc., 1965), pp. 208, 209.

36. H. Grattan Guiness, *Light for the Last Days* (London, 1886).

37. The others were 741, 738, 727, 713, 676, 650-647, and 598.

38. The Pastoral Bible Institute (P.B.I.) was headed by former board members of the Watch Tower Society who were dismissed by J.F. Rutherford in 1917 together with other prominent members.

39. *The Herald of Christ's Kingdom*, Vol. IV, April 15, 1921, p. 115.

40. *Ibid.*, pp. 115, 116.

41. *Ibid.*, p. 118.

42. *Ibid.*, p. 120.

43. *Ibid.*

44. *Ibid.*, p. 163. Interestingly, the November 1, 1921 issue of the *Herald* published an article prepared by another Bible Student in 1915, in which he presented evidence and conclusions practically identical to those of R.E. Streeter, although he dated the destruction of Jerusalem in 588 instead of 587 B.C.E. The 588 date was adopted by P.B.I. in subsequent issues of the *Herald*. As this man had no connection with P.B.I., he preferred to be anonymous, signing the article with the initials J.A.D. The Beraean Bible Institute, a Bible Student group with headquarters in Melbourne, Australia, accepted the conclusions of the P.B.I.

editors, also, as is seen from their *Peoples Paper* of July 1 and September 1, 1921, pp. 52, 68.

45. " 'Ancient Israel's Jubilee Year' Examined" in the July 1, 1921 issue of *The Present Truth*, pp. 100-104 and "Further P.B.I. Chronology Examined" in the September 1, 1921 issue, pp. 134-136.

46. *The Watch Tower*, May 1, 1922, pp. 131, 132. Other articles published during 1922 were "Chronology" (May 15, pp.147-150), "Seventy Years' Desolation—Part I" (June 1, pp. 163-168), "Seventy Years' Desolation—Part II" (June 15, pp. 183-187), "The Strong Cable of Chronology" (July 15, pp. 217-219), "Interesting Letters: Mistakes of Ptolemy, the Pagan Historian" (August 15, pp. 253, 254) and "Divinely-given Chronological Parallelisms—Part I" (November 15, pp. 355-360). "Mistakes of Ptolemy, the Pagan Historian" was written by Morton Edgar.

47. *The Present Truth*, June 1, 1922: "Some Recent P.B.I. Teachings Examined" (pp. 84-87); July 1: "Some Recent P.B.I. Teachings Examined" (pp. 102-108); August 1: "Further P.B.I. Chronology Examined" (pp. 117-122); November 1: "Sone Mistakes in Ptolemy's Canon" (pp. 166-169).

48. *The Herald of Christ's Kingdom*, May 1 (No. 9), 1930, p. 137.

49. *The Herald of Christ's Kingdom*, May (No. 5), 1935, p. 68.

50. *Ibid*., p. 69.

51. The year 1934 was still held to be an important date, occupying "a prominent place in chronological prophecy." In support of this conclusion, P.B.I. editors referred to a statement by Edwin C. Hill, a press reporter of international reputation, to the effect that "the year 1934 had been a most remarkable one. There had been many important occurrences and developments, he said, affecting the destinies of all the nations of the earth and marking the year as *one of the most significant of history*." *The Herald of Christ's Kingdom*, May (No. 5), 1935, pp. 71, 72

52. Earlier, in the writings of C.T. Russell and J.F. Rutherford, the Gentile times were also identified with the "seven times" of chastisement predicted in Leviticus 26:18,21,24,28. See *Bible Examiner*, October 1876, p. 27 and *Studies in the Scriptures* Vol. II, p. 89. This identification was still retained in the book, *The New World*, published in 1942, on page 77 although it seems to have been dropped soon afterwards. Since then the calculation of the 2,520 years is based entirely on Daniel 4. Some Bible translations use the expression "sevenfold" in Leviticus 26:18,21,24 and 28 instead of "seven times." See for example the Jerusalem Bible.

53. Dr. Frederic Louis Godet, *A Commentary on the Gospel of St. Luke*, 5th edition (Edinburgh: T. and T. Clark Ltd., 1976), Vol. 2, page 268. The *Com-*

mentary was first published in 1870 at Neuchatel in French. One may wonder whether Jesus used the phrase "times of the Gentiles" to describe a period, the length of which was known to himself at the time. Although this is stated to be the case in the book *"The Nations Shall Know that I Am Jehovah"—How?* (Brooklyn, N.Y.: Watchtower Bible and Tract Society, 1971), p. 233, the answer is very likely "no." Especially is this true if the termination date of this period marks the beginning of Christ's *parousia* as the Watchtower Society holds. In his last great prophecy Jesus repeatedly stated that the time of his second coming was unknown, even to himself. (Matt. 24:36,42,44,51; 25:13; Mark 13:32-37; Luke 12:40,46) Even after his resurrection, Jesus told his followers: "It does not belong to you to get knowledge of the times or seasons (*Chronous e kairous*) which the Father has placed in his own jurisdiction" (Acts 1:7 NW) This statement reasonably included the exact length of the times (*kairoi*) of the Gentiles, too, as it was given in answer to a question regarding the time of the restoration of the kingdom of Israel.

54. *Aid to Bible Understanding*, p. 95.

55. Young, p. 110.

56. *Aid to Bible Understanding*, p. 95.

57. *True Peace and Security—From What Source?* (Brooklyn, N.Y.: Watchtower Bible and Tract Society, 1973), p. 74.

58. *Aid to Bible Understanding*, p. 1213.

59. For a thorough refutation of the year-day concept, see pp. 111–126 of Samuel P. Tregelles, *Remarks on the Prophetic Visions in the Book of Daniel*, originally published in 1852. Reference here is to the seventh edition (London: The Sovereign Grace Advent Testimony, 1965).

60. Literally "sevens." *The New International Version* translates Daniel 9:24 "seventy 'sevens' are decreed..." etc., which is a very literal rendering of the expression. Seventy 'sevens' of what? "Seventy" most probably refers back to the *seventy years* in verse 2 which indicates the seventy "sevens" to be years. Thus the *context* indicates the new period introduced by the angel to Daniel to be 490 *years*. This conclusion may be drawn without applying the year-day principle to this text. See also the excellent comments on this prophecy by Tregelles, pp. 116-118.

61. C.T. Russell concluded that both periods were *years*, "for if three and a half times are 1260 days (years), seven times will be a period just twice as long, 2520 years." *Studies in the Scriptures*, Vol. II, p. 91.

62. *The Watch Tower*, May 1, 1922, p. 139.

63. See the article "The Setting Up of Christ's Kingdom" in *The Watch Tower*, June 1, 1922 which still has the 1878 date.

64. *The Bible on Our Lord's Return* (Brooklyn, N.Y.: Watchtower Bible and Tract Society, 1922), p. 93.

65. Christian commentators of several different denominations regarded this event as a sign of the times. It will be remembered that as early as 1823, John A. Brown, in his *The Even-Tide*, ended the "seven times" in 1917. In his opinion 1917 would see "the full glory of the kingdom of Israel...perfected." (Vol. I, p. xliii f.) Dr. Grattan Guiness, too, pointed forward to 1917 as a very important date: "There can be no question that those who live to see this year 1917 will have reached one of the most important, perhaps *the* most momentous, of these terminal years of crisis." *Light for the Last Days* (London, 1886), pp. 342-346. Aware of these predictions, eight well-known English clergymen, among whom were Dr. G. Campbell Morgan and Dr. G.B. Meyer, issued a manifesto which was published throughout the earth and declared: "(1) That the present crisis points towards the close of the times of the Gentiles....[and] (5)That all human schemes of reconstruction must be subsidiary to the second coming of our Lord, because all nations will then be subject to his rule...." (*Current Opinion*, February 1918) Although this manifesto has been cited several times in Watchtower publications in support of *the 1914 date*, it was actually issued in support of the 1917 date and resulted from Allenby's "liberation" of Jerusalem in the latter year.

66. *The Watch Tower*, 1931, pp. 253, 254; J.F. Rutherford, *Vindication* (Brooklyn, N.Y.: Watchtower Bible and Tract Society, 1932), Vol. II, pp. 258, 267.

67. *The Watchtower*, November 1, 1949, pp. 330, 331.

68. See *'Bablyon the Great Has Fallen!' God's Kingdom Rules!*(Brooklyn, N.Y.: Watchtower Bible and Tract Society, 1963), pp. 452, 453; *Aid to Bible Understanding*, p. 95; *"The Nations Shall Know that I Am Jehovah"—How?*, pp. 232-235.

69. *Aid to Bible Understanding*, p. 1004. The Watchtower Society took a similar view as early as 1953. See *"Make Sure of all Things,"* 2nd ed. (Brooklyn, N.Y.: Watchtower Bible and Tract Society, 1953), p. 233 under the subheading "Christ King of Christian Congregation Since First Presence."

70. *Aid to Bible Understanding*, p. 1004.

71. *Ibid.*, p. 94.

72. Gerhard Kittel and Gerhard Griedrich, eds., *Theological Dictionary of the New Testament* (Grand Rapids: Wm.B. Eerdmans Publishing Co., 1967), Vol. V, p. 859. The question about Christ's coming was evidently caused by his statement at Matthew 23:39: "Blessed is he that comes in Jehovah's name!" (NW) This is a quotation from Psalm 118:26, a prophetic psalm which deals with the coming King—the Messiah. See also Matthew 21:4,5,9 and Zechariah 9:9.

73. The Greek word for "sign," *to semeion*, is the same in both Matthew 24:3 and 24:30.

74. Robert Fleming, Jr., *The Rise and Fall of the Papacy* (London, 1849), p. 68. This work was originally published in 1701.

75. *Ibid.*, p. 64.

EPILOGUE

1. This has been thoroughly demonstrated by Karl Burganger in *The Watch Tower Society and Absolute Chronology* (Lethbridge, Alta.: Christian Fellowship International, 1981).

2. From 1955 up to about 1971, the date 539 date was termed an "absolute date" in Watchtower publications. See Burganger, p. 13. When it was discovered that this date did not have the support that Watchtower scholars imagined, they dropped this term. In *Aid to Bible Understanding* 539 is called "a pivotal point." (p. 333) Since 1971 this designation has been dropped too. Now it is stated only that "historians calculate" or "hold" the Babylon fell in October 539 B.C.E. *"Let Your Kingdom Come"* (Brooklyn, N.Y.: Watchtower Bible and Tract Society, 1981), pp. 136, 186. Yet the Society still anchors its whole "Bible chronology" to this date.

3. Personal letter to the author, dated August 9, 1981. The reason for uncertainty among scholars as to whether Jerusalem was desolated in 587 or 586 B.C.E. stems from the Bible, not extra-biblical sources. All scholars agree in dating Nebuchadnezzar's eighteenth regnal year to 587-6 B.C.E. (Nisan to Nisan). The Bible usually dates the desolation to Nebuchadnezzar's *nineteenth* regnal year (2 Kings 25:8; Jer. 52:12), but once to his eighteenth year. (Jer. 52:29) This discrepancy may be solved if a nonaccession-year system is postulated for the kings of Judah. See Appendix A. The 597 B.C.E. date for the earlier capture of Jerusalem and the deportation of Jehoiachin, says Dr. Campbell, is one of the very few *secure* historical dates recognized by scholars. The reason is the exact synchronism between the Bible and the Babylonian Chronicle at this point. See Appendix B, note 12 and the context, also Appendix C, comment No. 3.

4. Personal letter to the author, dated August 16, 1981. For a discussion of the question of 587 or 586 B.C.E., see note 3 above.

5. Gerhard Larsson, "When Did the Babylonian Captivity Begin?" in *Journal of Theological Studies*, Vol. 18 (1967), p. 420.

6. See Albertus Pieters' discussion in *From the Pyramids to Paul* (New York: Thomas Nelson and Sons, 1935), pp. 184-189.

7. Ernest Wilhelm Hengstenberg, *Die Authentie des Daniels und die Integrität des Sacharjah* (Berlin, 1831), p. 57. Translated from the German.

8. *Josephus' Complete Works* (Grand Rapids: Kregel Publications, 1978), pp. 678-708.

9. *Ibid.*, p. 684, para. 14.

10. *Ibid.*, p. 686, para. 19.

11. *Ibid.*, pp. 688, 689, para. 23.

12. On the seventy years, see A. Roberts and J. Donaldson, eds., *The Ante-Nicene Fathers* (Grand Rapids: Wm. Eerdmans Publishing Co., 1979), Vol. II, 119.

13. *Ibid.*, p. 120, ftn. 1.

14. *Ibid.*, p. 329.

15. In "*Let Your Kingdom Come*" (pp. 138, 188) the Watchtower Society discusses the possibility that Jeremiah 25:11 and the prophecy of the "seventy years' began to be fulfilled with the battle of Carchemish in 605 B.C.E. and that Jerusalem was indeed destroyed in 587-6 B.C.E. Such reckoning would, according to the Society, place the end of the Gentile times or "the prophetic 'seven times' in the World War year of 1916." This cannot be considered satisfactory reasoning, however, because it ignores Ezekiel 21:26, 27 which is used by the Society to mark the beginning of the Gentile times. That text deals directly with the *destruction* of Jerusalem by Nebuchadnezzar at the end of Zedekiah's reign, not an event which occurred nearly twenty years earlier.

APPENDIX A

1. Carl Friedrich Keil, *Biblisher Commentar über den Propheten Jeremia und die Klagelieder* (Leipzig, 1872), pp. 536-542. Dr. J.A. Thompson explains: "This concluding chapter to the book of Jeremiah is based on 2 K. 24:18-25:30....The section from Kings was probably included to show how Jeremiah's prophecies were fulfilled." *Book of Jeremiah* (Grand Rapids: Wm. B. Eerdman's Publishing Co., 1980), pp. 773, 774.

2. Albertus Pieters, "The Third Year of Jehoiakim," in *From the Pyramids to Paul* (New York: Thomas Nelson and Sons, 1935), p. 186.

3. *Ibid.*, p. 184.

4. Dr. Jack Finegan, *Handbook of Biblical Chronology* (Princeton, N.J.:

Princeton University Press, 1964), p. 208. J. Philip Hyatt says: "It is obvious that Kings uses a system which reckons the accession year as the first year of a king's reign, whereas Jer. 52 employs the Babylonian system which does not count the accession year, but reckons as the first year of a king the year beginning with his formal coronation in Nisan following his accession." "New Light on Nebuchadnezzar and Judean History" in *Journal of Biblical Literature* 75 (1956), p. 278.

5. For a detailed discussion of Daniel 1:1f and 2:1 see Appendix B.

6. Dr. Edwin R. Thiele in *Bulletin of the American Schools of Oriental Research*, No. 143, 1956, pp. 22-27.

7. *Aid to Bible Understanding*, p. 279.

8. "In the Hebrew Scriptures the months are numbered from Nisan, regardless of whether the reckoning of the year was from spring or fall." Edwin R. Thiele, *The Mysterious Numbers of the Hebrew Kings* (Chicago: The University of Chicage Press, 1951), p. 31. In footnote 11 (p. 31), he gives many examples of this.

9. See for example J. Morgenstern's review of Parker and Dubberstein's *Babylonian Chronology 626 B.C.-A.D.45* in the *Journal of Near Eastern Studies*, Vol. 2, 1943, pp. 125-130. More recently, Dr. A. Malamat has strongly argued for a Tischri reckoning of regnal years in Judah, for example, in his article "The Twilight of Judah: In the Egyptian-Babylonian Maelstrom," in supplements to *Vetus Testamentum* (Leiden: E.J. Brill, 1975), Vol. XXVIII, p. 124, including ftn. 2. See also K.S. Freedy and D.B. Redford, "The Dates in Ezekiel in Relation to Biblical, Babylonian and Egyptian Sources" in *Journal of the American Oriental Society*, Vol. 90, 1970, pp. 464, 465.

APPENDIX B

1. The first edition was published in 1912 and 1913 and was distributed by the Watch Tower Society. It was re-issued in 1924, with some additions by Morton Edgar. (John Edgar died in 1910.) The quotations here are from the 1924 edition.

2. *Ibid.*, p. 31 and p. 28, ftn.4. That this "solution" was taken from an earlier writer is seen from the fact that Dr. E.W. Hengstenberg refers to it in his work *Die Authentie des Daniels und die Integritat des Sacharjah* (Berlin, 1831), p. 54. Dr. Hengstenberg rejects the idea because (1) there is no evidence indicating that Jehoiakim's regnal years were counted in this curious way, (2) that it is an unfounded hypothesis with no support in the Bible, or elsewhere, that Nabuchadnezzar's first siege of Jerusalem occurred in Jehoiakim's eighth year, and (3) that the "solution" is in inextricable conflict with Daniel 2:1.

3. John and Morton Edgar, *Great Pyramid Passages,* Vol. II, p. 32.

4. *Equipped for Every Good Work* (Brooklyn, N.Y.: Watchtower Bible and Tract Society, 1946), pp. 225, 226.

5. *Ibid.*, pp. 226, 227. This, too, was an earlier idea. Hengstenberg (p. 54) rejects it because there is "not the slightest trace" of any such reckoning of Nebuchadnezzar's regnal years anywhere.

6. *Equipped for Every Good Work*, p. 227.

7. D.J. Wiseman, *Chronicles of the Chaldean Kings* (London: Trustees of the British Museum, 1961), pp. 69-71.

8. *Ibid.*, p. 71.

9. "This battle must lie back of Jehoiakim's change of allegiance, when he withheld tribute from Babylonia, probably making an alliance with Egypt." J.P. Hyatt, "New Light on Nebuchadnezzar and Judean History" in the *Journal of Biblical Literature* 75 (1956), p. 281.

10. A.K. Grayson, *Assyrian and Babylonian Chronicles* (New York: J.J. Augustin Publisher, 1975), p. 102. The chronicle is in complete agreement with the description of this siege given in the Bible. See, for example, 2 Chronicles 36:9,10.

11. The Babylonians had a second Ululu (an intercalary month) in the seventh year of Nebuchadnezzar, thus making Kislev and Adar the tenth and thirteenth months respectively that year, although they were normally the ninth and twelfth calendar months. This fact does not affect the discussion above.

12. If the Babylonian army left Babylon some time after Jehoiachin had ascended the throne, the siege was of very short duration, two months at most and probably less, as the time the army needed to march from Babylon to Jerusalem has to be subtracted from the three months from Kislev to Adar. Such a march took at least one month. It is possible, however, that a part of the army had left Babylon earlier, as 2 Kings 24:10,11 indicates that Nebuchadnezzar arrived at Jerusalem some time after the seige had begun. The reason for the short duration of the siege was Jehoiachin's surrender to Nebuchadnezzar on Adar 2 or March 16, 597 B.C.E., Julian calendar. (2 Kings 24:12) For an excellent discussion of this siege, see William H. Shea, "Nebuchadnezzar's Chronicle and the Date of the Destruction of Lachish III" in *Palestine Exploration Quarterly*, No. 111 (1979), pp. 113f.

13. A brilliant discussion of this problem may be found in the article by Albertus Pieters, "The Third Year of Jehoiakim" in *From the Pyramids to Paul* (New York: Thomas Nelson and Sons, 1935).

14. This way of counting time periods is often termed "inclusive reckoning." The best example is the period of Jesus' death, from Friday afternoon to his resurrection on Sunday morning. Although, chronologically, this period was a little more than one day and two nights, Bible writers refer to it as "three days" (Matt. 27:63; Mark 10:34), even "three days and three nights." (Matt. 12:40) The Watchtower Society correctly applies it to mean "a portion of each of three days." (*Aid to Bible Understanding*, pp. 428, 429) Another example is the period of the siege of Samaria, started at 2 Kings 18:9, 10 to have lasted from the seventh to the ninth year of Hoshea; yet the siege is said to have lasted for "three years." For additional examples, see Edwin R. Thiele, *The Mysterious Numbers of the Hebrew Kings* (Chicago: The University of Chicago Press, 1951), p. 31, ftn. 12.

15. Edward J. Young, *The Prophecy of Daniel* (Grand Rapids: Wm. B. Eerdman's Publishing Co., 1949), pp. 55, 56.

16. Gerhard F. Hasel, "The First and Third Year of Belshazzar" in *Andrews University Seminary Studies*, Vol. XV, No. 2, 1977, p. 167.

APPENDIX C

1. Edwin R. Thiele, *The Mysterious Numbers of the Hebrew Kings* (Chicago: University of Chicago Press, 1951), pp. 158-165.

2. D.J. Wiseman, *Chronicles of Chaldean Kings* (London: Trustees of the British Museum), p. 63. See also Hayim Tadmor's article "Chronology of the Last Kings of Judah" in *Journal of Near Eastern Studies*, Vol. XV, 1956, p. 228.

3. A. Malamat, "The Twilight of Judah: In the Egyptian-Babylonian Maelstrom" in *Supplements to Vetus Testamentum* (Leiden: E.J. Brill, 1975), Vol. XXVIII, p. 125, ftn. 5.

4. Wiseman, p. 73.

5. "*The Nations Shall Know that I Am Jehovah" —How?* (Brooklyn, N. Y.: Watchtower Bible and Tract Society, 1971), pp. 285-287 argues for a siege of eighteen months.

6. *Ibid.,* p. 286.

APPENDIX D

1. Alfred Plummer, *A Critical and Exegetical Commentary on the Gospel According to St. Luke*, p. 483 as quoted by John F. Walvoord in "The Times of the Gentiles," *Bibliotheca Sacra*, January 1968, p. 4.

2. C.I. Scofield, *The Scofield Reference Bible* (New York, 1909), p. 1345.

3. "The term 'nations' or 'Gentiles' translates the Greek word *éthne*, which means 'people' or 'nations' and was used by the Bible writers to refer specifically to the non-Jewish nations." *Aid to Bible Understanding* (Brooklyn, N.Y.: Watchtower Bible and Tract Society, 1971), p. 94.

4. *The Kingdom Interlinear Translation of the Greek Scriptures*, p. 393.

5. This opinion is held by many expositors. "Most expositors bring the times of the Gentiles to a close with the second coming of Christ." John F. Walvoord, *Bibliotheca Sacra*, January, 1968, p. 7.

6. This is the simplest and most logical conclusion indicated by the context of Luke 21:24 and confirmed by subsequent history. Any attempt to avoid this conclusion has to ignore both the context and historical facts. For example, in *The Watchtower* of December 15, 1981, page 29, Watchtower Society President F.W. Franz was reported to have discussed with missionary graduates whether the "Gentile times" were connected with the "literal city of Jerusalem," explaining that "some have claimed that 1914 meant nothing and that Jesus had in mind a trampling on the literal city of Jerusalem." The consequences of such a view, he said, are that the "Gentile times" ended in 1967, when "Israel gained control of the West Bank, including the old walled city of Jerusalem. 'Yet,' Franz asked, 'has that resulted in the glory of Jehovah God? Has that resulted in the coming of the Messiah to establish the kingdom of God over there in earthy Jerusalem? The clear answer is, No." Thus, instead of dealing with the arguments developed above, Franz, according to this report, introduced completely extra-contextual procedure for approaching biblical texts. There is nothing in the context of Luke 21:24 to indicate that the ending of the "Gentile times" would immediately result in "the glory of Jehovah God" or the "coming of Messiah to establish the kingdom of God." Besides, the report indicates that he completely ignored the fact that the old temple site still, after 1967, is trampled on by Gentiles. Only by ignoring the context and historical facts, then, was he able to defend the view that the Gentile times ended in 1914 and refer to *heavenly* Jerusalem.
